The Democratic Marketplace

THE DEMOCRATIC MARKETPLACE

How a More Equal Economy
Can Save Our Political Ideals

LISA HERZOG

HARVARD UNIVERSITY PRESS
Cambridge, Massachusetts
London, England
2025

Copyright © 2025 by the
President and Fellows of Harvard College
All rights reserved
Printed in the United States of America

First printing

Library of Congress Cataloging-in-Publication Data
Names: Herzog, Lisa, 1983– author.
Title: The democratic marketplace : how a more equal economy can save our political ideals / Lisa Herzog.
Description: Cambridge, Massachusetts; London, England : Harvard University Press, 2025. | Includes bibliographical references and index.
Identifiers: LCCN 2024042058 (print) | LCCN 2024042059 (ebook) | ISBN 9780674294516 (cloth) | ISBN 9780674299894 (pdf) | ISBN 9780674299900 (epub)
Subjects: LCSH: Economics—Political aspects. | Democracy—Economic aspects. | Capitalism—Moral and ethical aspects. | Equality. | Economic development.
Classification: LCC HB74.P65 .H478 2025 (print) | LCC HB74.P65 (ebook) | DDC 330—dc23/eng/20250117
LC record available at https://lccn.loc.gov/2024042058
LC ebook record available at https://lccn.loc.gov/2024042059

To the train drivers who let me explore the world

Contents

Introduction: Democratizing Democracy, Democratizing the Economy   *1*

1. Markets, Corporations, and Their Alliance against Democracy   *25*

2. Workers: Underlings or Citizens?   *52*

3. Inequality: Why Democracies Need Less of It   *76*

4. From Growth to Functions   *100*

5. Time for Democracy   *123*

6. Repairing Democracy on the Open Sea   *148*

Notes   *169*

Acknowledgments   *221*

Index   *223*

The Democratic Marketplace

INTRODUCTION

Democratizing Democracy, Democratizing the Economy

Democracy and capitalism—for a long time, this was seen as the formula for the success of "the West." A political system based on individual voting rights and an economic system based on individual consumer choice: together, they seemed the best possible way of running large-scale, modern societies. But in recent years, this marriage of capitalism and democracy has been ridden by conflict. Anti-democratic forces are on the rise in many parts of the world. The *ur*-capitalist and *ur*-democratic countries, Great Britain and the United States, seem to be wavering in their commitment to democratic values. While a lot of soul-searching and analysis takes place, the question of how capitalism relates to democracy still has not received enough attention.

This book argues that Western societies have a choice to make.[1] They need to reform their economic systems or they will lose their democracies. They need to embed democratic values in their economic systems. Right now, the value that officially reigns supreme in the economy is efficiency, which is supposed to lead to economic growth. But efficiency and growth are not, per se, democratic values. Taken on their own, they can have deeply undemocratic implications.

The kind of capitalism we got in their name has led to soaring inequality, environmental degradation, and, in the United States and the United Kingdom, even falling life expectancies for certain demographic groups.[2] It is an economic system that serves the few, reintroduces a class society, and leaves the most vulnerable members of society to their fates.[3] These consequences are widely discussed as problems in themselves. But we also need to consider that such an economy is incompatible with a stable and flourishing democratic life.

A certain understanding of capitalism and markets has colonized the very way in which we think about, talk about, and practice democracy. It is understood in terms of a thin notion of "choice" and evaluated for its ability to efficiently cater to individuals' preferences. Public policy is expected to serve the god of efficiency as well, crowding out other values such as equality or dignity.[4] But democracy is about much more than "having a choice" on election day or being efficiently served certain public goods. Democracy starts from the premise that all members of a society have the same moral status; no one is, per se, more or less important than anyone else.[5] In a democracy, all members of society are granted a broad range of freedoms and opportunities. They "govern themselves" on the basis of equality. This means that capitalism and democracy are fundamentally in tension. Capitalism, at least in the unregulated version of the last decades, prioritizes property rights and distributes power according to ownership. Democracy, in contrast, focuses on equal personal rights and liberties, and on holding all power to account.[6] We urgently need to return to what the political scientist Sheri Berman has called a "primacy of politics"—the condition that prevailed in earlier societies where, as she writes, "markets were embedded in broader social relationships and subordinated to politics."[7] But we must also go beyond the old social-democratic recipes that fell short of recognizing the equal moral standing of citizens of all backgrounds. To do so, we need to reimagine democracy as being about more than choice. As the philosopher John Dewey famously put it, we must understand "democracy as a way of life."[8]

Democratic governments once had the upper hand in setting the rules of the economic game and deciding which values it would embody. In the post-WWII years, these values were translated into concrete policies: macroeconomic stabilization; provision of public goods in areas such as health care and education; and a welfare state to support the poor and provide safety nets. To some extent, this worked, at least for a certain demographic of white, male breadwinners and their families. The commitment to broad prosperity was implemented through various public institutions that complemented markets and private companies.

But as is well known, especially since the elections of Margaret Thatcher and Ronald Reagan in the 1980s, this democratic taming of capitalism, imperfect as it was, has unraveled.[9] Helped along by financial support from business elites, arguments about free markets as the paragons of efficiency won the day.[10] Rules and regulations meant to combine efficiency and growth with other values were rejected as outdated, prone to capture, and standing in the way of innovation and progress. Financial markets and international capital movements were deregulated, unions were smashed, and many public institutions were torn down or defunded.[11]

This has allowed economic systems to spiral out of control, away from any credible claim to deliver prosperity for all. And it has weakened democracy by subjecting more and more areas of life to the logic of capitalism. Many members of society are now, as workers, treated more as underlings than as citizens, and as consumers exposed to market behavior, often by powerful corporations, that can only be described as exploitative. Soaring inequality undermines the fair setting of the rules of the economic game. And citizens who are anxious and exhausted from trying to navigate this hostile economic environment, having no time and energy left to rebuild democracy, instead fall prey to populist snake-oil vendors. Welfare state institutions, to the extent to which they have survived, are badly in need of reform, to make sure they serve all members of society instead of privileging certain groups over others.

Of course, criticism of the current economic system is not rare. Many thinkers have pointed out the wrong assumptions on which some core policy recommendations have been based. The adoption of austerity measures, for example, to reduce public debt by spending less on social services, can have the opposite effect if consumer spending drops as a result and economic contraction leads to lower tax revenues.[12] Few of the wealth gains made at richer levels of society "trickle down" to the poorer ones—and therefore those gains increase the concentration of wealth and with it, economic power.[13] In recent years, another criticism has become louder, and rightly so: the deep concern with capitalism's harms to the environment. The term *Anthropocene* has been introduced to mainstream the idea that humanity has had such a massive impact on biogeophysical systems that it defines its own geological and climatic era. But some commentators argue that the term should really be *Capitalocene*, because it is the current form of capitalism that is to blame.[14] As calls for a directional shift have accelerated, we have seen a mushrooming of "heterodox" economic approaches rejecting the growth-driven, extractive, and exploitative capitalism that has taken hold in many Western countries.[15]

These criticisms are correct, yet they do not answer the question of what should come next in terms of values, or offer practical guidance on rethinking the relationship between democracy and the economic system. What values other than efficiency should guide economic policy, and how could these values be implemented? The problems, after all, go beyond the failure to deliver broad prosperity and beyond the environmental harms. Also at stake is the survival of democracy. These three problems are intertwined: it is unlikely that the current social and environmental issues can be successfully addressed unless democratic values win over capitalist profit-seeking.

For democracy to be stabilized, citizens need opportunities in their everyday lives to be heard and to be in control of their own decisions and actions. The economic system crucially affects both voice and agency. If it socializes individuals into non-democratic values, by casting them as rivals in Darwinian competitions or as underlings in steep hierarchies, it undermines their abilities to be good democratic citizens in their scarce free time.[16] If, instead, they encounter each other as citizens with equal dignity as they participate in markets and go to work, they are better prepared to interact with others in democratic civil society. This must be the horizon of values against which to evaluate and reform our economic system.[17]

This leads us to ask new questions, which are orthogonal to those typically asked by economists. Concerning markets, we need to ask not only whether a given market achieves an efficient equilibrium in its allocation of goods or services, but also whether it does so by attracting genuinely voluntary participation—rather than compelling submission, through sheer desperation, by people who lack alternatives. With regard to work, we need to ask not only how well it is compensated (although that question remains important, of course) but also what social relations prevail in it. To what degree are workers treated as equal citizens, with a say in the governance of firms? With regard to socioeconomic inequality, the question is not only whether it might at some point stifle innovation, but also whether it undermines the ethos and the institutions of democracy, making them mere puppet shows, public spectacles in societies best described as "post-democratic."[18]

Turning the economic system around and bringing it in line with democratic values also requires rethinking the orientation toward GDP growth that has dominated macroeconomic thinking and policies in the last decades—and challenging it not only for environmental reasons but also because the very *functions* an economic system serves must be actively determined by democratic politics. It is old news that profit-seeking individuals are not "led by an invisible hand" to act in ways that serve the common good. But democratic societies have not asked explicitly enough what it would mean for an economic system to serve the public well. Reviving democracy will require that citizens devote real time to such matters—but that can happen if productivity gains are translated into reduced working hours and people are encouraged and supported to spend the found time on civic participation. Reforms in this direction are not utopian dreams, but well within the realm of the possible—if there is enough political will to wrest democratic life from the grip of capitalism.

These are the themes explored in the following chapters. I write as a philosopher whose interdisciplinary background also includes a degree in economics and work in the social sciences. My intellectual upbringing is rooted in the (admittedly very Western) classics, an intellectual tradition of thinkers from Plato to Hegel, Arendt, Rawls, and Habermas, all exploring what a human society is and how it could be organized in a just way. It was out of curiosity, and as a backup in terms of employability, that I also studied economics— but this was a clash of worlds, both in terms of the pedagogic approaches and the implicit and explicit values embedded in these disciplines, that left me disappointed with the narrow visions of both fields.

Economics, in particular, radiated an arrogant sense of being better than all the other social sciences and humanities, because it used mathematical tools (at least, before the 2008 economic crisis).[19] I encountered it as a field in which abstract models reigned supreme and little attention was paid to actual economic life. Of course, there is nothing wrong with models per se. The problem is that, especially as used in undergraduate teaching and public discourse, they convey simplistic pictures that come with implicit value judgments, or with assumptions about what is feasible institutional design, without laying these assumptions open to discussion.[20] Economic models thereby distort and limit the imagination of how economic life could be organized, and how it could be brought in line with democratic values. The history of Western economic thought, which would help contextualize these models, is rarely taught; they are often presented as if they were universal truths. This is a kind of intellectual parochialism that can pose as universalism only because colonial and neocolonial power relations have spread this way of thinking all over the globe.[21]

On the philosophical side, the school of thought with which I have come to identify most is the pragmatist tradition that includes such thinkers as John Dewey, Jürgen Habermas, Axel Honneth, and Elizabeth Anderson.[22] What unites them is a strong belief in the moral dignity of all human beings and a rejection of the many forms of domination, exploitation, and refusal of recognition that mar our societies. Each of these thinkers envisions a society in which human beings consider themselves to be equals, across all lines of identity, ideology, and geography. Achieving this equality requires, among other things, holding power—political, economic, cultural, and in all its forms—in check through democratic control, and having a democratic culture that supports democratic institutions. As Lord Acton famously observed, "power corrupts, and absolute power corrupts absolutely."[23] Rather than starry-eyed hopefulness, this view of democracy reflects an understanding that human beings are no angels, and often not even particularly altruistic. But it also recognizes that human beings interacting with each other, on equal footing and under favorable conditions, are capable of amazing feats of social collaboration and can find ways to overcome past and ongoing injustices.

Across an academic trajectory that has taken me through several European countries and the United States, with shorter stays in Northern Africa and several Latin American countries, I have learned to appreciate the varying forms democracy takes in different places, and seeing the different socioeconomic conditions under which people live has inevitably shaped my thinking. But philosophy should not only contemplate existing social systems and compare their desirability. It must also dare to be a bit utopian, in the sense of imagining new directions that societies could take to move beyond what currently seems possible.

Developing such proposals requires "big picture" thinking of a kind that has gone out of fashion in the academic world, with its premium on ever-narrower specialization. This is what this book tries to offer, tying together a number of themes that have already generated detailed academic discussion (with apologies to those colleagues whose years-long efforts may be honored here with just a summary sentence or paragraph). The aim is to show that organizing these themes around a specific question—how to democratize the economic system—can provide a fresh orientation and show a way forward after the exhaustion of the neoliberal paradigm and its focus on efficiency alone. It can yield a vision, moreover, of how humanity, by moving from the relentless competitiveness of capitalism to the solidaristic relations of democracy, can reconcile its progress with its planetary boundaries.

Why Efficiency Alone Cannot Be the Answer

Efficiency, in the abstract, certainly sounds like a good idea: why waste things (or energy, or time) if that can be avoided? This is obviously important when it comes to the use of natural resources. It has also been assumed that increasing efficiency naturally serves other goals valued by policymakers, such as economic growth, job creation, or business cycle stability.[24] However, when elevated to the highest value that an economic system as a whole should serve, efficiency can become a highly dangerous ideal—even a deadly one. It typically translates into the imperative to keep costs low, regardless of whether the costs in focus are of raw materials or safety equipment for workers. It focuses exclusively on the means, never on the ends.[25] This can allow it to masquerade as "value neutral," while creating a dangerous blind spot with regard to the *ultimate* values that an economic system is meant to embody, and the functions it is supposed to serve.

Maybe efficiency appeals to us because it has deep roots in the evolutionary history of humanity, with its many periods of material scarcity. In times when societies are challenged by scarce resources, it makes a lot of sense to give priority to efficiency, as the imperative is to make the most of them. But just as our natural appetite is not well adjusted to a situation in which sugary and fatty foods are constantly available—inclining us toward obesity and related illnesses—our focus on efficiency does not serve us well in an era when the problem is not material scarcity as such.[26] Rather, the problems of modern economic systems are maldistribution, unfairness, lack of ecological sustainability, and insufficient mental space for even asking what one wants from the economy, as individuals and as society.

The concept of efficiency most widely used in economic theorizing is that of *Pareto efficiency,* but as a target for optimization it is actually a rather weak criterion: an allocation of resources is Pareto-efficient if there is no way of improving one agent's position without worsening the position of another.[27] Nothing is said about the equality of the resource distribution; an allocation can be extremely uneven and yet be Pareto-efficient. Another concept, known as Kaldor-Hicks efficiency, is less strict and says that a change that leaves someone worse off can still result in optimal efficiency if the side suffering the loss can (at least in theory) be *compensated* by the side making the gain. In the policymaking realm, this could mean redistributing gains made by the "winners" from a policy change to the "losers."[28] But because Kaldor-Hicks efficiency requires only that there be the theoretical possibility of such compensation, the question then is whether such compensations are actually paid. And there are always political choices to be made about *what kind* of efficiency should be pursued and through what strategies, since a given strategy may benefit some groups more than others.[29] Achieving efficiency may sound like a purely technical undertaking, but any decision about a specific way to do it is very much a matter of politics. Finally, the rhetoric of efficiency too often seems like a smoke screen being put up to obscure what is really driving the actions of parties (say, multinational corporations), which may be greed pure and simple.

Another failing of classic concepts of efficiency is that they make no distinction between efficiency gains with regard to the use of natural resources—which are of course urgently needed—and efficiency gains in other areas. These models all assume that every good has a price that adequately reflects its value, and that its use gets regulated by supply and demand. By this logic, questions about the environment translate into efforts to assign prices to environmental goods and services—but the various methods of doing so are highly controversial, and raise questions that cannot be answered by referring to efficiency alone.[30] Rather, democratic societies need to make conscious decisions about how they see the *value* of the environment, informed by environmental sciences and the best evidence on short-term and long-term effects of human behavior, but ultimately also guided by value judgments—for example, regarding justice between generations. The same holds for other areas in which the rules of the economic game need to be readjusted—for example, concerning the voice of workers within companies.

Sometimes, proposals to achieve greater efficiency are presented as trade-offs: choices to enhance efficiency at the expense of some other value. But, as the economist and public policy expert Julian Le Grand has argued, this is not a valid framing, because efficiency is not an ultimate value.[31] Economic policy is indeed often about trade-offs—for example, between the welfare of individuals and the protection of the environment. Efficiency is orthogonal to this, in that whatever trade-off of conflicting values is deemed to be the best possible balance can be achieved with greater or lesser efficiency. Le Grand also notes that it is not always clear what is meant by efficiency, the interpretation of which is "as much a complex and value-laden business as the interpretation of equity."[32] Different evaluation schemes for the environmental effects of, say, different food products, prove this point.[33]

Thus, to understand what should be done (in terms of economic policy or decisions within companies), one also must always ask: Efficient with regard to what, and for whom? If efficiency is construed as an ultimate value, it can legitimate any action designed to achieve a certain output with less input, no matter how much it harms other people, society, or the environment. In practice, one person's efficiency can be another person's loss of income, security, or quality of life—for example, when it is more efficient for a company to outsource its cleaning services to another company, and the cleaning staff (maybe even the very same individuals) find themselves in a considerably lower wage scale, with fewer benefits and longer hours. Whether or not this is a good thing, from a societal perspective, is not at all clear. The reference to efficiency can all too easily hide strategies that are ultimately deeply undemocratic, in the sense that they ascribe a greater worth to some individuals' interests than to those of others.

The values embedded in the economic system matter because they shape our thinking and our social relations. We spend so much time in economic contexts that this is almost inevitable. If these contexts are governed by efficiency alone, then other values are crowded out. Today, the average day of a normal citizen in Western countries is, arguably, shaped to a far greater degree by economic pressures than by democratic freedoms—and this is especially true of those individuals who are less privileged along the lines of gender, race, class, and their intersections. Individuals often meet others in relations of either hierarchy or competition; these hierarchical and competitive institutions are justified by their alleged efficiency (despite no serious consideration of whether they really are the most efficient arrangements). But they create a social environment that can be deeply inimical to a culture of democratic equality. Democracies need democratically minded citizens who defend and sustain democratic institutions. If the economic system provides no space for learning democratic habits, where is that learning supposed to happen?

Another reason that efficiency is a dangerous ideal for democratic societies is that it neglects questions of power. The highly unequal amounts of societal influence and political power that we see today are incompatible with the principle of equal political influence that is at the core of democracy.[34] To be sure, money's influence on politics can be reduced in various ways—for example, by regulating campaign donations—and democracies should certainly use such strategies. But democracy can bear only so much economic inequality without becoming a sham. We need to stop focusing on efficiency alone, and explicitly ask how much inequality we want to tolerate, from a democratic perspective.

Is this a call to abolish capitalism? It depends on what one means by capitalism, and what one sees as alternatives. We do need massive changes, and we need a reassertion of the power of democracy, undistorted by financial interests, over the rules of the economic game. Some changes proposed here overlap with the rejection, on the left, of "cannibal capitalism."[35] Others align with libertarian criticisms of "crony capitalism."[36] What the libertarians fail to appreciate is the power of human beings to coordinate action and solve problems in ways that go beyond markets—including through interventions by government institutions. This is certainly not to say that all markets should be replaced with large-scale, undemocratic bureaucracies with authoritarian features, like those of the Soviet bloc. Just like capitalism, socialism can take many different forms, and different commentators mean different things by it.

Politically speaking, the framing of the debate in terms of capitalism versus socialism is distinctively unhelpful, first because of this vagueness, but also because it derails so many practical and needed changes on which reasonable people from different ideological camps can agree (a point that Chapter 4 will explore, particularly with regard to discussions about "green growth" and "degrowth"). The contrast between "free" capitalist economies and "unfree" socialist systems stems from the Cold War period and was a propagandistic simplification even then.[37] That framing does little to illuminate today's challenges. More helpful is a focus on democratic values, not least because this can allow coalitions to be built across traditional party lines. And no matter what label we use, the resulting economic system needs to be compatible with human life on a finite planet, given that climate change is real and is only one of many environmental crises we face.

This book will suggest various changes to the economic system to achieve more democratic regulation of markets and more democratic participation by workers in companies, to embrace the democratic imperative to reduce inequality, to shift the focus from *growth* to democratically determined *functions*, and to move more of people's time away from capitalist wage labor and toward democratic collaboration. The proposed reforms, together with the learning processes along the way, would add up to true change in the relation between our political and economic systems.

Which Democracy Should We Want?

The argument set forth here proceeds with a vision of democracy very different from the one criticized above—the currently widespread vision that reduces democracy to individual choice.[38] That latter understanding of democracy has a venerable history, going back to the Austrian economist Joseph A. Schumpeter, and is sometimes described as a "realist" view. Schumpeter had a negative view of human nature: he assumed individuals to be egoistic, impulsive, and fickle.[39] The exceptions for him were the few truly outstanding entrepreneurs, the bringers of "creative destruction," whom he celebrated in his economic writings.[40] Moreover, it was his assumption that all societies have elite groups the members of which hold more power than ordinary people. What differentiated democracy from other forms of government, in his view, was that democracies had various elite groups competing for votes, and could, through regular elections, effect peaceful changeovers of elites without bloodshed. This may sound normatively undemanding, but it does presuppose that the different elite groups accept basic democratic principles, and relinquish power when they are voted out.

In this tradition, the competition for votes is seen as analogous to competition in markets, and hence it is not surprising that theorists have used the formal tools of economic theorizing to model democratic behavior. This "economic theory of democracy" mostly focuses on elections.[41] It has affinities with "social choice theory," which analyzes the aggregation of individual preferences with similar methodological tools.[42] There is nothing wrong with using such tools. But like all models, they create blind spots and throw light on certain aspects of reality at the cost of others. For example, their methodological individualism suggests that individuals' preferences and varying levels of information are among the most crucial parameters for understanding democracy, but neglects questions about preference formation, the collective provision of information (knowledge is a public good, after all!), intermediary institutions, and the social and cultural dimensions of democracy.

In recent years, such a thinned-out, purely procedural understanding of democracy has led to deeply undemocratic proposals, such as to give up the basic principle of "one person, one vote," and to give more weight to more "competent" voters.[43] But if we understand democracy as just another opportunity for individual choice, like any other market, we lose sight of all deeper questions about democratic values, democratic institutions, and a democratic culture.

In defense, an adherent of such an account of democracy might say that at least it does not put heavy burdens on individuals, and might also, by being so minimalist, be more stable. But this argument is problematic for several reasons. If democracy is understood as nothing but elections and representative institutions, it remains at a distance from the everyday lives of people and can all too easily be perceived by citizens as just another sphere of power. Other aspects of society can, in such an understanding of democracy, follow completely different logics. But this would mean that individuals were not embedded in social environments in which democratic values were a lived experience. And that in turn raises the question of how stable democratic institutions can be if they are not populated by individuals who understand the importance of democratic principles and are willing to defend them because they are imbued with a democratic ethos. In a proper understanding of democracy, the *social relations* between individuals matter as well: people need to be able to relate to each other as equal participants in the project of governing their common affairs. This has implications for how much difference in status and material wealth a democratic society can admit, as later chapters will explore.

Moreover, elections are one of the most antagonistic elements of democracy: they are about winning and losing, and attacking one's opponents is part of the game, up to a point that can be debated. But this combative dimension of democracy needs to be balanced by other democratic values such as cooperativeness, mutual respect, and willingness on all sides to uphold democratic institutions and procedures. If public attention focuses on election campaigns alone, citizens will likely come to see democracy as just another kind of public spectacle, on a par with sports leagues or Olympic games—and it is a sad irony that critics of democracy then disparage it for reducing politics to the equivalent of sports rivalries, with citizens just cheering for their opposing teams.[44]

For democracy to be stabilized, it needs to be thickened. Democratic values need to be present in society as a whole and on people's minds consistently, not just on election day. And these values need to be broader than the competitiveness that surrounds elections. First and foremost, they need to include a commitment to the moral equality of all citizens and the willingness to govern society together in a democratic way. Doing so requires the willingness to listen to each other, but also to accept certain basic facts, as established by solid methodologies, rather than sticking to one's own wishful thinking. For it is only if one is willing to acknowledge that there is a shared reality out there, on which one's own perspective is but one among many, that one can start to think about how to *govern* this shared reality together.[45]

Honoring these democratic values requires, at the very least, that other spheres of society do not *undermine* these commitments—as is, arguably, currently the case in the economy. But if a democratic ethos is not actively fostered anywhere in society, one wonders from where it is supposed to come. Noted above was John Dewey's description of democracy as a way of life. Such an understanding of democracy implies that democratic values should be embedded in all spheres of life that can be described as public—that concern several individuals or groups, that is, with potentially conflicting values or interests. As should be obvious, the economy is such a sphere, and one in which the distance to democratic values is at this moment particularly great.

This approach also has a dynamic element: it implies that one always needs to ask how democracy can be improved, or where it needs to be repaired because hostile forces, or the simple ravages of time, have made some of its institutions or its ethos brittle.[46] Arguably, many democratic societies are currently going through a phase in which their formal institutions have aged. Democracy was taken for granted for too long, with not enough attention being paid to the need for maintenance work. It is by keeping up this attentiveness, and by doing that repair work, that democracy can, today, be stabilized and defended against its open and covert enemies. Given my interest in the economic system, my focus will not be on, for example, defending equal voting rights (though even these are under attack in some countries) but on repairing the economic institutions and practices that currently undermine the material conditions and social status of equal democratic citizenship. In this area, reform is possible through changes in social norms and democratic majorities, in a much more straightforward sense than when it comes to, say, changing certain elements of "culture" directly.

Putting labels from political science on these arguments, I am here arguing for participatory democracy, with a strong deliberative element. *Participation* means the active involvement of citizens, while *deliberation* means that citizens exchange opinions, perspectives and arguments, and are willing to give in to the "persuasive force of the better argument."[47] Deliberative democracy has, in recent years, become the dominant strand in theorizing about democracy.[48] It can go hand in hand with, and normatively undergird, the mechanisms of representative democracy, but it is more demanding. It requires a certain culture of public discourse and a specific approach to institutional power. Take the example of parliaments: their members must be willing to respect the voice of others and to find solutions that all sides can live with. This is certainly not always easy. It is exhausting to listen to those with whom one disagrees, and it often takes time to figure out compromises. But it brings much stronger legitimacy to democratic decisions. They are not just pushed through by the winners of elections; rather, different parties have grappled with the problems at hand and tried to find the best solution.

I accept these normative arguments, but I worry that by focusing on deliberation alone, one relies on an overly intellectualist account of human nature (always a temptation for philosophers). It is not enough for citizens to discuss things—in private, in public, on social media or in person—and for professional politicians to then try to channel these discussions into policy proposals through further discussions in governmental bureaucracies and parliamentary committees. In addition, citizens need to be able to actively participate in processes of democratic decision-making, together with others.[49] Of course, not everyone can sit in parliament. But such decision-making processes can also take place at many other levels and in many other areas of life: in local government, but also in civic society associations, or (as Chapter 2 will argue) in workplaces. With democratic participation in various spheres of life, a real redistribution of power, away from elites toward normal citizens, can be achieved.

This can help build a democratic culture from the ground up, and it also creates opportunities for individuals to get engaged and to meet those "others" who are their fellow citizens, in concrete real-life settings. And if the different levels and venues of democratic participation are interlinked, then ideas and arguments can travel more easily between them, making the whole system more responsive to the concerns of citizens.[50] Given that people are differently situated and that opportunities for putting political issues on the agenda are contingent on various factors, "equality of opportunity for political influence" may remain an aspirational ideal.[51] And yet, we can certainly do better than we are doing now. Offering more, and more varied, opportunities for democratic participation is an essential strategy for improvement. This also means that talented individuals can be spotted and recruited in a broader variety of settings, and representative institutions can become more representative of society as a whole, rather than consisting predominantly of rich, highly educated individuals from the dominant ethnic groups.[52]

Such a participatory vision of democracy requires a complex institutional framework, and also complex checks and balances between institutions. Together, they need to hold the powerful to account, guarantee the rule of law and the equal standing of all members of society, ensure an open public discourse in which different voices and perspectives can be heard, and create opportunities for citizens to get involved in running their common affairs. These institutions need to be considered from a systemic perspective, because their interplay matters: how one specific institution works, and whether it succeeds in realizing specific democratic values, can depend decisively on how other institutions work. To take two brief examples: labor markets can take on very different characters with or without the presence of unions; legal systems work differently in more or less socioeconomically divided societies.

This is certainly a more complex view of democracy than a rational choice model of voter behavior. But given how complex modern societies are, with their extreme division of labor and their broad pluralism of values, this should not come as a surprise. Complex societies need a complex set of institutions to strike the right balance between individual rights and the common good, between the values of specific communities and more broadly shared principles, and between so many other poles that democratic politics need to navigate.

This is not a view of democracy based on *community*, in the sense of a close-knit social fabric that connects everyone to everyone else and that is backed up by a shared national culture or even nationalist pride.[53] Instead, it is a view that takes seriously the plurality of communities within our societies, with their different worldviews and daily practices. But it assumes that there is a sufficient overlap of values between these groups—in John Rawls's phrase, an "overlapping consensus."[54] The various groups share a commitment to upholding the democratic structures that create the conditions for their peaceful coexistence. The revolutionary socialist Rosa Luxemburg famously insisted that freedom can only be understood as freedom for those who think differently.[55] Certainly, a plurality of perspectives is needed in any democracy, and along with a shared willingness to grant the same rights to others that one claims for oneself.[56]

My view also differs from another way of thinking about democracy, which has become popular among the left in recent years. In this approach, sometimes derided as "identity politics," there is a strong focus on matters of culture and language—for example, an inclusive use of gender pronouns—to express one's concern for democratic values. The ways in which we see each other and talk to and about our fellow citizens are hugely important for democratic life. If, despite formally equal rights, certain groups are not seen as belonging to "us," or if our language fails to take seriously the dignity of all human beings, this is a grave problem for democracy. And yet, the focus of discussion in these approaches has been too narrow. The culture and language that develop between individuals cannot be decoupled from the power relations between them—and these power relations in turn have to do with more dimensions of social life than just culture and language, and notably with economic relations.[57] Cultural changes without changes in economic power relations risk staying at the surface, and thus always remain vulnerable to backsliding. The fights for more justice for non-white and non-male individuals have received a lot of attention in recent years.[58] They need, however, to include a socioeconomic dimension and join forces with those who fight for changing economic power relations.

Maybe in other societies, or in other periods, one would have to think about other threats to a stable and flourishing democratic life. Religion can be such a threat, and maybe we can also imagine scenarios in which, say, certain artistic practices could create risks for democracy—for example, because they promote deeply undemocratic ideas about the divide between "the geniuses" and "the masses." But today, it is the economic system that poses the greatest threat to democracy. And contrary to what some people might think about religion or art, you cannot abolish the economy: all societies need *some* way to organize the human metabolism with nature and to allocate goods and services. The current way is undemocratic and unsustainable, and if we do not reform it, we can save neither the environment nor democracy.

How to Democratize the Economy

The following chapters will spell out what democracy can mean with regard to different aspects of the economic system. The aim here is to guide the uninitiated through the arguments that economic philosophers have discussed in recent years—but also to provide food for thought for those already familiar with these debates. Inevitably, my own position will shine through in how the discussions are presented. I also provide some new arguments—most notably, for shifting the current discussion of "green growth versus postgrowth" to a more fruitful one about economic functions and democratic power; and for focusing more attention on "time politics," with the objective of reducing working time, not only as an aspect of individual welfare but for the sake of democracy.

The paragraphs below provide a high-level preview of the chapters to follow. First, however, a few elements that are *not* to be found in this book should be noted. Left out, for reasons of space, are changes in political systems, such as campaign finance. Much has already been written about them, and doing justice to any of these proposals would require detailed engagement with the political institutions and cultures of specific countries.[59] Neither is there discussion here about the role of media organizations and their interplay with economic interests.[60] Instead, the focus is on the connection between democratic values and economic institutions, and even within this realm, topic choices are somewhat selective. There is, for example, no engagement with possible reforms of the monetary and financial system.[61] Ideas with potential to make the *international* economic order fairer and more democratic are also out of scope.[62] And the reforms needed in specific economic sectors, such as education, the housing market, and the health care system, are not spelled out. The book is forward-looking, in the sense that it does not provide an analysis of how we got into the current situation.[63] Rather, it proceeds from the assumption that the neoliberal paradigm has exhausted itself, and that we need a new understanding of the values that orient economic policy.

The chapters that follow will develop the broader argument for democratizing the economy, looking at different core concepts of economics and dimensions of economic reality. The text will challenge many existing arguments and assumptions, often based on economic theorizing, as to why certain institutions should be organized the way they currently are. The hope is to show that our institutions can and should be organized differently, in line with democratic values.

Up first for examination is a key institution of current economic systems—the market—with a focus on the variety of forms it can take on and why democracies need to prevent markets from turning extractive. As will be shown in Chapter 1, it is misleading to think of the current economic system as only a "market economy," because it is dominated by corporations, which follow a rather different logic. The combination of markets and corporations has resulted in a refeudalization of the economy in which economic and political power are ever more closely intertwined. Aligning markets with democratic values is therefore an urgent task. With this established, the work of Chapter 2 is to open up the internal social relations of corporations and other workplaces, and to ask how democratic citizens should understand their role as workers. The short answer is that they need to be able to relate to each other and to their employers not as underlings but as equals, and there are strong arguments and concrete proposals for democratizing work.

Democratic relations at the workplace are not enough, however, and unlikely to make a real difference, if material inequality remains at the levels at which it stands today. Therefore, Chapter 3 turns to inequality, first by rejecting some arguments that seemingly justify an unequal distribution of income and wealth. It then explores the dangers for democratic societies: inequality leads to an unequal distribution of power, it invites the formation of different social classes, and it pushes citizens into a never-ending rat race of status-seeking. More egalitarian societies not only have better chances to preserve democracy, but also allow for more socially useful forms of innovation.

These arguments about reforms of markets, workplaces, and mechanisms that generate inequality explain how our economic systems could be brought better in line with democratic values, but they do not yet explain what the orientation of economic policy should be. In the past, this orientation was toward GDP growth, which has led to criticisms especially from an environmental angle. Therefore, Chapter 4 turns to the question of whether democratic societies should pursue "green growth" or "degrowth." It turns out that the proponents of these camps are less distant from each other than is often thought, at least when it comes to concrete policy proposals. This chapter argues for a decisive shift away from today's prevailing, undifferentiated commitment to GDP growth—and a reorientation to a democratic politics that determines the sustainable social functions of the economy.

All these proposals, however (and more generally speaking, the democratization of the economy), will be difficult to achieve if citizens are caught in endless hours of work. Chapter 5 takes up a topic that is crucial for the realizability of reform: the politics of time. Not only do democracies need to find a better balance between paid and unpaid work, they also need to give citizens more time to do work that will not yield profits in markets but is needed by society. A four-day workweek could be a concrete step in this direction, freeing up energies for the renewal of the democratic project. Finally, Chapter 6 reflects further on the possibilities of reforms substantial enough to change the fundamental power structures of the economy. It discusses the role of social norm change, and highlights the reasons that, despite all challenges, there is hope for democracy.

The reforms proposed in this book are urgently needed to stabilize democracy, but their importance goes even beyond that: they also offer an opportunity to *deepen* democracy and to fulfill democratic promises that have so far remained unmet. We do not need a perfect blueprint of the best possible economic system ever; we can start with those areas in most dire need of repair and study other countries' approaches to discover what might work.[64] The greatest promise of the changes described here would be to make average citizens, and especially those most disadvantaged by the current economic system, freer and more able to flourish in very tangible ways, and in ways that allow them in turn to do their bit to strengthen democracy.

1

MARKETS, CORPORATIONS, AND THEIR ALLIANCE AGAINST DEMOCRACY

At first glance, markets may seem the perfect way for democratic citizens to regulate their economic affairs. People meet, maybe in a town square, some with wares and some with needs to fill, and after a bit of consideration and haggling, goods and money change hands and all leave happier than before. When described in this way, the market mechanism seems as if nothing could ever be wrong with it.

Occasionally, one finds such markets in real life. A few years ago, I was looking for a new dress, hoping to buy one that was organically sourced and fairly produced. I found a shop in a hip neighborhood of Berlin that offered an amazing range of organic and fair-trade clothes. After trying on a few things, I settled on a red summer dress. The elderly guy at the checkout, apparently the owner of the shop, smiled when I handed it over to him. "I sewed this myself," he said. "See the sewing machine over there? That's where I made it." I couldn't but mirror his smile. And I realized that this was a rare moment—I could not remember ever before having met in person the producer of a piece of clothing I had bought.

This discussion of democratization of the economy starts with markets because it is a widespread assumption that we live in "market economies." Moreover, markets seem to be a natural match to democracy: both are often described as being based on individual freedoms and as allowing all members of society to get involved in social systems as equals. And yet, many markets we see today are a long way from this vision. The unwholesome effects of corporations on markets, in particular, have deeply undemocratic implications. In many markets, the people who produce goods disappear behind long supply chains, and consumers see only impersonal brand names—the shop in Berlin was an exception. And of course, not everyone is privileged enough to have the leisure to stroll around looking for clothes, and money to buy what they want.

A similarly happy example of market exchange appears in a book about the role of markets in society: it describes a woman using her "economic freedom" to open a dog-grooming business. The example is presented as if all markets had the same harmless features.[1] But markets can also show a very different face, one that is incompatible with democratic values. For many producers, markets mean competition: relentless pressure to lower costs to please and keep customers. For consumers with little purchasing power, markets are often realms from which they are excluded: while others have a lot of choice, they stand at the margins, sifting in cheap outlets or secondhand shops through the metaphorical breadcrumbs that fall off the table. Markets are also, for all the choice they offer, often confusing and exhausting. With so much choice, how does one find the right product, and make sure there are no treacherous clauses in the fine print?

Critics see markets as one of the causes of the social ills our economic system produces: environmental pollution, high inequality, and financial insecurity. Often decried as the loss of traditional bonds, "marketization" may have had a liberating dimension at first, but also throws individuals into a cold, gray world of grim competition. "All that is solid melts into air," the authors of the *Communist Manifesto* wrote, and the unleashing of market forces was one of the catalyzing factors they had in mind.[2]

What, then, should one think about markets from a democratic perspective? This chapter's first argument will be that democrats cannot be "for" or "against" markets in the abstract. Markets can take on very different forms, some of which are in line with democratic values while others are in deep tension with them, or even undermine them. Their form depends on how they are regulated through legal and social norms.

This, in turn, leads to the question of who determines market regulation: the citizens of society, through democratic politics, or those who are meant to be regulated—the currently powerful players in the economic system? Anti-democratic distortions in the regulation of markets typically come about because there are imbalances of power. The collective organizations that could speak for workers and consumers have been massively weakened, and as for the natural environment, it has no systematic representation at all. Corporations are the most powerful collective agents still standing after half a century of neoliberalism.[3]

The chapter's second argument, therefore, is that we cannot understand the role that markets play in today's societies unless we also take into account the role of corporations—not because there could not also be imbalances of power and exploitative relations among private individuals, but because the imbalances of power among corporations and individuals are so much greater, and the risk of violations of democratic values, therefore, is much higher. Corporations, as they are currently set up, are legal entities created to maximize value for shareholders—and despite all criticisms, this is still the principle most corporations live by. And all too often, they create profits not by creating genuine value for society, but by engaging in extractive social practices that are incompatible with democratic values.

Corporations often attempt, moreover, to bend markets in their own favor. They have the financial firepower to influence the rules more effectively than other market participants. This is how markets that are supposed to be competitive can easily become feudal bastions of unequal market power. Historical research confirms this pattern, raising the vital question of where the relation of markets to democracy stands today.

These arguments do not amount to a complete rejection of markets. Paradoxically, it is when they are embedded in a rich array of non-market institutions that markets can function best, from a democratic perspective. And this brings us to the chapter's last argument: markets need to be embedded in a broader institutional framework, and oriented toward the public good. Most of the time, this does not even make them less efficient in an economic sense, because unregulated or badly regulated markets typically fail to deliver the mutual benefits imagined by friends of markets.

The discussion starts by describing the logic of markets, and then moves to the very different logic of corporations. It is especially from their interplay that risks for democracy arise: marketization, by increasing inequality and thus also unequal political influence, can lead to forms of refeudalization that are deeply at odds with democratic values. To avoid this, democratic societies need to design markets according to their own values. Ultimately, however, democratic societies can give only so much space to markets and must draw strict limits around them. They cannot understand themselves as "market societies" or allow markets to be the ultimate ordering principle of social relations.

The Logic of Markets

Markets are a specific way of organizing social interactions, with their own institutional logic. Central to them is the price mechanism: it brings together those who want to sell goods or services, and those who want to buy them, mediated by money.[4] Sellers typically have a minimum price below which they cannot sell without incurring a loss, and they would prefer to sell for a higher price. Buyers typically have a maximum price up to which their willingness to pay extends; the lower the price, the more likely they are to buy. These, at least, are the behavioral assumptions that go into the classic understanding of markets.[5] After some haggling and bargaining, an equilibrium price forms, at a point at which all possibilities for mutually beneficial exchanges are exhausted.[6] Other theories of markets put more emphasis on their dynamic aspects: from that perspective, their advantage is the constant adaptation of prices to the changing conditions of supply and demand.[7]

This logic of interaction can take place only if certain other institutions are in place. Almost all theorists of markets agree that property rights need to be legally enforced and socially accepted—otherwise, one gets robbery, extortion, and piracy instead of peaceful exchange. Moreover, institutions for the enforcement of contracts and the resolution of conflicts are needed. Most markets that exist today in Western countries are embedded in complex legal structures that regulate, for example, what happens if a product is not delivered as promised. To be sure, some markets have long existed below the radar of the legal system—black markets, as they are often called—and may always exist.[8] Without belittling the problems (and maybe sometimes opportunities) of such markets, the focus in what follows will be on markets that operate within the frameworks set by legal rules.

In addition to property rights and contract enforcement, numerous other legal rules impact the regulation of markets: the tax system (including the subsidies that are paid to certain industries or individuals), health and safety standards at work, the legal forms that are available for businesses, and so on. Some theorists—and maybe even more so, lay people not familiar with economic theorizing—are suspicious of any such regulations. They see them as intrusions into what would otherwise be a pure realm of property rights in which individuals trade with each other free from government interference. But this is a misleading picture. The property rights in market goods are themselves part of the regulatory framework that exists thanks to, and whose details are shaped by, government.[9]

A critic might reply that property rights must have greater normative weight than, say, health and safety standards in fast food restaurants. The government has no right to interfere with people's private homes or other private items, she might say. But the form of private property for which this intuition is most plausible is *personal* property, not *productive* property that one invests to earn money (and individuals might very well decide *not* make money with personal property because this would feel like a degradation).[10] What individuals, and in particular corporations, typically make money with in markets are different types of items: buildings, machinery, or intellectual property. Property rights for them can exist only as part of complex social structures in which—at the very least—the costs for their enforcement through legal institutions need to be recuperated through tax contributions.

Property rights can be carved out in very different ways, moreover, which are more or less beneficial for the owners themselves, but also for other members of society and *their* rights.[11] For example, the property in a piece of a land need not be understood as entailing the right to pollute it so much that adjacent communities suffer health problems. What can be done with productive property is a question of the rules that a democratic society gives itself, weighing the interests of different groups, both owners and non-owners.

In addition to legal rules, social norms can also play a role in determining the character of markets. Market participants obey them because they do not want to be frowned upon by others or cause public outcry.[12] Social norms are often imagined as the "soft" counterpart to the "hard" framework of coercive legal rules. But some social norms are extremely tenacious, for better or worse. They can rule out behavior that would violate democratic values and thereby make markets better—for example, if such behavior is seen as incompatible with the "honor of a merchant."[13] But they can also entrench inequalities and insider-outsider dynamics in insidious and undemocratic ways, as when individuals from certain social backgrounds are not considered as potential business partners in markets.[14]

This is why one sees a broad variety of markets, across history and across geographies, some of which look harmless and beneficial from a democratic perspective, and others highly problematic. As the economic sociologist Neil Fligstein puts it, markets are "social constructions that reflect the unique political-cultural construction of their firms and nations."[15] From a democratic perspective, this variety needs to be taken seriously.

It is telling that the defenders of markets often use examples of small businesses whose founders, embedded in local communities, depend on the continued goodwill of their customers. The example of a woman opening a dog parlor mentioned earlier comes from John Tomasi, a US-American philosopher defending a market-based vision of society. He affectionately depicts the imaginary case of "Amy," who opens "Amy's Pup-in-the-Tub."[16] Such a business will be a success only if Amy delivers genuine value to her customers (although most dog owners probably wouldn't mind there also being regulations governing how dogs are handled in the grooming process, to prevent mistreatment). There is little Amy could do to exploit others because, presumably, no paying customer is existentially dependent on her services. But it is highly misleading to generalize from Amy's dog parlor to all other forms of market activity. The transactions between Amy and other market participants can be described as genuinely productive: both sides benefit, and no third parties are harmed (although she might well harm competitors, a point explored below). Many market transactions are not like this.

Exploitation will here refer to the unfair treatment of individuals (typically, workers) and *extraction* will refer to the profit-driven use of natural resources in ways that harm the environment and often, as consequence, also local populations. In exploitative market relations, individuals or companies take advantage of their power over certain groups to subject them to their one-sided will and to extract benefits from them.[17] The transactions can appear "voluntary" at first sight: workers take on jobs even though the pay is low and the working conditions are abysmal.[18] And yet, they are problematic from a democratic perspective because they are based on unjustified power rather than on genuine consent: these workers simply have no alternative source of income.

The use of the term *extractive* here draws especially on strands of thought from Latin America reflecting these countries' experience with foreign corporations entering their markets.[19] Such companies have often perpetuated patterns of racist, colonial exploitation and subjected local populations to miserable working conditions. They have appropriated land and other natural resources on a large scale, overexploiting them for export and destroying not only the natural environment, such as by replacing rainforest by soy plantations, but also the livelihoods of local communities, such as by polluting water supplies.[20] These neo-extractive patterns can happen because companies are in cahoots with local officials; resistance has often been met with violence.

Amy's happy dog parlor, and strip-mining operations in the Brazilian rainforest that irreversibly harm the environment and exploit the local workforce—both are instances of markets. And yet, with regard to their compatibility with democratic values, they are completely different. This illustrates the argument that, from a democratic perspective, one needs to look at markets not in the abstract, but in the (admittedly dazzling) variety of forms they take on in real life. And of course, exploitative and extractive practices do not exist only in the Global South but also in many markets in the Global North. Laws and regulations that are meant to prevent them, by protecting vulnerable groups and the environment, have often been

Markets, Corporations, and Their Alliance against Democracy 33

slashed, or continue to exist on paper but go unenforced because public authorities are underfunded.

Lying between purely productive and purely exploitative or extractive markets are what economic theory, since David Ricardo, calls *rents:* payments that the owners of scarce assets such as land can extract from others because their assets are scarce and their owners have market power.[21] Rents can arise because of insufficient market competition, or because of regulation that creates artificial scarcity. For example, many legal theorists argue that the way in which the regulation of intellectual property (IP) rights functions today creates rents: their owners can extract higher profits from other parties than would be needed for ensuring the production of the IP-protected products.[22] The greater the imbalance of power between the parties, the more transactions shift to the rent-seeking and exploitative end of the spectrum, at which even the most basic interests of market participants are no longer sacrosanct, as for example in the payday lending industry in the United States.[23]

It is not helpful to frame this debate in terms of *how much* regulation there is for different markets. Instead, the right question to ask is: Who benefits from the regulation, and whose rights and interests are protected by it? It is true, as friends of markets often hold, that a complex tangle of rules can make it more difficult to do business—but such rules are often necessary to protect the environment and the rights of individuals and groups. Without them, market participants are given license to collect rents or to use exploitative or extractive strategies, instead of creating genuinely productive business models. And the players that do so are often sufficiently powerful to do so, because they are not individual owners of dog parlors, but representatives of a very specific kind of entity: the corporation. Because, in today's world, corporations shape the reality of many markets, and often for the worse, it is necessary to understand their logic, which is quite different from that of markets.

The Logic of Corporations

Amy's happy dog parlor is a family business: as the owner, she is liable with her private fortune if the business goes bankrupt (which is why a shrewd Amy might in fact opt for a different legal form). Many other market participants are not like this: they are not human individuals, but legal entities that can employ thousands and millions of human beings, and possess huge amounts of assets. As such, it should not come as a surprise that they often have immense power: financial power in the first place, which they can translate into legal power (by paying for the best lawyers) or political power (through lobbying and campaign contributions). It is a curious fact that these huge collective entities have been embraced by many commentators who think of themselves as "pro market," even though they follow a completely different logic.

Legally speaking, corporations are a curious construct: they are entities of their own, with their own internal governance structures.[24] Their shareholders do not actually own the corporation and its possessions (premises, buildings, machinery, and so on). Rather, they own their shares. There is a legal firewall between the corporation and the private property of the shareholders; if a corporation goes bankrupt, its shareholders are not liable and their private fortunes are not at risk beyond the loss they will take on that investment. Conversely, if a shareholder declares bankruptcy, the corporation is not affected, because the shares held by that person will simply change hands.

The shareholders, as a group, have some power over the management of the corporation: they can issue a vote of no confidence and require a new leadership to be installed. But this is a very different kind of right than the right one has over private property in a family business or partnership. In these cases, ownership comes with the flip side of full liability. In the case of corporations, the risks for owners are massively reduced, and not only because of the legal separation of the corporation. Shareholders also typically manage their risk by diversifying their portfolios, holding shares in many different corporations.

Why do such legal constructs exist? Corporate legal personhood has a long history, covering, for example, medieval cities and universities.[25] But the modern corporation arose for the more specific purpose of amassing large amounts of money for risky commercial enterprises. In the colonial age, joint-stock companies were the legal vehicles for shipping expeditions.[26] In the United States, the construction of railroad lines in the nineteenth century led to a boom in incorporations. Early corporations had to explicitly ask the government for the privilege of incorporation, which they usually did with a specific purpose in mind. Over time, the process was standardized and was made accessible to companies of all kinds, without any questions being asked about their purpose.

Corporations have certain advantages. Few individuals would be willing to take on private liability for large, complex business operations, and such business operations have the potential to bring great benefits to societies—at least in principle. Internally, corporations function by planning, not by coordination through market prices. But this is very often needed: as economist Ronald Coase has famously argued, the transaction costs (of getting information, negotiating a deal, and so on) for many exchanges are too high for markets to develop.[27] Instead, employees are integrated into hierarchical organizational structures in which their tasks can be discussed as they go along, and they can collaborate in teams to solve the problems at hand. This creates the conditions for gains from collaboration and economies of scale.

But corporations also create great risks. They contribute to the concentration of capital, which reinforces the risk of one-sided power relations.[28] And in recent decades, they have been understood more and more as single-mindedly oriented toward one goal: increased profits for shareholders.[29] Gone are the days, if they ever existed, in which corporations understood themselves as a broad alliance of interests—of shareholders, but also workers, suppliers, local communities, and so on—and saw it as their task to find mutually beneficial outcomes.[30] Instead, the logic of profit-maximization means that, in the words of critic Joel Bakan, corporations are "externalization machines": they try to pass on costs to, and extract profits from, other parties wherever they can, not because of the evil character of their members, but because this is what they are programmed to do, and what their members are incentivized for.[31]

Why does this matter for understanding the character of markets? It matters because in many markets, the "participants" are extremely diverse; some are human individuals or small family businesses, others are corporations. Therefore, the distribution of bargaining power is highly unequal: most of the time, corporations depend much less on specific workers or suppliers than those workers or suppliers depend on the job or the commission from the corporation. The picture changes somewhat if workers are also collectively organized—the role historically played by unions—but this is often not the case. The worst forms of exploitation and extractivism often arise in situations in which governments do not protect individuals, communities, and the environment, against corporations.

Economics textbooks sometimes use the term *homo oeconomicus* for the model of human behavior that students should learn: a figure that is single-mindedly interested in maximizing their "utility," understood in monetary terms.[32] Many critics have pointed out that this is not how human beings behave in real life: they are motivated by a much broader range of factors, including their reputations among peers and their altruism toward loved ones.[33] The irony of how *corporations* currently function, however, is that they, as legal entities, are often the perfect *homo economicus:* they are programmed to do whatever maximizes their profits.

Recognizing the role of corporations is crucial to understanding the processes by which the rules for markets are set. In an ideal

Markets, Corporations, and Their Alliance against Democracy 37

world, these would be determined by the forces of democratic discourse: by public discussion, which then gets taken up by policymakers and results in laws and regulations that steer businesses in directions deemed justified and useful by society.[34] But given the money at stake when the rules of markets change, those with much to gain or lose do not sit idle. They work to influence the democratic process, whether by swaying public discourse or by lobbying politicians.[35]

Of course, other lobby groups do the same, from unions to NGOs to rich individuals. But often, corporations are simply the most powerful players in this game. Moreover, they benefit from the fact that their interests are concentrated, while those of consumers or workers are more dispersed. This is an old argument, often associated with the name of institutional economist Mancur Olson.[36] But already Adam Smith had noted the tendency of "people of the same trade" to collaborate in what ends up being "a conspiracy against the public, or ... some contrivance to raise prices."[37] Today, this often happens not through direct collusion but by powerful players bending the rules of markets in their own favor.

Sometimes, corporations play this game in extremely dirty ways, leaving behind any expectation of truthful public communication. A famous case in point is the so-called tobacco strategy, first used by tobacco corporations in the mid-twentieth century to prevent the regulation of smoking when its harmfulness became more and more scientifically evident.[38] Sensing the dangers for their business model, the tobacco industry developed a counternarrative. In its center was the claim that the scientific results were still inconclusive, and that many other possible explanations for the rising numbers of lung cancer deaths could be found. This narrative was rolled out in public discourse, with thousands of leaflets being sent to doctors and public officials. Regulation of the market for tobacco products was painted in the darkest colors, as a kind of slippery slope toward Soviet-style authoritarianism—a trope that fitted the zeitgeist.

Such practices are not limited to tobacco. The list of corporate lies and crimes is long, and the less counterpower there is in a society, the more corporations can get away with. It is far from obvious that they should continue to exist at all in their current form. Why hand out the privilege of incorporation for the sheer pursuit of profits, rather than for specific, socially beneficial purposes? (And why not also grant that privilege only to companies with internal democratic structures? This point will be taken up in the next chapter.) For now, what is crucial to understand is that markets as we see them today are populated not only by human individuals as workers or consumers, and by cute family businesses like Amy's Pup-in-the-Tub, but by legally created behemoths that rightly raise fear in anyone who comes into conflict with them.

Marketization and Refeudalization

If one considers markets *together* with corporations, it becomes obvious why it is so important to govern them democratically. For otherwise there is a risk that the interplay of markets, market actors, and regulators will lead to a refeudalization of the economy.[39] In such a system, some players have power over others for which there is no counterpower, no accountability, and no checks and balances. This means that, for example, when a general shock happens, powerful players can shift the costs of adaption to weaker links in the chain. The most vulnerable individuals are hit hardest—as seen during the Covid pandemic in many Western fashion chains' dealings with suppliers in countries from the Global South, which harmed workers already disadvantaged by their low bargaining power.[40]

Let us assume that we begin with a more or less level playing field—a society in which, perhaps, most businesses are small and family-owned, there are no major economic inequalities, and no party is sufficiently powerful to tilt the market rules in its favor. But assume, too, that over time things change: socioeconomic differences grow, some businesses turn into corporations, and more financial power accrues to some of those corporations. At the same time, the processes of rule-setting become less democratic, beginning with bits of lobbying here and there, and gradually opening the door for the rich to have greater influence.

This means that the rules of markets shift in a direction that benefits the most successful lobbyists: their share of benefits from market transactions grows, while those of others shrink, with transactions turning exploitative and extractive. This allows the already privileged market participants to earn higher profits, which means that they have even more money available for influencing politics, while other market participants have less—for example, because impoverished workers can no longer pay union fees. In the next round of lobbying and rule-setting, the playing field is even less level. The merry-go-round of political and economic power spins faster and faster, and socioeconomic inequality takes on dimensions that resemble feudal societies much more than democratic ones.[41]

This is a stylized picture, but historical research shows that this pattern can be found in various epochs that saw the emergence of markets in land, labor, and capital—"factor markets," in contrast to markets in consumer goods. The historian Bas van Bavel and his coauthors have studied medieval Iraq, late medieval Italian city-states, and the early-modern Low Countries.[42] They found that when factor markets started to develop in these societies, they at first brought an increase in welfare and in economic and political freedoms for individuals. Over time, however, elites who benefited from markets bent rules and institutions in their own favor, which led to growing inequality and reduced the economic and political freedoms of normal citizens. Other historians have questioned whether the cases that van Bavel has analyzed are sufficient to establish a general model; there can certainly also be other reasons, beyond elite-capture, for why market societies can decline.[43] Moreover, the claim of inevitability sounds all too deterministic, leaving little space for the agency of human beings. And yet, this research makes a compelling case about a possible development of market societies.

The questions, of course, are where our societies stand today, and what can be done to prevent this threat of refeudalization. The first is an empirical question, and at least a few pieces of deeply worrying evidence provide a basis for arguing for a fundamental reorientation of market regulation.

Here is one noteworthy piece of evidence from the micro-level of contract law, concerning the practices of many corporations, in the United States and elsewhere, vis-à-vis their customers. As legal scholar Margaret Jane Radin has shown in painstaking detail, the boilerplate texts that accompany many service contracts, and that customers have little choice but to sign (or click on), have come to include more and more clauses that benefit corporations to the detriment of customers, even in ways that deny their fundamental rights, such as the right to go to court instead of accepting nonpublic arbitration.[44] Such terms shift legal risks to customers, away from corporations. This is another aspect of the externalizing tendencies of corporations: just as they duck responsibility for environmental and climate harms, they also shift other kinds of risk to other parties, especially when precautionary measures carry costs.

There is some sad irony in this: a key argument for having corporations is, after all, that they *can* carry risks, because shareholders are in danger of losing only their investments in shares, not the wealth they hold in other forms. The justification of corporate profits is that shareholders should be rewarded for risk-taking—they could otherwise just as well buy bonds with guaranteed returns. But if corporations shift more and more risks to other parties, what justifies the profits of their shareholders?

More evidence on where our market societies stand with regard to market regulation and corporate power has been put together in an impressive book by economist Thomas Philippon.[45] He argues that, in what he calls "the great reversal," the US-American economy has become less competitive in recent decades due to levels of industry concentration that have created oligopolies in many sectors.[46] In these markets dominated by a few companies, profits are higher and customer benefits lower; this holds, for example, for telecommunications and airline services.[47] The underlying reason? Philippon runs through a number of possible explanations—for example, changes in global market conditions—but finds that the most likely culprit is the interplay of regulation and intense lobbying pressures. This comes at a high cost for US citizens: a rough estimate is that, in the last twenty years, they have been deprived of $1.5 trillion of value that would have been created if US industry had remained as competitive as it was previously.[48]

Philippon may be more enamored than many others with market competition, equating competition with economic freedom in a way that overlooks the pressures that such competition also creates.[49] But his analysis of the link between lobbying and lacking antitrust enforcement is extremely plausible. Putting aside, for a moment, the question of how competitive one would want markets to be in an ideal society, the data clearly show that in the current US economic system, corporations get away with less and less competition, and thus worse offers for customers, because of an unholy alliance with political authorities. This is neither efficient nor democratic, and it also confounds the discussion: it gives markets a bad name, but for mechanisms that are based not on markets working as they should, but on vested interests undercutting their functioning.

Thus, distorted market regulation, while not often discussed in public, is one of the fields in which the erosion of democracy has, arguably, been most massive. The negative effects on citizens are often indirect, but they contribute to the loss of trust in the political-economic system as a whole, and make citizens susceptible to the siren songs of populists.

Democratic Markets

What kinds of markets, then, should democratic societies set up? It is helpful here to start with a thought experiment: What kinds of norms would one like to have in place if all trade were with friends, family, and other people one cared about? Surely the prevailing expectation would not be that people would be misinformed and therefore tricked into buying stuff they did not need, or that the deals struck would channel 95 percent of the benefit to one party and only 5 percent to the other. To be sure, markets transactions are not expected to factor in the kinds of charitable sentiments one brings to dealings with loved ones. Adam Smith made exactly this point in his famous observation that "it is not from the benevolence of the butcher, the brewer, or the baker that we expect our dinner, but from their regard to their own self-interest."[50] In modern societies, we have dealings with people far beyond those with whom we have personal ties, with markets coordinating these interactions. And yet, these strangers are also fellow humans, and we should expect, as Smith certainly did, that basic standards of justice will underlie market transactions.

The citizens of democracies must set the rules of markets in ways that are compatible with democratic values—and for many markets, this in fact means setting the rules in ways that also make sense from an economic perspective. Many of the moral problems that arise in markets have to do not with the functioning of markets as it should be, but with market failures: for example, with information asymmetries or with externalities. The most challenging externalities we currently face are in the realm of the natural environment; climate change, biodiversity loss, and other environmental damages bring huge societal harms and risks for current and future generations.[51] Market participants—again, often corporations—benefit from not having to pay a price for polluting the environment and harming the climate. This keeps socially inefficient modes of production in place,

Markets, Corporations, and Their Alliance against Democracy   43

whereas adequate pricing would shepherd markets toward more sustainable methods of, say, energy production and agriculture. But given the path dependency of today's system, such changes need to go hand in hand with other adaptations. These also need to take into account the distributive effects of reforms: simply putting high taxes on fossil fuel consumption, without asking how poor household can then afford heating and mobility, will not work.[52] And at the international level, richer countries cannot expect poorer countries to one-sidedly carry the costs of protecting biospheres. Rich countries have already extracted much value from these countries.[53] And they have already externalized many costs.[54] For the future, a fair sharing of benefits and burdens is called for.

But protection of the environment is not the only realm requiring democratic regulation.[55] The internal structures of markets must also be democratically regulated if citizens are to be treated with respect and fairness—including, for example, the rules for how information is used and presented in markets. The rhetoric in favor of markets emphasizes the "freedom" and "choice" they offer. But for freedom and choice to be meaningful, prospective buyers need sufficient, truthful information about product and service offerings and the options available to them. In practice, this also demands rules against misleading advertisements.[56] Democratic governments need to make sure that, the more that is at stake for consumers (given that some goods, such as housing, eat up larger parts of a household budget, and some goods are more vital to human health), the more is done to keep powerful players in markets from misleading buyers.[57]

There are also many questions about the ways in which market participants try to exploit the psychological weak spots of others—creating questionable offers to boost their self-esteem through luxury consumption, or undermining their self-control by putting tempting but harmful products under their noses just when they are least able to resist.[58] Such tactics would not be a problem if individuals were always rational and strong-willed. But, at least since

Aristotle's musings about *akrasia*, we have recognized the human weakness of will that so often prevents us from acting in our own best interests.[59] Modern-day behavioral economists have rediscovered this problem under the label of "time-inconsistent preferences."[60] Psychologists, alternatively, have distinguished between "system 1" and "system 2" thinking."[61] The citizens of democratic societies should not allow each other to exploit such weakness of will. Instead, markets should cater to our long-term oriented, reflective selves—they should enable us to act autonomously. This means, for example, creating cooling-off periods after online purchases that were made in the heat of the moment, in case they are regretted the next day.[62]

Yet another question concerns the distribution of benefits of market transactions—in economists' terms, the allocations of value to consumer surplus versus producer surplus.[63] Most individuals intuitively reject as unfair outcomes in which one party benefits much more than the other. This has been shown by a range of psychological experiments, especially those staging "ultimatum games." In a typical version, two participants are collectively promised a sum of money—say, a hundred dollars—but just one of them gets to say how it should be split between them. It is then up to the other to either accept or reject the proposed division. If the proposer's terms are accepted, both players are paid accordingly, but if the second player rejects the offer, neither party gets anything. The questions are: How selfishly will the proposer behave? And how much inequity will the responder abide? A purely income-maximizing proposer should propose a very lopsided distribution, knowing that an income-maximizing responder would accept getting *something*, as long as the amount is larger than zero. But as numerous studies have shown, offers below 30 percent are often rejected, even in "one-shot" games where actions will not influence subsequent rounds of play.[64] People are seemingly willing to pay a price to enforce a social norm of fairness, that windfall gains should not be exploited so greedily.

Markets, Corporations, and Their Alliance against Democracy 45

This intuition that gains should not be divided too unevenly also applies to markets. In markets for nonessential goods, individuals can simply refuse offers that they find too expensive, even though they would, theoretically, still deliver them small benefits. But in many markets, individuals cannot walk away so easily—think, for example, of the market for rental housing. When there is an imbalance between supply and demand in such markets, one side can often appropriate large benefits while the other side has to go to their threshold of pain, or even beyond it. Simply decreeing lower prices, however, is not a wise policy: it does not increase supply and might simply lead to under-the-table transactions in addition to official payments. Rather, what is needed is a broader strategy of how more housing could be provided, through public or private measures.

In other words, the question is how the framework of markets distributes their benefits to different groups, and whether this is in line with what society as a whole needs and wants. This question can, and should, replace, the simple (and often simple-minded) focus on whether certain policies support "efficiency" or "growth," without disaggregating which groups benefit from them.[65] Democratic societies can and should shape markets such that they reward those economic activities that are really valuable for society and distribute the gains equitably.

In fact, once one says goodbye to the misleading idea that markets would, simply by themselves, automatically be productive rather than extractive, societies *need* to ask which values orient market regulation. Efficiency, in a textbook sense, certainly matters—but as argued in the Introduction, it is a rather minimal condition, which aims to avoid waste while being compatible with very different types of markets. In today's situation, we need efficiency with regard to renewable energies, not with regard to oil extraction. Rent extraction is undesirable in all industries and needs to be prevented by keeping competitive structures intact, rather than allowing market concentration. This takes strong and independent market authorities that cannot be bought off by corporate money. And yet, the logically prior question is: Which markets do we want? Oil extraction or renewable energies? Governments do not have to answer this question by closing down factories and starting new ones themselves. Putting an adequate price on CO2 emissions would go a long way toward fueling demand for renewables and making oil extraction no longer worthwhile.

Last but not least, the markets that are most attractive from a democratic perspective will be those that provide enough options for all participants to fulfill their needs—instead of leaving some participants only the breadcrumbs that remain on the table after the powerful have feasted. Often, this has to do with a lack of purchasing power: the poorer some members of society are, the less likely it is that suppliers will find it worthwhile to cater to their needs or preferences. In the logic of markets, only the preferences backed up by purchasing power are visible—and the emphasis placed on those with high purchasing power can easily crowd out the attention paid to others. Many textbook models of markets make no explicit assumptions about purchasing power, seeming to suggest that it is distributed roughly equally among participants.[66] They do not ask questions about the *different* kinds of markets that often develop in highly unequal societies, and how these are—or are not—compatible with democratic values. This is another reason for being skeptical of high inequality (a point to be taken up in Chapter 3). In more equal societies, well-regulated markets can cater to the needs of all, not just the rich.

Beyond Markets

Is that all that democratic societies can and should do? It would certainly go a long way if changes along these lines were implemented. And yet, some doubts remain. Even when they are well-embedded and based on fairness and reciprocity, the logic of markets remains

Markets, Corporations, and Their Alliance against Democracy   47

one of individualism and the pursuit of financial advantage. I may be willing to pay *a bit* more to support Amy's local dog parlor, but how far does my willingness go if a cheaper alternative comes along? As a consumer, I have the freedom to switch to a different supplier—and that means that Amy can never be certain that she will not, in the future, be outcompeted by others. We may sound like friends when we chit-chat while my dog gets shampooed, but those are not ties that bind. I may wonder how much of Amy's friendliness is genuine, or whether she is just trying to build "customer loyalty." If I go through a phase with a tight budget, I may have to cut my visits. I may feel an urge to apologize to Amy in that case, but that is not because of the logic of the market, but because this specific market is embedded in the social norms of a face-to-face community.

The logic of markets requires a lack of commitment: customers *need* to be on the lookout for new offers, otherwise competition dies down and the price mechanism becomes inactive. This lack of commitment can be very dangerous when it eats into spheres of life that cannot flourish without commitment: personal relations, but arguably also the relations between fellow citizens who engage in public activities, such as through civil society associations.[67] And the more the market logic expands into various spheres of life, the more difficult it becomes to protect the different psychological mindsets and sets of social norms that are needed in other spheres of life, to realize different kinds of values in them.[68] The economic historian Karl Polanyi has suggested a distinction between "market economies"—societies in which markets play some role in the *economic* realm—and "market societies"—in which "instead of the economy being embedded in social relations, social relations are embedded in the economy."[69] Among the types of social relations for which this can happen are the relations between fellow-citizens: they may end up seeing each other merely as market competitors, not as co-legislators of the rules under which they live together.[70]

Paradoxically, it is precisely when they are embedded in a rich array of nonmarket institutions that many markets are likely to function best, from a democratic perspective. For example, if I know that Amy has, in case of need, access to a safety net or retraining opportunities, I will feel freer in deciding whether I truly want her services or not. If the housing market is well-regulated, renters will not be pitted against each other in ways that are difficult to reconcile with the basic sense of solidarity that a democratic society needs.[71]

In fact, imagine for a moment that, for all essential goods and services, individuals also had access to non-market provisions (say, in less fancy but still functional forms), so that their consent to market transactions would be truly voluntary. This would make markets much more likely to function in productive ways. Of course, some individuals will still choose to get the luxury versions of certain goods, sometimes driven by status anxiety.[72] Such feelings are ubiquitous in today's market societies, and can produce psychological afflictions that should not be belittled. But there is nothing democratic about them—they reflect and reinforce social hierarchies in which some individuals strive to occupy higher social rungs than others. In a society in which markets played a more limited role and all essential needs were taken care of by a stable safety net of welfare institutions, such feelings might be less widespread, freeing up energies for solidaristic civic action rather than competitive rat races in search of self-affirmation.[73]

The more the market logic pervades a society, the more personally we take it: we misread success in markets for a proof of virtue, and failure as a sign of vice. But markets rarely reward good deeds as such—even F. A. Hayek, one of their most passionate defenders, held that they reward the supply of matches, not that of virtue.[74] To be sure, the more their regulation is aligned with democratic values, the more they reward what a society needs—for example, the supply of affordable green energy—but that is *still* not the same as a judgment about an individual's character. Even in very well-regulated

Markets, Corporations, and Their Alliance against Democracy 49

markets, being a little bit ruthless probably pays off. And in many of today's rather badly regulated markets, you win by "moving fast and breaking things," as the Silicon Valley slogan holds. "Breaking things" may be justifiable if the breaking is morally justified and what is being broken is no longer needed by society—the market power of fossil fuel companies comes to mind. But the attitude of "breaking things" must be carefully contained and applied only in well-targeted ways. This can succeed only if the market logic does not take over all spheres of life.

One way of thinking about markets, inspired by the philosopher G. W. F. Hegel, is to understand them as the sphere of society in which change is allowed to happen that may threaten the interests of incumbents invested in the status quo, but that positively benefits society as a whole.[75] This means that a market can embody a brutal kind of social rejection; when others no longer like what I have to offer, they vote with their feet and stop patronizing my shop. I therefore have to stay on my toes all the time. But that is the price a society pays for the freedom of *others* to also try their luck—a next generation of shopkeepers, for example, presenting new offers.

A more positive way of framing this point is to say that markets, if well-regulated, can be a tool for decentralizing power.[76] Whatever market power is exerted by an individual, or more likely a corporation, that power can be challenged. Markets thus contribute to keeping economic power in check—that is, unless their framework becomes itself part of the game and the feudal spiral described above sets in. No matter how exactly democracies design their markets—and there can certainly be reasonable disagreements on how to weigh different values, or the interests of different groups—this is something they must not let happen.

What, then, are alternatives to markets, and how should one choose between them? Schematically, one can again follow Polanyi, who saw autarchic self-provision and centralized government distribution as the big alternatives to markets.[77] But this is really just that: a scheme for organizing one's thought. The institutional reality is much more varied, with many combinations between these principles that can coexist with well-regulated markets. Democrats need to ask for which goods and services markets, of the well-regulated kind, are permissible and function better than other forms of provision—and for which they do not.

Self-provision is particularly important for anything that would change its character if transacted on a market. This holds, in particular, for personal relationships, such as the ties between friends or between parents and children. Many individuals do not want to outsource the tasks required to maintain friendships and provide family care; they would rather have time off from market-based work to be able to do such work without being overburdened.[78] This translates into questions about *time politics,* a topic for a later chapter.[79] Public provision is particularly important for securing citizens' basic rights, and not only civic rights but socioeconomic rights—providing safety nets for those not successful in markets. And then there are the various public goods that markets are simply not very good at supplying—not only internal and external security, but also goods such as a clean and viable natural environment, and public health.

Talk of public provision may for some people bring to mind huge, centralized bureaucracies with endless forms to fill in and Kafkaesque decision-making procedures. But this need not be the case. Even when funding is centralized, implementation can happen on a local level. Institutions can receive feedback from citizens—perhaps not through "exit," as in markets where customers can take their business elsewhere, but also through "voice," in public dialogues and discussions.[80] A great advantage of "voice" is that it is, in principle, accessible to all citizens, instead of being mediated by their unequal purchasing power. Of course, subtle forms of social power can always creep into such processes. And yet, processes of voice can also offer citizens opportunities to encounter each other as equals, and to look for solutions that everyone can live with.

The best markets, ones that democratic societies can endorse, are thus carefully limited realms in which self-interested, but genuinely voluntary, productive exchanges take place, and in which new products and services can be experimented with. But markets can never be the only logic for organizing a society—and in fact they never are. Humans do not just exchange; they also collaborate in many other ways, and as indicated above, this often happens within hierarchical organizations. The next chapter turns to the role of citizens as workers within such organizations, where reforms along democratic lines are also urgently needed.

2

WORKERS

Underlings or Citizens?

In the winter of 2022–2023, when the Covid-19 lockdowns were finally over, something unexpected happened on social media: users started talking about labor relations. "Quiet quitting" became the catchphrase of the day: the idea of not working more for one's job than was absolutely necessary, rejecting the narrative that work required maximal engagement. Some commentators saw hopes for a new wave of resistance to capitalist norms and to the strong work ethic that is still part of the culture of many Western countries.[1] Others pointed out, however, that the phenomenon was not so new. Unions have long known that an effective form of protest is to have laborers strictly "work to rule," ruining productivity while technically adhering to workplace protocols.[2] Yet quiet quitting as an individualistic strategy, while maybe indicating a widespread dissatisfaction with excessive workloads, did not, or not yet, seem to amount to a social movement.

The discussion about quiet quitting was not just about working hours and material benefits. It raises deeper questions about the meaning of work, the boundaries between life and work, and about how employers and employees should relate to each other.[3] Working long hours, at low pay, just to maximize a company's shareholder value, can feel demeaning. Why should one sacrifice one's time and energy if work is understood not as meaningfully contributing to society, but as a tool for increasing the profits of those who are already privileged, as shareholders tend to be? Can work ever be a labor of love if its price is ultimately determined by nothing but the bargaining power of employers and employees?

Today, many workers in countries such as the United States face a dilemma: they can either work in traditional, bureaucratic institutions in which they must submit to the power of a boss without any counter power. Or they can try to earn their living through alternative forms of work, which are more flexible and can be wrapped around other responsibilities, such as family work, but which require giving up even the last bits of security that regular jobs bring.[4] Submission or precarity—is that the choice that workers should face? This chapter argues that such an organization of labor markets is unworthy of democratic societies, and that better alternatives are possible. The members of a democratic society can, and should, relate to each other as equals, not just when they act as political citizens, but also as contributors to the economy.

This chapter is about paid work, and thus neither about self-provision nor about all the unpaid work done in families, neighborhoods, and civil society organizations. Self-provision is not a realistic option for most individuals, and is unlikely to play a major role in the foreseeable future. Unpaid work, in contrast, is so important that it merits a separate discussion, in Chapter 5. The work in focus in this chapter takes place in organizations that range from small family businesses to large multinationals. It is almost never the kind of work that individuals would engage in to directly fulfill their own needs, such as growing vegetables for their own consumption. In modern societies, we work for other people's needs and others work for ours, but this fact on its own need not be a problem—or so this chapter will argue.

The question is, rather, how work is *organized:* Is it organized in ways that individuals, as equal citizens, can agree to? Or are work relations more similar to the medieval relations between feudal lords and their serfs—or the master-slave relations that freed up ancient Greek citizens to participate in democracy? The glorification of ancient Greek democracy, by the way, is an indication that the challenge of figuring out the relation between democracy and work has still not been resolved.[5] For this was a democracy mostly for those who could afford *not* to work. Today, we want democratic voice for all members of society, and most of them must work, in paid and unpaid ways. This makes the question of how to make democracy compatible with the way in which work is organized all the more pressing.

Work is currently the place in which adult individuals spent most of their waking time—and those in the United States put in even more hours than individuals in other Western countries.[6] Work-time reductions may be desirable (as will be argued in this book), but we should not expect this fundamental fact about the centrality of work for our lives to change in the near future.[7] As long as most normal days in the life of normal citizens mean going to work, we need to ask: Are the social relations they experience at their workplaces compatible with, and maybe even conducive to, the realization of democratic values? This question might be crucial for overcoming the current crisis of democracy. As evidence from Europe shows, the quality of social relations and freedom of opinion at work are correlated to individuals' democratic attitudes.[8] Bad working conditions, and the frustration and resentment they cause, may thus be recognized as some of the underlying causes of citizens losing trust in democracy.

Discussion of these matters starts out with the choice that many workers face today, between submitting to the hierarchies of large organizations and experiencing the precarity of seemingly independent work. A section is devoted to the phenomenon of "fissured" workplaces, in which outsourcing is used to lower wages.[9] Another lays out a suggestion for how work can be understood from a democratic perspective: as a matter of social contributions that connect one to one's fellow citizens. This requires protection from work-related harms, fair conditions, and opportunities for changing jobs throughout one's life, but also workplaces that are in line with democratic values. This is why the chapter concludes with a discussion of the democratization of workplaces, which could not only make work better, but make societies more democratic.

Between Submission and Precarity

Modern work is divided work: it is an eminently social phenomenon in which different individuals play different roles and, ideally, contribute with their specific interests, perspectives, and skills to something that is much more than the sum of its parts. The joy of creating something together with others is one of the goods that work can, in the best case, deliver.[10] But because work is such a social activity, it needs to be coordinated—and this immediately raises questions about its organization and about the power relations between workers and employers.

As discussed in the previous chapter, the internal structures of workplaces—whether private companies or public administrations—do not follow the logic of markets, but of hierarchies. Instead of haggling and bargaining about single tasks, employees receive a specific type of contract: they sell their labor power, for a certain number of hours, in exchange for a salary.[11] As employees, they are bound by the commands of their bosses: about what to do, how to do it, and when and where to do it. To be sure, much depends on their individual bargaining power: a highly sought-after IT expert can negotiate to work mostly from home, and even if they are regularly late for meetings, their boss may swallow their anger because they know that this employee is difficult to replace. But for most workers, the balance of power is inverse: they depend more on their jobs than their employers depend on them. They have to submit to orders, or risk losing their incomes. Even if they may find another job, this costs them time and money, and alternative jobs may come with no better conditions. So typically, it is the employee who needs to bite their tongue—sometimes even in cases in which it would be better for everyone, including their employer, if they spoke up.

The organizational structures of work, as they currently exist, are often a mixture of the functional logic of collaboration, and power structures that reflect this imbalance of power between employers and employees, which is, moreover, often intertwined with factors such as gender, race, class, or migration status. The logic of collaboration requires people to show up at the same time for meetings, do their tasks as agreed, and stick to deadlines. Someone who fails to do so without good reason is a bad colleague, forcing others to pick up the slack. A good test question for sorting out whether something is a matter of collaboration or power is how the same issue would look among, say, a group of friends fixing an old house together, as equals and volunteers. Coordination can take time and we often have to deal with the all-too-human vices of obliviousness or procrastination. That is why it can make sense to introduce some level of hierarchy: someone gets the task of keeping the team together, reminding everyone of their tasks, resolving conflicts, and, ideally, keeping up everyone's good spirits. But this role does not have to be permanent: it can rotate between people or be split it into different sub-tasks. If one person is particularly good at it, the group can decide to assign it to this person on a permanent basis, but on the understanding that if she fails to deliver as leader, the roles will be reconsidered. This is how "hierarchy" can also play a role among equals, but in a very limited, purely functional way.

In many workplaces, the role of hierarchy is different. Bosses are not elected but appointed from above. And they often decide about much more than just the allocation of tasks in teams: about whether someone keeps a job at all, or about bonuses or promotions, often without accountability to workers. This is why bosses often have far more power over employees than would be needed from a functional perspective. Many employees fear their reactions, and do not dare to speak openly to them. As Kathy Weeks puts it, "the work site is where we often experience the most immediate, unambiguous, and tangible relations of power that most of us will encounter on a daily basis."[12]

Adding to this power, hierarchical structures have deep roots in our collective cultural imagination. The idea that someone needs to be at the top, and others need to submit to their power, can be traced back at least to the medieval idea of a "great chain of being" in which all creatures, from God and the angels to humans and animals, were seen as forming part of one overarching cosmological hierarchy.[13] This idea justified not only the patriarchal order of households but also the feudal hierarchies in which most people could only be underlings. Today, the organizational charts of many workplaces still have the same pyramidal shape, with a gradient of power from the top to the bottom, and no counterpower.[14] The result is that, as Andrew Cumbers puts it, "under liberal democratic capitalism, democracy and human rights effectively stop at the workplace."[15]

In such structures, seeing work as something one does with others to fulfill a social purpose becomes rather difficult—even though organizations often like to present it as such, in their cynical attempts to exploit individuals' intrinsic motivations. The ultimate end for many organizations is to make money, and workers constitute inputs to their production process, alongside raw materials and other resources. And often, the work is chopped up into such separate, abstract activities that workers struggle to see the contribution their efforts make to a greater whole. The demotivating effect of this has long been a complaint about assembly line work and "paper shuffling" in bureaucracies, but it is not limited to those types of jobs.[16]

During some decades of the twentieth century, however, the integration into organizational hierarchies brought at least some security for workers. Precisely because they had to motivate employees, employers often provided at least slightly better conditions than workers could find elsewhere.[17] Bosses knew that lowering wages or arbitrarily dismissing people could have a hugely demotivating effect on all employees, and tried to avoid this.[18] It is true that working with the same colleagues day in and day out can create a sense of solidarity and provide psychological safety. And yet, the price that many employees pay for this arrangement is to be constantly submitted to the power of others, in ways often not justified by functional requirements. This holds in particular for workers whose lack of specific skills makes them, in employers' eyes, easily replaceable. In some infamous cases, workers were not even allowed short breaks for using a bathroom.[19] In other cases, workers' lives were routinely disrupted by erratic scheduling, including back-to-back shifts with insufficient time to rest in between.[20] Such jobs subject workers to constant orders from others, give them no say in how their work is organized, add nothing to their skill sets, and offer no prospects of expanding their opportunities.[21]

Having to endure such conditions to feed one's family is not a fate that democratic societies should impose on their citizens. And yet, the picture drawn so far is downright rosy compared to the phenomenon that has since the 1980s spread far and wide: the splintering of work relations across different companies that employ individuals for specific tasks, even though the final product comes under a different trade name. Those working in offices are probably accustomed to the fact that the cleaners, caterers, and security guards moving through their buildings are not on the payroll of their same organization—as was usually the case in earlier decades—but are employees of external contractors. Management scholar David Weil calls this phenomenon the "fissured workplace."[22] A lead company, such as a hotel chain, outsources cleaning and maintenance services, but also payroll administration and other services, to other companies, which compete for these contracts. These companies are typically smaller and less stable and offer less generous working conditions.

Outsourcing can be productive in some cases—for example, if a company only occasionally needs specific skill sets.[23] But it can also be a way of making contracts more exploitative, by pitting subcontracting companies against each other and thus creating downward pressure on wages. For integrated companies, it makes sense to pay somewhat consistent wages to all employees; otherwise, perceptions of unfairness might demotivate workers.[24] Another solution, however, is to outsource certain tasks to other companies, which may in turn outsource them to yet other companies or independent contractors.[25] This happens in industries from mobile communication to mining, in various organizational forms, but very often at the cost of workers, in the sense that the working conditions become more precarious and health and safety standards receive less attention.[26] In other words, and returning to an argument from the last chapter: this is a way in which labor markets become more exploitative: because of one-sided power relations, companies can extract higher benefits from workers and outsource risks to them.

And then, there are the newest versions of precarious work in which individuals do not even have a boss but take orders from algorithms: they take on specific tasks that are posted on a platform.[27] Labeled "platform work" or "microwork," such forms of work may, at first glance, seem tempting because they come with the promise of flexibility and autonomy. The tasks to which this organizational principle has been applied vary: they can take place in the online world (such as labeling pictures for training algorithms), or in the offline world (with the most visible examples being the bicycle couriers that deliver food). Individuals register on an online platform to get access to such tasks, and all the data about the business processes become the property of the company that owns the platform.

The absence of a real boss who could shout at you or reprimand you may seem enticing, as does the ability to decide flexibly when to work. But platform work often takes individuals out of the frying pan, into the fire. Legally speaking, they are not employees—and many legal battles are currently being fought, especially with regard to the ride sharing service Uber, about their status. As independent contractors, workers have no right to a secure income or to payment for the time that they spend searching and preparing for tasks.[28] A recent report focused on UK-based online microworkers showed that their pay is almost always below the minimum wage, and often less than £4.00 per hour.[29] This should not come as a surprise if one considers that digital microwork is a global business, with low-wage countries such as India, Bangladesh, and Pakistan having the largest online shares.[30]

At the moment, platform work, whether online or offline, is still a somewhat marginal phenomenon. In the UK in 2021, for example, it was estimated that roughly 4.4. million people took on some kind of platform work at least once a week.[31] In the United States, an estimated 16 percent of the population earned money on online platforms that year.[32] Many individuals take on microwork assignments as a complement to other, steadier sources of income, sometimes approaching them in rather a playful way, as a kind of online hobby that adds a bit of cash.[33] But about 20 percent of the participants of the UK study spent many hours online and depended on this income to a considerable degree.[34] The demographic profile of microworkers varies from study to study; what this study noted, in particular, was a relatively high rate of Black workers and of individuals with disabilities and other health issues which presumably prevented them from taking on other forms of employment.[35]

The social technology of platform work is at odds with how work has traditionally been organized and regulated in the West, and this raises new challenges. How can at least a minimum of fairness be ensured for such contracts? What about pensions, health insurance, and vacation days? How can the imbalance be overcome between platform owners, who can access large amounts of data about workers, and workers, for whom the platform is a black box?[36] There is no shortage of policy proposals, to be sure.[37] They fall short, however, in addressing the bigger questions that arise when, thanks to platforms, work gets ever more fragmented. Will the "workplace" even be a concept in the future, or will work be done at home—or in varying locations to which one is assigned by anonymous algorithms? What, then, about the possibility of encountering others at work, not just in the fifteen seconds it takes to hand over a takeout order but in more meaningful, long-term forms of collaboration?

It is not technology as such that is to blame—at issue are the legal and social systems in which the technology is embedded. Platforms for coordinating tasks can also be publicly owned or owned by workers themselves in cooperatives.[38] It is the power relations that matter: who owns the data, who decides about the wages, and who benefits how much? In this respect, online and offline work do not differ so much. For let there be no mistake: workers who do digital microwork are probably *not* the most vulnerable ones in today's societies. The latter are often those in the least formal jobs: migrants without papers, or day laborer jobs below the radar of official regulation. In a recent study, political theorist Paul Apostolidis and his team interviewed such workers—Latin American immigrants in California—and observed their daily struggles.[39] For them, getting *any* kind of work, on any given day, is a matter of luck, and they run massive physical risks when working in landscaping or construction without training and safety equipment. And this, of course, is just one of the many forms of informal work that happen worldwide.[40] Across them all, precarity is the rule rather than the exception. For such workers, platforms could, in principle, provide a huge opportunity to coordinate and to gradually formalize their working relations—but only if it empowers them, rather than subjecting them once more to one-sided power dynamics.

Work as a Democratic Contribution

Work—understood in a broad sense as using one's energy to change the world in ways that are potentially useful for oneself or others—does not have to be something that makes human life miserable. To be sure, some forms of work are intrinsically demanding: they require forms of physical or psychological exertion that are hard to endure. But even in these cases, a lot depends on how such work is organized. For how long does one have to do it, under what conditions, and does one receive appropriate support, remuneration, and recognition? There are good reasons to think that if the conditions are fair, healthy grown-up individuals have a duty to contribute in some way to society through work, in exchange for benefiting from the work of others.[41] But most people do not need to be told that they have such a duty: they *want* to contribute, for their own sake and that of others.[42] Not having *anything* to do is, after all, a state that is bearable for only limited amounts of time. And it is typically only after long years of frustration, oppression, or exploitation that individuals fall into the attitude famously captured in Melville's story of Bartleby the Scrivener, "I would prefer not to."[43]

In a democratic society, socially necessary work should be distributed fairly among all capable individuals.[44] But this is easier said than done. Adam Smith, for one, imagined that in an ideal labor market, work would receive higher remuneration for being demanding, unpleasant, or carrying some risk or stigma.[45] He thought that employers needed to pay employees a premium for anything that made a job less attractive than others—a kind of inbuilt fairness. But this optimistic assumption holds only where the options available to employees are sufficiently attractive. Many workers in today's labor markets have little choice but to swallow the conditions offered to them. This is why labor-market dynamics often develop in the opposite direction, toward a clustering of advantages and disadvantages. On the one hand, there are intrinsically interesting professional jobs that enjoy high social standing and good pay (even though they often also come with long hours); on the other hand, there are physically demanding rote jobs with little intrinsic reward that hardly pay a living wage and do not carry much social recognition.[46] The latter jobs are the ones that often end up being done by structurally weaker groups, whether women, minorities, or migrants. In 1963, Martin Luther King Jr. famously called for respect for the sanitation workers of Memphis, whose work was vital and, like all work that serves humanity, had dignity.[47] One wonders, in terms of society's regard for its garbage collectors and cleaners, how much progress has been made since then.

But trash still needs to be cleared, one might object. This is true, and fires must also be put out, houses have to be built, and produce needs harvesting. The need for the work does not imply that it could not be organized differently, however. There is a distinction between the *technical* division of labor—the splitting of jobs into tasks—and the *social* division of labor—the distribution of these tasks onto different individuals, and the way in which they are embedded in organizational and social structures.[48] Many forms of "bad" work would not have to be so bad if they were organized differently and if those who did them received appropriate rewards. The same argument applies to the problem of routinized worker: thinkers from the eighteenth century onward have decried its stultifying effects on the human mind, and its harmful effects on the human body.[49] But the more routinized tasks are, the more easily they can be taken over, or at least supported, by robots and algorithms. For those tasks for which this is difficult, practices such as job rotation or different forms of job design—for example, partly routine, partly more varying tasks—can go a long way in taking the dehumanizing sting out of them. At the turn of the twentieth century, the French sociologist Emile Durkheim pointed out that divided labor typically also requires workers to interact with those who do other specialized tasks, and that these interactions can enrich their work and support social cohesion.[50] He added an important qualification, however: this mechanism will not function well if the positions of individuals are too unequal, because then power and domination, instead of mutual complementarity, structure their relations.[51]

How, then, should a democratic society organize paid work? The first demand must be the seemingly minimal one that paid work should not harm individual workers. Rules about health and safety and maximum working hours must be consistently enforced to keep employers from making cost-cutting moves that harm workers. This may sound trivial and obvious, at least in Western countries, and yet the social reality is at quite some distance from it. In some cases the existing rules are insufficient, and in other cases it is the enforcement that falls short. As Weil reports, the problem is particularly great in fissured industries, where the likelihood of a US federal or state labor standards investigator visiting a workplace in any given year is one in a thousand (in contrast to well below one in a hundred for all industries).[52] Lead businesses that design the contracts for subcontracting firms need to be held responsible for workplace quality and safety, Weil argues, and must use monitoring tools to ensure compliance with not only product quality standards but health and safety regulations, too.[53] Workers who lack formal status as employees simply have no one looking out for their well-being. Day laborers like the ones Apostolidis interviewed call themselves lucky if they are able to connect with a charity or NGO willing to advance their calls for safe work equipment or complaints about wage theft. It is not hard to see what policy measures could be taken against this—the challenge is mustering the political will to enact them.

Beyond that, working conditions in democratic societies need to fulfill basic standards of fairness, which must be implemented through labor market regulation (and, in the case of other legitimate employment forms, through regulation of their contractual conditions). To start again with a normative minimum: there must not be discrimination along lines of gender, race, or class. This is another case of "obvious in theory, difficult in practice," with one challenge being the collection of enough evidence of violations to take an employer to court. But discrimination-free work environments are crucial for democratic societies: they can be places of encounter beyond all the dividing lines that mar our societies. Workplaces stand out as spaces in which individuals can interact with others they would never meet in their private lives. This is true with regard to race.[54] It also holds with regard to political orientation.[55] The experience of working together can allow individuals to get to know each other and to come to appreciate certain qualities in others who would, from a distance, be nothing but stereotypical personifications of the loathed "other side."

Of course, fairness concerns wages, and minimum wage legislation is a crucial tool for democratic societies to prevent competitive spirals down into hunger wages.[56] But it also concerns many other, nonmaterial dimensions of work. While it is difficult to define "good" or "bad" work in the abstract, it is clear that some jobs have features that many individuals appreciate, while others carry risks such as exposure to toxins, or require individuals to endure irregular work patterns or exposure to bad smells and physically revolting items. What Smith thought the market would do on its own can be achieved through regulation—new rules both to minimize the harmful dimensions of jobs and to provide extra benefits in compensation. To be sure, money cannot buy everything and for some harms it is hard to imagine any fair compensation.[57] Yet, if such jobs came with fair compensation, as well as social recognition, many would be less bad than they currently are.

One of the great injustices of today's labor markets, however, is that workers often get stuck in bad jobs for longer periods than they ever imagined, with their chances of moving into better jobs seemingly cut off. (And some jobs could be better simply by being different and offering new challenges.) There are huge path dependencies in how individuals find their ways into different occupations, with few opportunities to start afresh later in life.[58] That is the case despite the fact that on average, people live longer and are also healthy for more years than many generations before them.[59] It would thus be natural to expect that people might want to try out different things in their lives, even if this means that they have to give up some of the benefits that skillfulness and experience can bring. But the opportunity to, say, take some time off work and get trained in a new field is currently a privilege for those with sufficient private savings. Much more could be done to support individuals who may have started working in an unskilled job early in life, to get advanced training or a college education later on. Such policies are no mere utopia, not least because governments start to realize what a waste, in addition to an unfairness, it is not to allow people to change jobs over the course of their lives. Austria, for example, has introduced the possibility of taking a "training leave," that is, taking time off work while receiving a subsistence income, to allow individuals to retrain for a different job.[60]

Protection from harms, fair conditions in inclusive workplaces, and the opportunity to reconsider one's occupational opportunities later in life—is that all that one can expect from work? It would, at least, improve the fate of millions of workers who are currently forced to earn an income under far worse conditions. Labor market regulation is crucial to get there, but an additional instrument is also worth endorsing: a public job guarantee that provides jobs at the minimum wage and under good conditions, in socially useful activities. It can serve as a minimum floor below which the conditions in private employment cannot fall, because otherwise individuals would switch into these public jobs.[61] It also has further advantages: it prevents people from falling into unemployment, which is often extremely harmful for individuals and their families, and it stabilizes the macroeconomic cycles of the economic system. This idea is gaining traction, and several countries run experiments with job guarantee programs.[62] Through experiments, one can learn how to design such programs without undesirable side effects. The experiences made so far provide reason for optimism that in the future, a job guarantee can be a very valuable instrument in the toolbox of labor market policies. (And remember: it does not have to be perfect to be better than the status quo.)

But there is more. Democratic societies should not consider labor markets as just another type of market that needs to be regulated well. Work has a deeper impact on our lives, and shapes our character in a more thoroughgoing way, than other market transactions. For many individuals, work is not just a job, it is part of one's identity. And while this may be more true for some kinds of jobs than others, and more pronounced in Europe than in the United States, this identification with one's job can be traced back centuries in Western intellectual history.[63] For many people there is some truth in the claim that they are what they do. This makes one vulnerable: losing one's job is then not just a matter of exchanging one activity for another, but a matter of giving up something that is deeply tied up with one's identity.

For this reason, but also because *all* workers have weighty interests tied to their work, democratic societies should give individuals a say in how their work is organized: in the structure of daily activities, but also in the broader strategic questions that shape their workplaces. At the moment, in many workplaces the only chance to express one's opinion is to resort to quiet quitting. But as so often, there is a socioeconomic gradient: in "better" jobs, individuals typically have more of a say, whereas in many manual and unskilled jobs they are expected to remain silent no matter what, at the threat of dismissal. To be sure, companies often put up little boxes, digital or physical, in which one can put suggestions or feedback. But all too often, what workers have to say ends up making no real difference— because it is the managers and shareholders that hold more power. This needs to change: work organization needs counterpower, and ultimately truly democratic structures. This is a question of protecting workers' interests, but also of creating structures in which individuals can learn the attitudes and skills of democratic citizenship.[64]

Organizing Democratic Work

The debate about "workplace democracy" has gained momentum in philosophy and the social sciences.[65] Yet it is often met with astonishment and resistance outside of the academic world. Shouldn't work be oriented toward efficiency? Wouldn't it make work processes far too complicated if everyone had a voice? Wouldn't that, in the end, mean that everyone would end up poorer? Such worries deserve to be taken seriously, but there are arguments to meet them. If one understands work as a contribution to society, then this work indeed needs to be organized in ways that are not completely dysfunctional—this would come at the cost of those whom the work is supposed to serve. And it is also a frustrating and deeply demotivating experience for workers to try to deliver a contribution in dysfunctional structures (and this experience is all too well-known even to employees of supposedly efficient private companies).

But is it true that democratic work is less "efficient"? Efficient for whom, one is tempted to ask back. It may be less efficient for shareholders alone.[66] But this does not mean that it would be less efficient for the work organization as a whole and for its ability to produce goods and services for society in truly productive ways.[67] For one thing, "democracy" can be implemented in different ways that allow for different combinations of small and large teams of decision-makers, more or less veto-points, more or less feedback loops—and what is "efficient" in the sense of finding good solutions to practical problems, and fair compromises between different groups and individuals, is likely to vary between organizations. A plea for the democratization of work is not a plea for a one-size-fits-all organizational solution, and to be sure, different ways of implementing democratic norms are likely to work better or worse for different types of organizations.[68] (In fact, what one might find more surprising is that *shareholder theory* assumes that one organizational logic would work efficiently for all kinds of different organizations, from bakeries to hospitals).

One great advantage of democratic structures at work is that they are likely to better motivate individuals to bring forth their knowledge and skills in ways that are productive for the organization.[69] Hierarchies are inimical to open communication, because the lower echelons are vulnerable to retaliation. "The boss only gets the good news," the saying goes, and many organizations, and organization scholars, struggle with the question of how to create a better feedback culture.[70] What they often do not consider, however, is power: the imbalance of power between those who rule over teams or whole companies and those who are subjected to them. In such structures, efforts to elicit more feedback and input from employees are likely to stay at the surface. What would really allow for honest conversations would be changes in the rights and responsibilities of the different parties.

Defenders of workplace democracy can grant to their critics that democratic decision-making processes are likely to take longer than autocratic ones—but they are also likely to lead to better decisions, which can in turn prevent problems and delays down the line. Even if managers are well-meaning, they may not be able to convince employees that they have sought a fair compromise if decisions are taken in a purely top-down manner. Employees are all too easily left with the nagging feeling that there could have been a better solution, but that they had no chance of suggesting it (and hence also no chance to hear other perspectives that might convince them that their proposal would *not* have been a good solution). Democratic participation can, in the best case, lead to solutions that all parties can live with, and this, together with the deeper understanding of issues that comes from an open, multi-perspectival discussion, is likely to facilitate the implementation.

The European experiences with participatory models in companies, such as board-level codetermination and works councils, show that such models can work—even in a globalized economy in which these companies have to compete with non-democratic firms.[71] A recent study on Norwegian firms found a positive effect of union density on firm productivity, which the authors explain as probably driven by the formalized arrangements of bargaining and consultation that highly unionized workplaces have.[72] Of course, not all is perfect in the European model. Union membership has declined, and the polarization of labor markets is happening there, as well. Moreover, many models of codetermination do not deliver *fully* equal standing to workers compared to shareholders.[73] And yet, the fact that companies with such governance structures are successful undermines claims about alleged competitive advantages of purely capitalist firms. Worker cooperatives, another model of democratic workplaces, can be very stable over time; in them, workers as owners have full democratic control over the fate of their companies. Cooperatives neither go out of business at higher rates than comparable non-cooperative firms, nor do they all devolve into traditional hierarchical business models. (Some do, but most do not.[74])

One might well ask: Why do we not see *more* democratic firms? Shouldn't they have outcompeted non-democratic firms if they have so many advantages? The nineteenth-century economist and philosopher John Stuart Mill, for one, expected this: as humanity progressed, he thought individuals would prefer to work in cooperative structures rather than hierarchies.[75] But this optimistic prediction has not yet come to pass. Scholars have discussed various possible explanations, such as the lack of access to capital for cooperatives.[76] What very likely plays a role as well is path dependency; with most firms being purely capitalist, democratic firms remain condemned to niches, not least because their model is not well known. What is taught in many universities around the globe is the Anglo-

Saxon model of the shareholder-driven corporation. In recent years, "shareholder value" has been declared "the dumbest idea in the world" by business leaders.[77] Surveys show broad public support for more voice for workers.[78] Yet even today the discussion of alternatives gains ground only slowly.

How, then, can workplace democracy be realized in concrete forms? In the United States, the first thing many people would probably think of, apart from worker cooperatives, is the unionization of workplaces. Battles around such unionizations are currently being fought all over the country.[79] Many researchers emphasize the importance of unions for the fight against inequality and the political participation of workers.[80] While they are important instruments for securing workers' rights and negotiating fair wages, company unions have a decisive disadvantage: from a structural perspective, they cannot avoid competitive races to the bottom within industries, especially fissured ones. In this respect, sectoral bargaining is more advantageous, because it sets the same rules for all companies of an industry.[81] And because collective bargaining provides the same conditions for all employees in a certain category, it can benefit more vulnerable individuals, such as women with care responsibilities or members of minorities, who, individually, have weak bargaining positions. Unions can decisively shift the power relations between employers and employees; in many European countries, they also play a key role in the codetermination system.

Codetermination means that elected worker representatives hold a number of seats on the advisory board of a company, depending on the size of the company.[82] For firms to be fully democratic, however, they would have to have the right to occupy at least 50 percent of the seats. Historically, this has rarely been the case—the German steel and mining industry is a notable exception—but for the future, this is a promising way forward. Sociologist Isabelle Ferreras argues for a bi-cameral model, that is, two separate chambers of representatives for workers and shareholders, which have to jointly agree on all major strategic decisions of the firm.[83] In this way, workers' interests are represented at the highest level of corporate decision-making. For companies that have more stakeholder groups, however, it makes sense to have even more chambers, or advisory boards, drawn from these groups, such as patients in a hospital or users in a social media company.[84] Some researchers also suggest panels of randomly drawn citizens as additional supervisors of firms, especially with regard to social and environmental sustainability.[85] The task, thus, is to reinvent corporate governance in a way that protects *all* relevant groups and finds fair compromises between them, while ensuring the proper functioning of organizations with regard to their social purpose.

Such *representative* forms of democracy in workplaces are crucial for shifting the balance of powers toward workers and other stakeholders. And yet, in large organizations even worker representatives may be at quite some distance from the everyday work of employees. There is a risk that representative democracy, on its own, may run into a problem that it also encounters in political life: that a class of office holders forms, who are meant to be the voice of citizens, but who develop interests of their own. To prevent this, and to implement truly democratic principles in workplaces, representative democracy must be complemented by *participatory* forms of democracy—formats of decision-making and of collaboration in which individuals are not voters but real participants.

Participatory democracy is often criticized for being cumbersome and slow, but this need not be the case, especially in the context of work. Employees need to collaborate anyway—so the real question is whether this happens in hierarchical or egalitarian relations. To be sure, in larger groups some distribution of roles is often needed, but especially in smaller teams, egalitarian decision-making seems possible. In fact, companies have experimented with team-based work structures since the 1970s, often with success—but the ideological waves and the fears of global competition of the 1980s and 1990s have ended many of these experiments.[86]

In recent years, the revolution brought about by digital communication has brought new momentum to questions about organizing work in more horizontal ways—although, interestingly, this movement had little to do with the traditional forms of codetermination in Europe, and many unions are slow to embrace it. The new technical possibilities tie in nicely with calls for better working conditions. Under the slogan of "new work," ideas such as self-determination and self-realization, but also flexibilization and innovation, have been taken up widely.[87] The origins of these ideas were highly political; today, they are often used in watered-down versions that do not challenge existing power structures. "Agile work," for example, was first introduced in software engineering and entails teams working together in self-organized ways, not to empower employees but to raise efficiency.[88]

The hope here is not for progress coming from digital technologies alone.[89] But such technologies help address one serious challenge for participatory forms of democracy: the costs of coordination are massively lowered if information can be shared quickly, and ideas can be collected from groups of people who do not even have to be in the same room. Algorithms might, for example, help to put together assemblies of random but representative samples of employees, thus bringing the principle of "lottocracy" to the world of work.[90] Lottocracy belongs to the representative camp of democratic practices, but if it is practiced on a regular basis, all workers get a chance to be involved in such assemblies. And it is this kind of involvement that really makes a difference: as a recent meta-study on the psychological effects of democratic work found, what matters is that individuals have a perception of being able to participate.[91]

How far does one get with such practices? There is debate among advocates of workplace democracy as to whether changes in the rights and responsibilities of different groups within a work organization will make a meaningful difference, or whether the real requirement is for changes in ownership, so that a workplace is ultimately accountable to the workers themselves, or perhaps to a local community.[92] The case may be stronger for focusing on reallocating rights and responsibilities within organizations—not least because restructuring ownership is just one of many ways to do this, and ownership rights in their modern form do not always confer more power. But of course, this position is compatible with urging democratic societies to experiment with new forms of ownership and firm governance to discover what functions well for what kind of organization.[93]

What might well make a massive difference, however, is another institutional proposal already mentioned above: the provision of a public job guarantee as a fallback option for any individual who, for whatever reason, wants to step back from private-sector work.[94] An additional positive effect of such a policy is to strengthen workers vis-à-vis employers, and thus also to influence the *internal* dynamics of workplaces. While most workers probably prefer to keep their jobs, with a job guarantee in place they would no longer be vulnerable at the existential level of losing all income (and, in the United States, often also their health insurance), and this would provide a better starting point for honest, open conversations at workplaces. Exit from particular jobs would also become easier in cases in which there are deep value conflicts between different members of an organization—which, in a pluralistic society, is something that one must expect to happen from time to time.

Democratic workplaces would change not only the character of work, but also the role of corporations in society, bringing their purposes better in line with democratic values. Those who hold power in them would be held to account not only by shareholders, but also by employees and other stakeholders. Empirical evidence provides reason for optimism that more democratic firms do better on social and environmental counts.⁹⁵ This is not the only step that needs to be taken to rein in the power of corporations.⁹⁶ But democratization could be an important contribution and change their nature from within. Democratic work will not come overnight. Even if legal changes are introduced quickly, getting used to democratic practices will take time. After all, many workers have had to obey, and bite their tongues, for years on end. It will take some time to unlearn practices of submission and to relearn practices of citizenship at work.⁹⁷ Step by step, teams need to develop cultures of listening to each other and showing respect, even in moments of stark disagreement. And it takes experimentation to discover the practices, organizational structures, and forms of technological support that work best in different work contexts. One should also not expect that once a system has been found it can remain the same without requiring any further discussion. Working together always requires meta-discussions about *how* to work together—but it is better by far to discuss these questions openly, among equals, than to force those who disagree to resort to quiet quitting. As democratic societies, we can do better than that, by treating each other as fellow-citizens, not as underlings, when we are at work.

Such reforms, however, need to go hand in hand with others to fight our societies' massive inequalities of income and wealth. It is hard to imagine how individuals, as coworkers and colleagues, could run their affairs democratically if their material situations remained as uneven as is currently the case. This, therefore, is the topic to be taken up in the next chapter, turning to the broader question of inequality and its incompatibility with true democracy.

3

INEQUALITY

Why Democracies Need Less of It

If you meet another person on the street, can you tell how poor or rich they are? Sometimes there are unmistakable signs: expensive shoes or accessories, or, on the other side, cheap clothes from second-hand stores and bags from discount shops. And yet you might think that we have overcome the time in which the rich paraded in their expensive carriages and the poor went in rags. Jeans and t-shirt—that's what everyone wears when going for a stroll on a sunny Sunday afternoon. But then again, do the rich and the poor even meet on such strolls today? Is there a public space in which they would have a chance to meet one another? Those who are really poor probably have to work another job on Sundays to make ends meet. The really rich, in contrast, would not stroll on a public street, if only because they are worried about their safety, preferring private venues that are closed off to the public.

We like to think of our countries as societies in which equality is still a widely held norm, at least as an ideal. But the numbers speak a different language. For about two decades, research on inequalities of income and of wealth by Anthony Atkinson, Thomas Piketty, Gabriel Zucman, Emanuel Saez, Pavlina Tcherneva, and others has shown that inequality in many Western countries has grown massively since the 1970s.[1] A much-cited number is that the ratio of CEO pay to average pay in big US companies is now almost 300:1.[2] The gaps that are opening up between different tiers of the economic spectrum are even wider for wealth than for income, with the rich getting richer faster than anyone else.[3] And while these developments may be most extreme in some Anglophone countries, they also mar other Western democracies. One way in which they have become very tangible is their impact on home purchases. Wealthy families can support the next generation in buying property, through direct financial support or through guarantees for loans. Without such support, it has become extremely difficult for young people to buy housing in metropolitan areas. A new divide is opening up between those who can and those who cannot afford to do so.[4]

Material inequality is known to have many negative effects. For example, more unequal countries have higher rates of mental illness, both among the rich and among the poor.[5] This chapter, however, focuses on what is wrong with inequality from the perspective of democracy. Already discussed (in Chapter 1) are the ways in which unequal market power can lead to refeudalization.[6] Here, the focus is on the broader societal implications of inequality. Before turning to them, however, two counterarguments need to be addressed. Some commentators, even on the political left, argue that it is not inequality as such that matters. What matters most is to get everyone out of poverty. This argument is powerful: deprivation in the midst of rich countries is obviously a problem, and thwarts equality of opportunity for the next generation. Nonetheless, looking at the lower end of the distributive scale is not enough—it is its overall shape, including the upper end, that matters for democracy.

This leads to a second set of arguments that are sometimes used to justify inequality: arguments from desert. It is popular to think about economic outcomes by asking: Do people deserve them? If poverty is deserved, maybe there is no duty of justice to alleviate it (even though there might be a duty of charity). And if riches are deserved, society has no right to redistribute them—or so the argument goes. But can the notion of desert even be applied here? The argument here offers a contrasting view, based on considerations about the nature of desert and the function of markets, thereby clearing the way for arguments against inequality from a democratic perspective. The focus is on three such arguments: the arguments from unequal power, from class formation, and from wasteful rat-races. By avoiding these, more egalitarian societies not only strengthen their democracies but also create more space for socially productive innovation. This chapter concludes with some practical ideas for reducing inequality—concrete policy proposals with the potential to be broadly endorsed by those who care about saving democracy.

The Anti-Poverty Intuition

Many people share the intuition that what matters most for justice is that everyone has enough resources for a decent life. Philosophers call this approach "sufficientarianism," because it focuses on how much is sufficient for everyone.[7] Where exactly to draw the line for this threshold differs depending on what reasons stand behind it: it can be rather low if one focuses on basic physical needs, or higher if one grounds it in, say, a conception of human beings as social creatures who need resources for social participation. It makes eminent sense to think of disadvantages not just in terms of money, but in terms of a broader set of resources that one needs for leading a decent life.[8] In practice, these theoretical differences find expression in how welfare systems are designed: do those who need public assistant just receive enough to get by, or do they also receive—material or immaterial—support for, say, retraining for another job or participating in society in other ways? But in any case, those who endorse a sufficientarian approach hold that it does not matter for justice what happens above this line. If some have ten times, or a hundred times, what others have, this is not a matter of justice. The argument that one should prioritize the fight against poverty may seem strong at first glance. After all, there is enough work to do to convince those who do not want to offer *any* support to those in need. Thinking about justice beyond that point may even seem to have an illiberal smell: Why not simply let people earn as little or as much money as they like, in the higher echelons of the socioeconomic ladder? Even if one believes justice does require looking at overall patterns of income and wealth, that may not be a wise *political* strategy. Many societies are currently so far from doing justice to the poor that it may seem imperative to give priority to the fight against poverty.[9] This also makes sense from the perspective of equality of opportunity. One can hardly create fair equality of opportunity if some kids grow up in poverty, sleeping on moldy mattresses in decaying apartment blocks, their parents always short of money and time, and hence unable to meet their needs.[10]

I shared these intuitions for quite some time. I was moved much more by the misery of some fellow human beings—and especially the injustice of children growing up in deprivation—than by abstract calls for "equality." However, one argument always seemed very strong: "poverty" is not a concept that can be set in stone once and for all, across all historical periods. Even what counts as "basic need" changes over time. Think, for example, about the availability of running water, and about how social norms about personal hygiene have shifted. What it takes to be accepted as a "normal" member of society has a historical index. Adam Smith wrote about the "linen shirt" and "leather shoes" that every worker was expected to wear or else be "ashamed to appear in public" in his time.[11] This standard, to appear in public without shame, seemed a good heuristic for how much even the poorest members of society need to have. For example, today, admitting that one does not have a smartphone would be shameful for many people, and would also mean exclusion from many practical and social contexts and thus create very concrete disadvantages.

By acknowledging that poverty is relative, one already moves a step away from a hard sufficientarian line. For it means acknowledging that if something happens in the higher echelons of society—for example, if the use of new technologies becomes the norm—this has implications for how to draw the line below which nobody should fall. In other words, one needs to look at the character of society as a whole to determine what justice requires, even if one then focusses on providing enough for the poor. I have come to think, however, that acknowledging the relativity of poverty is not all that justice and democracy require. For even individuals who have enough in the sense of sufficientarianism can often not be fully equal members of society. Democracy, as a commitment to the equal standing of all citizens, requires more, as will be argued in some detail below.

Social theorist Albena Azmanova recently put forward an interesting argument that can be understood as similar in spirit to sufficientarian arguments.[12] She argues that, instead of focusing on inequality, more attention should be paid to economic insecurity, which in today's system of "precarity capitalism" afflicts not only the poor but also many members of the middle class.[13] The parallel with sufficientarianism is the plea to get people *out* of something—out of poverty, and out of insecurity. This is an important dimension of the discussion about social justice: What safety nets do people have, individually and collectively? Surveys regularly show that many individuals do not have the means to deal with any emergency requiring an outlay of a few hundred dollars.[14] This is particularly alarming in a society such as the United States, where many medical expenses need to be paid out of pocket even if one has health insurance.[15] Reducing economic insecurity, and the stress that it creates for individuals and families, is an urgent imperative.[16]

But the question remains of whether insecurity can be eliminated *without* addressing the enormous inequalities that cripple societies, turning also to the upper end of the distribution. It seems clear that ensuring a decent minimum and security for all will not be possible without more massive changes in the current distribution of income and wealth—because this distribution is also one of power. Before engaging with the positive arguments for more equality, however, there is another argument to be addressed. It is often used to advocate *against* equality, but as will be shown, it cannot be used in this way, and in fact pulls in the opposite direction.

Deserved Inequality?

Arguments for limiting inequality are sometimes met with resistance because individuals feel that incomes are, in some sense, "deserved." Often, this is no more than a vague intuition, based on everyday examples such as the idea that someone who works longer hours should also get a higher income. It is quite an argumentative jump to move from such basic fairness intuitions to views about the super-rich. But such jumps are being made, with an explicit reference to "desert": Harvard economist Greg Mankiw recently argued that the incomes of the super-rich are deserved if they reflect what they "contributed to society."[17] This, he claims, has its basis in the intuitions of many people, who seem to resent not so much the high incomes of successful innovators or artists, but the outsized earnings of those they believe "manipulate the system," such as CEOs who lobby for government bailouts.[18] In another paper, he also argues that most CEOs' incomes are likely based on their high contributions to company value, and therefore deserved.[19]

Mankiw puts forward his arguments without any detailed consideration of what "desert" actually is or can be.[20] His claims do not stand up to scrutiny, and it is worth discussing in some detail why—not so much to criticize his views specifically, but to clarify the moral force of the intuition that desert must play some role in the distribution of income, which is widespread. Many people seem to think that markets prices express social contributions, and that market incomes are therefore deserved, rewarding those who are particularly productive. But this picture is misguided in many ways.

Desert always describes a three-part relation between a subject (*who* deserves something), an object (*what* they deserve), and a desert basis (*why* they deserve it).[21] There is a broad consensus among desert theorists that it must describe something about the person for which that person is responsible—for example, some action she took.[22] This is how the concept is applied, say, in the context of legal judgments, when it is said that someone "deserves" a punishment or an acquittal.

But can this notion be applied to how much income and wealth individuals have? A first challenge is that it cannot be applied to anything that people are not responsible for. This straightforwardly excludes inherited wealth: it is a matter of luck, not something one has worked for, and so it does not make sense to say that one "deserves" it.[23] But the question is what else, beyond inherited wealth, people can or cannot be held responsible for. One does not choose one's family's social networks, or where one grows up, so any benefits one gains from them cannot be deserved either.

So, the discussion needs to focus on what individuals *can* be meaningfully held responsible for. And to make meaningful statements about who deserves what compared to others, one needs to start from a fair baseline of comparison. At a sports race, everyone starts at the same moment, and the conditions are the same for everyone. In our economic system, however, things are different: people start from vastly different positions.[24] Nor, in fact, is it precisely clear what the "race" would be, given that individuals work in vastly different jobs, all (or most) of which are needed for society, but which involve very different activities or outcomes that could, theoretically, serve as bases for desert claims. We must assume, for the sake of argument, that there is a common currency to compare them, maybe the "social contribution" that they are making.[25]

If, counterfactually, there were a level playing field, what would be the basis of desert for incomes? Presumably, it would be the success of people's work in making social contributions. But here one immediately runs into new challenges: two people may make the same kind of effort, but with very different outcomes. This can be a matter of external circumstances, or sheer luck, or it can have to do with different talents. Talents, however, are again not something one can deserve.[26] They are the outcome of a "natural lottery," as some theorists have called it.[27] Or to be more precise: it is the combinations of inborn talents and social circumstances that matter, because the latter determine which talents a society rewards. In many historical societies, for example, a talent for horsemanship provided a good income, but today such a talent is not in high demand.

From a philosophical perspective, it is thus dubious to make *any* arguments about "income" being deserved. How can we justify that the lucky ones whose talents are currently in high demand get so much more than others? But let's assume, for the sake of argument, that we *can* hold people responsible for what they do (at least as healthy grown-ups), and let us assume that we can cash out some notion of "social contribution" as the basis for desert. Let us also, for the moment, ignore questions about unequal talents. From this more pragmatic perspective, it is often held that market prices track social contributions, as Mankiw also assumes. But there are many reasons for why this cannot be right.

The first reason is that the rewards that individuals receive in markets depend on demand *and supply*. Take an activity that delivers a valuable social contribution, without imposing harm on others or the environment, such as making beautiful sculptures that contributes to people's good life. Let us also assume that the people who would like to buy sculptures have sufficient purchasing power to do so (without this assumption, the idea that markets could ever reward social contributions is stillborn from the start). The wages paid to sculptors will nonetheless depend not only on how many people see such work as a valuable contribution and would be willing to pay for it, but also on how many people want to be sculptors. In many societies, there are far more artists than there is purchasing power for art, which is why, for many of them, incomes are low. The major exceptions are a few superstar artists, of course, but this is another story; in a global attention economy, the income of someone whose name becomes a brand is determined by brand value, not social contribution.[28]

This is what markets do: they use the price mechanism to indicate scarcity and abundance.[29] And this matters in particular when the circumstances of demand and supply change. For example, in recent decades, the high demand (undergirded by purchasing power) for programmers has meant they could expect high wages for the social contributions they make, but as artificial intelligence becomes increasingly adept at writing code, human programmers will presumably face lower demand for their services, and the lower wages that follow will (according to economic textbook logic, at least) induce fewer people to seek employment as programmers. Whether all of this normatively desirable overall is another question—but for now, the important point is that labor markets, as they currently exist, do not reward social contribution per se. And this is not even to mention all the social contributions that are made *outside* of markets—but that, in many cases, make market contributions possible.[30]

There is also a slightly more technical argument against the view that markets reward social contributions, which has to do with the difference between average and marginal contributions.[31] The standard assumption about labor markets is that the marginal contribution of additional workers declines: the first worker you hire makes a massive difference, and as you hire more of them, the additional value each adds becomes less and less. Employers—at least those following the textbook logic—stop hiring at the point where the cost of bringing on an additional worker exceeds the additional value that workforce expansion would deliver. That point of equilibrium sets the wage that all workers get paid, but it is not the average of their contributions: the latter is higher because of the higher added value of the earlier workers. When one uses a concept of "social contribution" as a basis for desert, however, this needs to be a concept of average, not marginal contribution, because it is a matter of luck who gets hired first and who is added further down the line.

But these abstract considerations are of limited relevance for real-life markets. In those, it is often quite meaningless to ask what a "fair" starting point would even be. Those markets are often shaped by differences in bargaining power that have to do much more with individuals' gender, ethnicity, or legal status, than with their "contributions."[32] Moreover, it is not just the bargaining processes *within* markets that are shaped by unequal, and often unjust, power relations; the same is true of the frameworks within which markets take place.[33] One of the most visible expressions of these power relations is the fact that jobs that are understood as "female" and done mostly by women carry a lower market wage than those traditionally understood as "male."[34]

At a more fundamental level, however, it does not even make sense to focus on specific labor markets and the incomes generated in them as *separate* mechanisms in which social contributions would be made and rewarded. All these labor markets are embedded in an economic system in which the only reason an individual can specialize in one kind of work is because others take on other tasks. It is only possible to decide to earn one's living as a sculptor, a nurse, or a programmer because other people work to provide food and other necessities. Everyone's contribution depends on the contributions of others, including those who work in the public institutions providing public goods, and including those whose work, in families and elsewhere, is not paid at all. The value of each contribution depends on the total of these contributions. The features of the wider system also affect the compensation levels of certain jobs: the same kind of work can carry very different wages depending on the economic system and its general level of productivity.[35] Philosopher Tom Malleson cites the case of bus drivers in Sweden, who earn a salary about fifty times higher than their counterparts in India do.[36] This is not because of differences in the "social contributions" made by these nations' drivers, but because of the interrelations with different economic systems.

The upshot of these arguments is that intuitions about desert cannot deliver plausible counterarguments against reducing inequality. Many of the highest incomes and highest wealth levels are probably *not* deserved, because they are based on factors that individuals are not themselves responsible for. The fact that some of them stem from markets indicates the demand for them, not their "social contribution." From a desert perspective, instead of defending existing inequalities, one must critically ask why many individuals who *obviously* make important social contributions, from firefighters to nurses, are paid so miserably. There was some awareness of this fact during the Covid-19 crisis, but it quickly faded from view afterward.[37] A coherent theory of deserved incomes, if it can be developed at all, would probably come to the result that *they* deserve higher wages.

In fact, in a more equal society, with greater equality of opportunity and better regulated markets (for example, with fewer opportunities for rent-seeking), desert arguments might be *better* applicable. If all kids have access to sufficient resources and a high quality education, no matter which family they are born into, one can, with greater plausibility, say that a candidate "deserves" a certain job than in a society in which many kids never got a chance to compete for it in the first place. And inherited money is, on any plausible account of desert, *not* deserved, and should thus be taxed away, as some defenders of desert theories in fact hold.[38]

Does this mean that one should get completely rid of the notion of desert and the intuitions behind it? One can maybe grant that it can still play a role in specific social contexts, in which its basis is clear, but not as a moral notion that would describe some weighty entitlement, but rather in a functional sense, tied to different social roles.[39] If an organization defines criteria for filling a certain position and one has a choice between an outside candidate who clearly ticks all the boxes and an inside candidate who does not, but happens to be friends with the head of the search committee, then it is meaningful to say that the first, rather than the second, deserves the job. But this says nothing about the entitlement to their income of either of them.

Sometimes, we speak more loosely about "deserving praise," and this seems to be a somewhat more moralized understanding of the term. But again, it has little to do with markets or wages. We can express our admiration for achievements in various ways, and we have many social mechanisms beyond financial compensation for honoring them. In many occupations, there are prizes, medals, and various informal, community-based forms of recognition that celebrate quality of service, independent of monetary considerations. And yet, the questions raised above, about the bases of desert and the extent to which they are under individuals' control, remain in place even in such cases. What should be clear, however, is that the justification of the current inequalities of income and wealth cannot be based on such an account of desert.

The Democratic Costs of Inequality

Having cleared the way by addressing the misconceived objection from desert, we can return to the question left earlier: Why care about inequality, beyond the fight against poverty and economic insecurity? From a democratic perspective, there are three central reasons making it an urgent issue if democracy is to be stabilized: unequal power, class formation, and the endless, unproductive rat race to which highly unequal societies condemn their members.[40]

The first problem is that high inequality with regard to income and wealth spills over into other areas of life in which equality should be the norm—and the greater the economic inequality, the more difficult it becomes to maintain the institutional barriers between different spheres.[41] Chapter 2 outlined the problem of market rules being bent in favor of the most powerful market players, leading into a spiral of refeudalization. But the problem goes further, concerning not only economic policies but also all other areas of legislation. In a famous study, political scientists Martin Gilens and Benjamin Page show that decisions of the US Congress typically follow the preferences of industry interest groups and citizens in the top 10 percent income bracket.[42] In other words, money *does* buy political influence.[43] But only those with spare money can buy it—and those private individuals (in contrast to corporations or organized interest groups) making political donations represent for the most part a very small tier of well-off citizens.[44] Meanwhile, many average citizens have neither money nor time to spare for political engagement.[45]

Money buys many other things, as well. It buys better lawyers, better education, access to better healthcare—it is well established that the rich live longer and healthier lives than the poor.[46] Even just for that reason, they are able to play a greater role in political life, at least in societies in which positions of power tend to go to people above a certain age. Many working-class people cannot afford to take time off from paid work to run for political office.[47] Add to this the indirect influence that stems from the greater representation of well-off individuals in areas such as the arts, literature, or higher education, which in turn have an impact on politics.

A helpful way of thinking about this phenomenon comes from the French sociologist Pierre Bourdieu, who in the 1980s described a variety of types of capital beyond the conventionally understood economic capital.[48] *Cultural capital*, for example, means the mastery of cultural codes that give one access to certain positions of power and prestige. It typically rises with educational achievement—and while economic capital (or the economic capital of one's parents) is often needed to acquire it, the relationship also works the other way. Having cultural capital provides access, in turn, to jobs in which one can acquire economic capital. *Social capital* refers to social networks and reputation; like cultural capital, it can often be translated into economic capital and vice versa. By translating economic capital into social and cultural capital, rich individuals can access various spheres of power and exercise influence in them. What is probably most insidious, from a democratic perspective, is that they can thereby also influence the social norms of society in ways that serve their interests.[49] This need not happen consciously, in some kind of conspiracy—it can happen simply because certain messages get amplified, while others get downplayed or crowded out.

One often hears a counterargument that philanthropy is a force for good. Don't rich people contribute in manifold ways to society through donations, and isn't it a small price to pay to stick a mogul's name to a wall to encourage more of this to happen voluntarily, without the coercive force of the state? But this is indeed a point at which a purely economic, efficiency-based perspective and a democratic perspective diverge fundamentally.[50] Let's imagine a hypothetical setting in which the rich donated just as much as they would otherwise pay in a just system of taxation—an unrealistic scenario, to be sure, given how small the percentages of their donations typically are.[51] Even in that case, the power relations would be fundamentally different (and remember that many donations are tax-deductible, so money that gets donated does *not* get used for public policy). Rich individuals, corporations, or foundations can set their own priorities, which can range from odd and whimsical to eminently reasonable—and as such, there may well be a certain "discovery function" connected to philanthropy, as Robert Reich has argued, because it may fund projects that neither the market nor the democratic public would support.[52]

And yet, this gives rich individuals (or the administrators of trusts) a degree of power over public policy that is highly problematic, especially if it is combined with political influence through strategies such as lobbying and campaign donations.[53] It speaks to the ways in which our societies have gotten used to undemocratic forms of financial influence that philanthropy is today often simply taken for granted. In contrast, there was quite some resistance when, at the beginning of the twentieth century, super-rich industrialists began creating foundations, such as the Rockefeller Foundation.[54]

To be sure, in our non-ideal world, philanthropy *can* be a force for good. And those who have the power to spend philanthropic money can and should do so in more democratic ways.[55] They can, for example, let citizens from different backgrounds apply for projects instead of pursuing only their own agendas. They can choose publicity, and allow for public deliberation, instead of the hidden paths on which philanthropic money often travels today. But in a more democratic society, funds that perform the beneficial functions that philanthropy sometimes serves today could also be made publicly available, with public oversight. Both the use and the origins of the money would then be public, and trusts and foundations—were they still to exist—would be held accountable for the sources of their money as well as its use.

A second, related problem with high inequality, from a democratic perspective, is that money buys advantages that *cluster* in ways that lead to the formation of different social classes whose lives grow more and more apart from each other.[56] Class is about more than money—it relates to a whole set of habits, practices, and social norms, and a plethora of background assumptions about what one takes for granted in life. It shapes not only one's worldviews but also one's language and even one's body. Bourdieu's work is illuminating in this respect, as well: he suggested the notion of *habitus* to describe how class gets inscribed in bodily behaviors, such as postures and ways of speaking.[57] When people from the same class background gather, they feel comfortable and at home with each other. When members from other classes join, they quickly realize that what they usually take for granted does not hold in these circles. They have to self-monitor and adapt themselves, trying to fit in.[58] Individuals from rural backgrounds who move into professional lives in urban communities, for example, often wear different kinds of clothes and adapt their ways of walking, laughing, and speaking when moving between these different social realities.[59]

Such class structures are not only deeply unjust, they are also deeply undemocratic and probably explain a lot of the recent disenchantment with democracy. Individuals cannot relate to each other as equal, but instead fall into behaviors of domination or submission. Some take themselves to have the say, while others do not even dare to speak up, or are tired of being silenced again and again. Ultimately, all of them become more unfree. For sticking to the rules of one's class—and one better does so, at the risk of painful social sanctions—often reduces one's freedom. One has a more limited choice of hobbies and spare time activities, but also of friends and romantic partners. Businesses have fewer choices to hire qualified people because real requirements of skill are overshadowed by considerations about who "fits in" along class lines. Beyond democratic politics, society as a whole runs the risk of being paralyzed by rigid class boundaries.

To be sure, in liberal societies there will always be different communities, with different social habits and cultural codes, based on occupational groupings, ethnic and religious background, or shared interests. This is the kind of diversity that we cherish, but that also requires painful compromises and mutual tolerance in the face of deep value conflicts. Democratic societies do well to not let this positive form of diversity be overshadowed by the formation of socioeconomic classes. Precisely because of all the differences between their citizens, they need to remain societies in which, in the words of philosopher Elizabeth Anderson, "no one need bow and scrape before others."[60]

If a highly unequal society is *not* too paralyzed by class structures, then another challenge arises from the fact of socioeconomic inequality: the way in which it drives its members into futile rat races that undermine solidarity. This is a third argument against inequality. For in such societies, individuals always have to "keep up with the Jones": they have to run to stand still, because *everyone* is trying to move up. And the greater the distance between the rungs of the social ladder, the harder the struggle. This mechanism has been a blind spot for traditional economic theory, which assumes that the utility of goods is independent of individuals' social surroundings. But in reality, many of the goods we consume are "positional goods": their value depends on how they compare to similar goods that others have, and on their relative place in the ranking.[61] Or to be more precise: many goods have a positional *dimension,* in addition to some independent utility. I may feel perfectly fine wearing my old, worn jeans at home, but when I leave the house, I feel that I must wear something more "decent." What counts as decent clothes, as a decent home, or as a good education, however, depends on how much others spend on these items.[62] And it is impossible for everyone to catch up: only 10 percent can be in the top 10 percent.[63] It is a zero-sum game, or even a negative-sum game, because so many individuals spend money and energy just to stay on the same rung (a point to be taken up further in Chapter 4).

This is bad on many levels. It is bad for the environment because the resulting higher consumption often goes hand in hand with a greater environmental footprint.[64] It is bad for people's mental health because it creates anxieties about status and fears of being left behind even among members of the middle and upper classes.[65] From the perspective of democracy, what is particularly bad is that it creates unnecessary competitive relations between individuals. A society completely free of competition is probably an unrealistic dream—after all, democracy itself requires competitive structures that help to hold those in power to account and allow new political forces to emerge. But too much competition can be corrosive of the mutual tolerance and solidarity that democracy also needs.[66] If you feel that you always have to outshine your neighbors to win the economic game or the social popularity contest, how can you unite with them when it comes to fighting climate change, or an illegitimate power grab by a local politician?

But why couldn't there be inequality without the rat race, one may wonder. This is certainly a theoretical possibility, but it would require admitting that there is *no* equality of opportunity, and that there is no point in even trying to move up. In other words, it would require openly opting for a feudal society. But given the public commitment to democratic values—and given that many individuals would realize what an adverse class position they actually find themselves in—this is unlikely to generate legitimacy. Insofar as the current system is seen as legitimate at all, it relies on the fairy tale that everyone can make it to the top. And thus, everyone *trying* to make it to the top, against all odds, leads to the rat race. If you are a single individual or a couple without children, and if you are lucky enough to live in a country in which the welfare state still offers some safety, you might decide against it: you might opt out of the rat race, take an easy job that covers basic needs, and simply stop caring about social status. For many others, however, this is too risky a strategy, if only because they want their children to have a reasonable choice about how *they* want to lead their life. And if you belong to those who have to struggle to simply make ends meet, the idea of "opting out" must appear like a remote dream.

The result is a never-ending sense of having to push on, because someone is already closing in to overtake one from behind. If one is no longer rising, one will fall, and the fall will accelerate because one will be labeled a loser—or at least this is what one fears. Even taking a break seems a risk because there will be some others who will not take one. And there is no end to the pressure, no matter how successful one is, because there is always someone who is further up. The result is a sense of existential exhaustion, of wanting to press the stop button, for oneself and for society as a whole. During the Covid-19 pandemic, this sense of exhaustion intensified for many families.[67] But it is not specific to pandemics, it is built into the very structure of highly unequal, highly precarious societies with their constant imperative to keep up with others. If there is no security in sight, one never gets a chance to take a deep breath and to look at others not as competitors, but as fellow citizens.

Reducing Inequality, Enhancing Freedom

What, then, should democratic societies do? There is no shortage of proposals for inequality-reducing policies, apart from simply increasing taxes on high income and wealth (and closing tax loopholes).[68] One policy that could be a powerful counterweight to the inequality of wealth is a combination of an inheritance tax and a capital grant for young people who do *not* inherit, for purposes such as financing an education, starting a business, or making a down payment for a mortgage.[69] It could be designed differently depending on the specific needs of different societies, with variations in not only the amount of money but also the purposes for which it could be used. There is a tradeoff between individual freedom and paternalism here: on the one hand, giving people more leeway in what they want to do with the money sends a strong signal that they are seen as autonomous members of society. On the other hand, some restrictions on permissible uses might help sell the policy to the broader public, because it would reduce the fear of money going wasted. But in any case, such policies would work against the gulf that has opened up between those from monied families and those from other backgrounds, and that risks undermining democratic equality in the long term. In the context of the United States, where wealth is also extremely unequally distributed along racial lines, it would also be a way to contribute to racial justice and to help repair past injustices in access to wealth.[70]

Another strategy is to withdraw more of the goods that matter most to people's lives, especially education and health care, from market forces.[71] If such goods are publicly provided, conditions can be made the same for everyone, and people of different backgrounds can interact and form social ties in these public institutions.[72] Generally speaking, it is wise to use policies of *predistribution* instead of redistribution wherever possible, and set up the framework of markets and other institutions in ways that prevent the concentration of wealth in the first place.[73] This can head off resentments of wealth being "taken away" from richer individuals. Philosophically speaking, of course, that is not a valid complaint since there is no reason to think that people have an automatic moral right to their pretax income.[74] Still, it is a very real phenomenon, known to psychologists as the "endowment effect," that people cling to what they think of as "theirs."[75] "Predistribution" can also mean that all new economic policies are evaluated not according to their potential for "economic growth" in an undifferentiated way, but in their effects on different income brackets.[76]

Another element of egalitarian economic policies is a reliable and sufficiently generous safety net, which takes the character of social insurance *as insurance* seriously. Economic systems in which a certain degree of innovation and change happen bring risks for everyone: their jobs might become redundant because robots or algorithms get better at these tasks, or their region might enter an economic downturn because the goods that were produced there go out of fashion. And then, there are the many things that can simply happen, in all economic systems: illness, divorce, death, whatever life throws at you. Privileged individuals have many financial, social, and psychological support structures for such situations. For disadvantaged ones, such events can be the step into the abyss. Democratic societies have a duty of care toward their members, to make sure that they can get quick and unbureaucratic help in such situations. A job guarantee, as discussed earlier, could be an extremely valuable instrument in this context, but it needs to be supplemented by other instruments for those who cannot work or face additional challenges.

The greatest worry that many people have about such an egalitarian future is that it would lead to an economic system in which these elements are precisely missing: innovation and change. The concern is that without the chances to get rich, individuals would not take the risk to start a business, or would not even be motivated to work hard in existing jobs. The fear of economic failure, bad as it may be, is seen as having a positive effect after all, as the stick that accompanies the carrot of economic success. And, a critic might add, didn't many of humanity's greatest artists and inventors work under the most dire economic circumstances, in extreme insecurity, and yet create masterpieces? Wouldn't a more egalitarian economic system lead to bleak, grey homogenization, without any space for those risk-takers and innovators to whom we owe so much?

If this picture were true, a trade-off might have to be made between equality and innovative power—and it would still not be clear whether the way in which societies *currently* make this tradeoff would be justifiable. What is the point of technological and artistic innovation by the few if the many live in poverty and insecurity? But this claim should be challenged at a more fundamental level: it is *not* true that innovators can be motivated by riches alone, let alone that fear and insecurity are the best drivers of innovation (of the socially useful kind, that is). A more egalitarian society would be *more*, not *less* friendly, to innovation; it would give more individuals access to the conditions under which they can develop their creative and intellectual talents.[77] We have no idea how many Einsteins, Curies, and Kahlos humanity has lost because their scientific or artistic curiosity was nipped in the bud during childhood.[78] We also do not know how many more fantastic entrepreneurs might start socially useful businesses if more young people had a chance to even consider this. What we do know is that the founders of startups come predominantly from rich backgrounds, providing them with safety nets.[79] Also, it seems highly unlikely that financial considerations are the main driver of exceptional intellectual, artistic, or organizational work—such work requires focusing all energies on the task itself, and thinking about possible financial benefits is a mere distraction.[80]

When it comes to egalitarian economic policies, it is important not to be misled by outdated economic theories that are based on overly narrow accounts of human motivation, or that leave out important dimensions of economic reality. Take minimum wage legislation: it was, for a long time, rejected by economists with the argument that it would reduce the number of jobs available to poor people and thereby ultimately harm them. But empirical research found that its introduction did not have this effect. In 2021, the Nobel memorial prize in economics went to a group of economists who used empirical methods—so-called natural experiments—rather than theoretical models for understanding the economy. One of them was David Card, who had in the 1990s studied the introduction of minimum-wage legislation and had been chastised, together with his coauthors, for allegedly deviating from economic common sense.[81]

Of course, this does not mean that there could never be unintended consequences of badly designed policies. For example, if too many veto points are built into a system, innovation might indeed be stifled. Democratic systems, in which majority decisions play an important role, always need to watch out for the rights of individuals, especially of minorities—this is why the rule of law is so crucial as a counterweight to majoritarian decision-making. It probably would not be a good idea to require democratic committees to first approve of all proposals for new products or services. For economic innovation (of the kind that is really useful) to happen, there need to be spaces in which individuals, especially young ones, can experiment with new things. This also holds for other realms, especially arts and culture.

On the other hand, there are reasons to think that the members of a more egalitarian society might also be more *open* to innovation, and hence allow for a more dynamic economic and cultural life. After all, resistance to change often comes from fear. If individuals had more security—for example, if the specter of unemployment could be killed once and for all by a well-designed job guarantee—they might be more open to welcome change. What if one's social status were no longer tied to one's position in a financial rat race?[82] If instead it were firmly grounded in egalitarian citizenship, then one might be more tolerant toward those who experiment with different economic or cultural models. Of course, a complete end should not be expected to the distrust, and even resentment, of those who try out radically different things. But that is not necessary. An egalitarian democracy is not a like-minded community in which all dissident opinions would be stifled.[83] It is a society in which *different* communities, with *different* ways of life, can flourish, as long as they stay within the framework of shared democratic values.

How equal *exactly* should a democracy be, then? It is difficult to provide numbers in the abstract, because so much depends on the overall design of institutions. If institutions in areas such as education, health care, and pensions are publicly provided at a generous level, then somewhat higher inequality of income or wealth is tolerable. An interesting idea for funding such institutions is for an independent government fund to acquire shares in companies and to channel the income to public uses.[84] As discussed in Chapter 2, the ownership in companies can also be spread out more evenly through employee-ownership-plans or by encouraging the transformation of companies into co-ops that are owned and run by employees. Different measures could be combined in different ways, depending on the economic traditions in different countries. Overall, the unequal distribution of wealth needs to be brought back from the current excess, the ratio of lowest to highest incomes to something more in the ballpark of 1:10 than 1:300.

Ultimately, a more egalitarian society would be a freer society. If economic inequality could be regulated, then many other regulations that currently try to keep money out of spheres where it does not belong would be less necessary. If certain social spheres, such as education, were organized fully as public institution, there would be no need for additional support for poorer families in this area. There could be more cross-pollination between ideas and practices of people working in different fields, whose paths hardly ever cross in today's societies. And you really wouldn't be able to tell, when meeting someone on the streets, whether they are rich or poor—because they all belong to a solid middle class.

Such an egalitarian society would also have more opportunities for being a sustainable society, in the environmental sense: it would not have to rely on economic growth as the only way of producing a few breadcrumbs for the poor, without bothering the rich. Instead, it could focus on the economic functions that really matter to their citizens. But when it comes to growth, one currently finds a fierce battle between the proponents of "green growth" and those of "postgrowth." The next chapter turns to this discussion, arguing that their animosity is unnecessary. The more important question is whether democratic politics *can* shift the economy into a more sustainable direction.

4

FROM GROWTH TO FUNCTIONS

A few years ago, on a sunny spring day in a park in the Netherlands, I ran into an interesting artwork: yellow lines marked a square, running diagonally across an intersection and into the surrounding grass. A sign explained the meaning of the square: this was the amount of land surface you would get if you divided the entire surface of the Netherlands by the number of its inhabitants.[1] It did not feel particularly big—one immediately wondered how much food could be grown on it, and how much space would be left for living. How large would this square be for other countries—say, Bangladesh or Canada? How large had it been in the past, and what would it look like in the future? If you had to put solar panels on it, what would be left? The artwork reminded me of another visualization etched into the mind of anyone who has studied economics: the distinction between linear growth (a straight line that goes up at a fixed angle) and exponential growth (a line that bends upward with an angle that grows at every step). It has often been used to raise the question of how an economic system with an exponential expansionary dynamic can exist on a finite planet.

From Growth to Functions

Economic growth has returned as a topic of public and academic debate. If one sits between the academic fields of economics and philosophy, one quickly realizes that it is one of the topics on which one's colleagues from the two disciplines disagree deeply. Most economists embrace economic growth full-heartedly: they want to see more of it, to save humanity from poverty and to fuel "green" innovations.[2] Philosophers tend to be much more wary about growth—not because they would be happy to live in a barrel like Diogenes, but because they emphasize its negative features: the constant rush, the pressures on the natural environment and on the social fabric.[3] "I am not charmed with the ideal of life ... of struggling to get on," John Stuart Mill wrote in the mid-nineteenth century, which he saw as a matter of "trampling, crushing, elbowing, and treading on each other's heels."[4] Real happiness and a flourishing life are very different from what economic growth currently delivers, at least in rich countries—this is what many philosophers instinctively assume.[5] They thus tend toward the position of postgrowth, as "an era in which the societal project is redefined beyond the pursuit of economic growth."[6]

As this chapter will argue, the question of growth is an excellent test case for thinking about the relation between democracy and capitalism, both historically and with an eye to the future. Historically, economic growth has long played an important role for bringing together these two social logics of modern Western societies: a democratic political system, in which legitimacy is based on universal suffrage, and a capitalist system in which the spoils are distributed unevenly. How to combine the egalitarian values of the former with the inequality of the latter? The answer is to keep the economic pie growing, so that even those whose slices shrink proportionally enjoy gains relative to what they had before. At the same time, objections to redistribution can be milder in a growing economy, to the extent that people perceive it is the *additional* resources that are being more heavily taxed and redistributed.[7]

Maybe just as importantly, an overwhelming focus on growth allows avoiding deeper questions about what values an economic system should support. Especially in the era of the Cold War, this was a convenient strategy for liberal governments: they could position themselves as neutral, in contrast to the ideological indoctrination taking place in illiberal countries.[8] By using growth as a rationale for economic policies, one did not have to ask about the many other values that might inform them. Let economic policies focus on growth, and let private individuals decide what values to realize with the resources the economy delivers—that seemed a reasonable division of labor.

This model, however, is no longer tenable. We face climate change, biodiversity loss, and many other environmental problems.[9] Growth of the kind we have seen in the past is clearly part of the problem: it was, to a great extent, dependent on the exploitation of fossil fuels and other natural resources.[10] Moreover, the growth of the last decades has no longer been the metaphorical "tide that lifts all boats," but has disproportionally benefited the rich.[11] And apart from all discussions about the *desirability* of growth, many Western societies seem to have entered a phase of lower growth, a phenomenon described as "secular stagnation."[12]

This is why democratic societies need to rethink what they want from their economic systems, and what it takes to tackle the "green transition" to a low-carbon economy. Debates about postgrowth or degrowth, which were long a niche interest in heterodox economics, have begun to reach a wider audience. Heterodox economists have popularized notions such as Herman E. Daly's idea of the "steady-state economy."[13] Authors such as Tim Jackson and Jason Hickel have questioned the value of growth for human flourishing and for the sustainable coexistence of human and nonhuman life.[14] At least, that is, they do so for Western countries. In countries in which the basic needs of citizens go unfulfilled, economic growth is obviously still needed (and the debate is, rather, whether these countries might be able to "leapfrog" over the carbon-intense periods that Western countries went through and arrive directly at ecologically sustainable forms of development).[15] But with more space needed for poor countries to grow and hence, typically, to increase their CO2 emissions, the question about reducing CO2 emissions, and hence maybe also growth, becomes even more urgent for rich countries.[16]

This chapter argues that the debate about growth and its alternatives brings attention to the *values* toward which economic systems should be oriented—but also, that there are surprising points of agreement between the defenders of green growth and the champions of postgrowth. Instead of focusing only on their remaining differences, the two camps should focus on the question of how democratic politics can rein in capitalist forces in ways that lead to more sustainability. This requires shifting from a logic directed toward growth, whether green or otherwise, toward a logic in which the *functions* performed by the economic system are explicitly determined by democratic politics. The effect could be to end the stalemate between the defenders and critics of growth, and engage them in a search for the concrete measures that can increase the functionality *and* sustainability of the economy. This would also encourage explicit attention to the *social* dimensions of the transition, finding fair solutions in cases in which decarbonization creates winners and losers. Empowering citizens to get engaged in a more democratic economic system, which is less marred by power structures and rent-seeking, is the best bet for a sustainable and functional economic system.

The place to begin is with a brief explanation of what is actually meant when people talk about "economic growth." Once the limited explanatory power of GDP as a measure of growth becomes clear, one can focus on the actual policy proposals discussed in the growth/postgrowth debates, and can find, in fact, a lot of common ground. What they all presuppose, however, is that democratic politics is sufficiently powerful either to shift growth in a green direction (for the pro-growth camp) or to move the economy into a direction in which things other than nominal growth matter (for the postgrowth camp). This chapter will also draw on the British philosopher R. H. Tawney to illustrate the functional logic that this requires, and discuss the connection to the need for a *socially* as well as environmentally sustainable economy. It concludes with a discussion of how democracies can indeed redirect their economies in this way.

Growth, Conventionally Measured

At the beginning of many discussions about economic growth stands bewilderment about the gap between public discourse—in which the desirability of economic growth, measured as positive change in gross domestic product (GDP), is rarely questioned—and the reality of what GDP actually captures.[17] As a composite figure, GDP sums up the economic output traded in markets, measured in prices, of a country over a period of time, typically a year. The idea of measuring economic output goes back to the seventeenth-century polymath William Petty, who made the first attempts at calculating the annual national income of England. In their modern version, such measurements were pioneered by economists Colin Clark and Simon Kuznets, who, in the first half of the twentieth century, used statistical methods to understand the economic developments of different countries. The political interest in their approaches grew in the context of the Great Depression, the Second World War, and the postwar efforts at reconstruction, which required an empirical basis for economic policies.[18] During the war, the United States, Canada, and the United Kingdom harmonized their approaches.[19] The Marshall Plan was instrumental for bringing them to Europe, and over time they spread to more and more countries.[20]

Initially, there was a lot of debate about different methodologies of calculating the national product, and doubts about how accurately any of them could capture the economic well-being of a country.[21] Kuznets described GDP as "a concept... that implies answers to problems over which social philosophers have wrangled from time immemorial."[22] The statistic says nothing about the *distribution* of resources, and thus hides questions about inequality.[23] It is silent about nonmarket phenomena; only what has a price and changes hands for money is included.[24] This means that, for one thing, public goods, but also goods traded in other currencies (for example, in exchange for access to digital data) are not counted. For another, it means a lack of distinction of different types of goods: not only is there a neglect (by definition) of market externalities because these do not have a price, there is also no differentiation between, say, the weekly grocery shopping of a family and the private jet bought on a whim by a billionaire. Productive and extractive forms of exchange are treated alike.[25] If you compare a scenario in which an environmental disaster, say an oil spill, is avoided, with one in which it does take place and leads to costly clean-up activities, then all else being equal, the latter scenario implies a higher GDP.

Now, one might think that there is nonetheless nothing wrong with making statistical calculations about economic transactions; maybe they can serve as a proxy for other things that really matter, such as public health. But the problem to which critics point is this: if you produce such measurements, and use them in public life, they can take on a life of their own.[26] This is an old problem in the governance of social systems: you measure certain things, and people start changing their behavior to look good in the statistics. Here is an example, discussed by Cathy O'Neil in her book *Weapons of Math Destruction*.[27] In the 1980s, American magazines introduced university rankings. Originally, these were based only on surveys among academics; they got more and more sophisticated over time. Of course, universities wanted to look good in the rankings.[28] "Great," one might think, "they're working harder to do a good job for students." But—and cutting a complex story short—doing so costs money, and while the rankings increased the number of dimensions they considered, one thing that they did *not* consider was costs for students (this held for a long time; today, some do). So, universities faced perverse incentives to add ever more costly facilities to their campuses, to score higher on the central variable of "student satisfaction." This, O'Neil argues, is one of the reasons that tuition fees in the United States have gone up so dramatically, at a rate four times that of inflation.[29]

For critics of GDP, the situation of Western countries is a bit like this: they have put all their energies into pursuing growth, measured in terms of GDP, without considering the costs.[30] In the process, critics hold, they have forgotten what really matters. As Jason Hickel puts it, "growth has come to stand in for human well-being, and even progress itself."[31] In response, defenders of growth have often made two arguments. One is that, even if GDP is not itself a goal, it is an indicator that correlates with many good things, or at least did so in the past, with richer countries having happier and healthier citizens living longer lives.[32] To this, critics respond by pointing to countries that have lower GDPs but high ratings in terms of other outcomes, such as health and happiness.

The second argument by defenders of GDP is that it has not really played such a decisive role in determining policy objectives: it was never the only lodestar and societies can, and maybe should, combine it with other indicators such as health and longevity.[33] The idea that "what gets measured is what gets managed" has never been the whole truth.[34] Societies are certainly capable of pursuing other goals as well.

Thus, GPD as such may not be the culprit. And yet we need to keep in mind how little it says about the performance of a society's economic system. This raises the question of *what else* democratic societies should focus on. Later in this chapter that topic will be taken up, but it is helpful first to explore in more detail what policies the critics and friends of growth in fact defend.

Green Growth, Postgrowth, and the Need for Democratic Policies

The debate between defenders and critics of growth is fierce, and often quite polemical, with mutual accusations of ignorance, naivete, and illiberalism. What is fascinating, however, is that when one starts reading texts from the different camps side by side, one quickly realizes that there is much more agreement than disagreement between them. No reasonable commentator today denies that, whatever is permitted of our economic systems, they must not be allowed to violate the "planetary boundaries" set by the biophysical conditions of the earth system. These boundaries represent the limits beyond which our natural world cannot be strained by human impact and still be able to recover, in areas including climate change, biodiversity loss, ocean acidification, and various forms of pollution.[35] Alessio Terzi, for example, who is an economist and fervent defender of economic growth, acknowledges in a recent book that it is "now widely accepted in climate science and economics that economic growth, in its present form, based on fossil fuels and unfettered carbon emissions, cannot be sustained for much longer."[36]

There may be some disagreement on the details, but commentators also accept, by and large, that purely technical solutions, based, for example, on more efficient devices, are insufficient. What prevents this—apart from the question of whether technology could ever be efficient *enough*—is an effect associated with the name of nineteenth-century economist William Stanley Jevons.[37] According to this effect, which environmental economists also call the "rebound effect," increased efficiency can lead to higher, rather than lower, demand for energy. If I get a new washing machine that uses less water and electricity, I might let it run more often. To prevent such behavioral shifts, the prices need to change as well, expressing the real-world costs of the behaviors in question. If the prices of all goods and services reflected their true impact on planetary boundaries, *then* technological innovation could indeed lead to a more sustainable economy.

It is, hence, no surprise that the necessary reduction of environmental externalities is another point of agreement between friends and foes of growth. The tools they suggest differ in some respects, but they all push in the same direction. Writers in the postgrowth and related literatures often recoil at the economists' language, which puts a price on everything and might thus risk understanding the value of nothing.[38] They suggest that we need to develop a completely different attitude toward nature, one of care, relatedness, and reciprocity.[39] But this requires a long-term cultural shift, and arguing for it is compatible with holding that in the shorter term we need to change the behavior of individuals, and in particular of corporations, by drawing on the language that they currently understand: money.

It is also worth noting that the tools suggested by both camps are compatible with democratic values and the rule of law—contrary to a few strawman-ish arguments that they are inherently illiberal.[40] The most obvious of these tools are bans of certain harmful activities and discouragement by taxation. Herman Daly, one of the pioneers of the contemporary postgrowth debate, captured this point prosaically: "Value added is a good thing, so it should not be taxed. Depletion and pollution are bad things and should be taxed accordingly."[41] Terzi, the pro-growth economist, wants to put a tax on carbon emissions, as well.[42] Hickel, on the anti-growth side, also endorses this point, and suggests a number of additional measures that can also be understood as reducing environmental externalities. For example, he wants to legally require companies to stop practices of "planned obsolescence," and place limits on advertising. He also supports a shift from "ownership to usership" (to reduce the use of material resources), an end of food waste, and measures to "scale down ecologically destructive industries."[43]

There is nothing wrong with these suggested measures. But appropriate pricing of environmental harms—not the insufficient measures currently in place, but a true reflection of costs to nature and society—would, in fact, push in the same direction. For example, the environmental burdens of the beef industry, one of Hickel's examples, imply that there should be a high tax burden on beef products—or more generally on CO_2 emissions and other environmental harms, which would include beef products. It is likely that, in response, consumers would shift their consumption. If all raw materials were priced according to environmental impact, and if companies or consumers had to carry the costs of waste recycling (for example, of electronics), then planned obsolescence would also quickly become a thing of the past. With regard to food waste, the cost-of-living crisis of 2022–2023 has already shown, in many countries, that instead of wasting food, for example, because it is past its formal expiration date but still safe to consume, it is better to hand it over to food banks. And as to advertising, there are many reasons to suppress messaging that appeals to short-term, irrational desires and leads us into overconsumption. But I would not argue for a limit on advertisements for innovative heat pump technologies that could nudge me to replace my old gas boiler, and I doubt that Hickel would.

For here is another point on which the green growth and postgrowth proponents agree. They all want to keep the "good" kind of innovation: technologies that allow for genuine efficiency increases ("genuine" in the sense that they do not reduce pressure on one planetary boundary at the cost of higher pressure on others). Such innovation can be technological, but it can also be low-tech and social, based on behavioral change. For example, providing a safe and comfortable biking infrastructure—as cities in the Netherlands have done for decades—enables much larger parts of the population to go about their daily business on foot and bike, with no need for cars. Combine this with sustainable energy provision for public transport and lots of feedback opportunities for citizens about their mobility needs, and you get to a point where a future with far fewer cars is no longer utopian.

So, what to make of the battle between the friends and foes of growth? At least when it comes to concrete policy measures, it would seem to boil down to question of labels. Do you call the direction in which our economic systems need to move *degrowth,* because a rising GDP is no longer what matters? Or do you call the goal *growth* but emphasize that it must advance in a "green" direction through efforts to "harness the forces of capitalism"?[44] To be sure, when it comes to the deeper values and the underlying ontologies, the two camps may need to agree to disagree. But for political purposes, they could join forces.[45] And as to the use of specific tools, why not take a pragmatic approach and see what works best, learning from the experiences in different countries? All sides in the debate agree that what is needed is a mix of public and private initiatives.[46] One is tempted to ask: Shouldn't they put aside their differences and spend their energy finding out which measures work best?

A striking point about the debates over growth, however, is that everyone assumes, rather unproblematically, that it is *possible* for democratic policies to determine the rules of the economic game. Democratic policies need to force the productive sector to engage only in business that is compatible with, and ideally supports, the transition toward a system that remains within planetary boundaries. This is indeed what matters more than whether we call the result postgrowth or green growth: *Can* democracy succeed in this project, either to tame economic growth, or to channel growth into a "green" direction, or some combination of these? This shifts the axis of the debate toward the power relation between democracy and capitalism.[47] Are democratic politicians able and willing to stand up against the power of corporations and other economic actors, and prioritize the long-term public good over short-term profit interests?

A critic might object that this line of thinking exaggerates the need for *political* steps to stir the economy onto a sustainable path. Can't we get there without coercive measures, such as bans, limits, or taxes? It is certainly true that voluntary action by citizens can play a role as well, especially if they use their role as consumers, buying sustainable goods and refusing to buy unsustainable ones. If they have bargaining power in the labor market, they can also push their employers to invest in sustainable practices and production processes, from showers for bike commuters to the use of responsibly sourced materials.[48] The more the economic system is understood as obeying democratic principles, and the more exploitative practices and unaccountable power relations are reduced, the more likely it is that citizens are empowered to make such demands.

But this is unlikely to be sufficient—we need to act on environmental issues not only as consumers and employees, but also as democratic citizens and by means of democratic rule-setting. Many changes will only come about if laws change or if the cost structures for companies change, for example, through the consistent taxation of externalities. Active economic policies are also needed to break from the current, path-dependent course that the availability of cheap resources, with no attention to their environmental costs, has set us on, in areas from transportation to heating to agriculture. This may sound daunting, but there is no shortage of ideas and practical proposals—many already tried and tested in some countries, but yet to be adopted elsewhere.[49] With stronger political support, and taxation that makes the use of fossil fuels financially unattractive, a lot seems possible. The big question is whether the political will to move in this direction is strong enough to overcome the resistance from those who benefit from the status quo.

Political action is also needed to encourage innovation—for example, with regard to renewable energy provision and the use of circular or recyclable materials. As noted above, this is what all commentators want: creativity, new ideas, technical and social innovations. There is some disagreement on whether, and to what extent, one needs financial incentives for fueling such innovation, and how exactly to divide the tasks between private and public organizations.[50]

Recognition from others, together with the intrinsic joy of exploring new things and putting solutions into practice, could, in principle, go very far in motivating individuals to become "green" inventors and innovators. But as long as we still live in capitalist times, recognition that is not expressed in monetary terms may feel shallow to some people. So, to manage the transition, it may be wise to not exclude financial incentives—while working toward a more democratic understanding of the economic system, in which the need for such financial incentives (for what is, after all, often highly interesting and satisfying work) can be reduced over time.

In many countries, the public debate about green economic policies is in full swing. There are subsidies for "green" investments.[51] International organizations push for "green jobs."[52] The European Union plans to raise the price of CO_2 emissions.[53] And thinking about postgrowth is no longer taboo in Brussels.[54] But what is missing is a deeper discussion about what functions an economic system is actually supposed to fulfill. The growth/postgrowth debate goes into this direction, as do other heterodox approaches.[55] But the fundamental shift in the economic logic that this requires is often left implicit. The next section turns to this new logic.

From Growthmanship to Social Functions

What if we looked at our economic systems in ways that go beyond "growthmanship"?[56] This would mean that one could not simply define one aim for the economy—namely, growth—and avoid all other questions. Instead, one would need to be explicit about the *functions* that the economic system is supposed to serve, which need to be compatible with the planetary boundaries and in line with democratic values. This is a shift away from the conventional understanding of the economy, which leaves the determination of goals or purposes to individuals as consumers alone (or to state institutions that use tax money for providing certain goods and services), and hopes that markets will deliver them, through companies that see profit-making as their main purpose. Instead, the approach of democratic institutional design means that one first defines the functions that an economic system (or subsystem) is supposed to deliver, through democratic deliberation and decision-making. Then, one designs economic institutions to achieve these goals, of which markets, appropriately regulated, can be an element, but of which public organizations—for example, municipalities that provide new energy infrastructure—can be part, as well.[57] Profit-making may still have some role to play, but it can at best be a secondary purpose that is used to incentivize the production of certain goods or services.[58]

One might call such an approach "functionalism," if "functionalism" were not used in so many, confusingly different ways in different academic disciplines.[59] It is certainly not "functionalism" in a pre-modern sense that would assume some predetermined natural essences for all beings. Rather, it is a view that sees economic institutions as what they really are: man-made structures that can and should be put into the service of society, to create the conditions under which all individuals can lead free and flourishing lives.[60] This has nothing to do with Soviet-style central planning; it fully acknowledges that, often, decentralized decision-making structures—whether in markets, civil society organizations, or local political constituencies—are the best way to decide about concrete functions. But importantly, this approach does not shy away from discussions about values: about the values that govern our economic practices, and about their compatibility with democracy. It thereby also acknowledges that there is no value-neutral territory in institutional design, because, whether we like it or not, our economic system *will* embed certain values. So, we had better talk about them!

One thinker who made such a functional logic explicit was R. H. Tawney, a British thinker, educationalist, and important figure in the British Labor Party in the twentieth century. While some of his ideas are outdated, it is fascinating to reread his 1921 book *The Acquisitive Society* and to see how many of the arguments resonate with today's situation. Tawney was highly critical of the unequal property distribution that he saw in his day—and of the fact that property rights, and the ensuing economic developments, were simply taken for granted: "The enjoyment of property and the direction of industry are considered . . . to require no social justification, because they are regarded as rights which stand by their own virtue, not functions to be judged by the success with which they contribute to a social purpose."[61] Tawney rejected all "functionless property," which is divorced from productive work and creates a class of rentiers who have a say about productive processes without having any direct connection to it.[62]

Instead, Tawney wanted to see a restructuring of economic relations such that the "acquisition of wealth" would be "contingent upon the discharge of social obligations"—the functions, that is, that society requires.[63] A "functional" society, as he called it, would honor all forms of work: it would "honor even in the person of the humblest and most laborious craftsman, the arts of creation."[64] Tawney was not so idealistic to think that humans would work simply out of altruism, and he took seriously questions about how to organize work efficiently. But he held that it is not financial incentives that create the strongest motivation to do a good job, but rather *esprit de corps* and "the public opinion and tradition of the little society in which the individual moves."[65] Influenced by guild socialism, he proposed forms of work organization in which the workers, together with those they serve (for example, the customers), have the strongest voice.[66]

These ideas are as relevant today as they were in the 1920s. What needs an update is the question of how societal functions are to be determined. Tawney seemed to take for granted that individuals would agree on them. Today, we have a better sense of the deep disagreements that can arise about economic policies—but also of the many ways in which democratic forms of decision-making and legal procedures for conflict resolution can address them. One may well ask, however, whether *all* areas of economic policy should be determined in this way. Modern societies are deeply pluralist, after all—and there is no reason to expect that this would change with the transition toward a greener economy. There need to be spaces in which individuals can agree to disagree and live according to different conceptions of the good life. Allowing this, despite the interpersonal tensions it can stoke, requires clear legal rules and protected rights for individuals, together with a culture of tolerance.

Critics of postgrowth are sometimes worried that *everything* would have to be decided democratically, leading societies into irresolvable conflicts.[67] But there is no such pressure. If the rules are set in a functional way, there can be a lot of space for individuals to take different decisions, based on their different values, and in cases in which this makes sense, mediated by the price mechanism. Herman Daly, in his vision of a steady-state economy, is clear about this point: the imperative, he holds, is to "provide macro stability while allowing for micro variability, to combine the macro static with the micro dynamic."[68] This, however, is very different from allowing market participants to destroy the environment, or to extract profits from others rather than create mutual value. Talk of "economic freedom" all too often covers up such forms of behavior instead of supporting a plurality of lifestyles and economic practices within the framework of planetary boundaries and of the basic values that democratic societies agree on.

What, then, are ways in which such a functionalism would work today? How should democratic societies realize the transition to a sustainable economy? A key point is that environmental and social policies need to go hand in hand, carefully orchestrated with each other, so as not to undermine the social cohesion that democracies need. A reduction of inequality, and better conditions for those who need to earn an income, will be crucial to maintain support for technological change.[69] Simply increasing taxes on fossil fuels, without additional measures, would lead to a cost-of-living crisis for large swaths of the population, and therefore to understandable resistance.[70] Hence, a green transformation that is not also a social transformation is unlikely to be successful. What are also needed are fair solutions for those who lose out in the transition—not, that is, for the CEOs and shareholders of fossil fuel companies, but for the workers whose livelihoods will be on the line, and who will need support in retraining and moving to different jobs.[71]

The most basic function of an economic system, ultimately, is to provide for human needs in ways that maintain social cohesion and allow all individuals to flourish. Many defenders of growth have in fact held that *social peace* is the most important argument in its favor. In times without growth, social tensions have often been on the rise, and resentment against minorities has grown.[72] If the pie shrinks, the scramble for resources gets rougher—or so the argument goes.[73] This is an important argument for democrats, especially in today's time in which the tensions between different groups in society already run high: one would not want to recommend any policies that might trigger more resentment and us-versus-them thinking.

But economist Benjamin Friedman, who analyzed this pattern in a detailed historical study of Western countries, has shown that there was one notable exception: the New Deal era in the United States did *not* bring such social tensions.[74] In this period, bold measures were taken, such as the "job corps" created for the unemployed. What matters, thus, is that if the economy does not grow, individuals' needs, especially those for meaningful work and a decent income, continue to be secured. Such steps must also be taken today, if talk of a "Green New Deal" is to be more than just rhetoric.[75] This is another reason to endorse the idea of a job guarantee, as advocated in earlier chapters.

A good starting point for operationalizing this social dimension of sustainability—and as such, a good successor to GDP—is the so-called capability approach, developed by economist and philosopher Amartya Sen and philosopher Martha Nussbaum.[76] It assumes that all human beings have certain basic functions that they need to be able to fulfill for a flourishing life. These include physical needs (for food, clothes, shelter, medical care, and so on), but also skills and opportunities for social engagement and participation in society (for example, literacy and basic numeracy). While Nussbaum bases her approach on the Aristotelian tradition and proposes a fixed list of functions, Sen chooses a different approach: he suggests proceduralizing the question of which capabilities matter, and in what ways. This means that citizens use democratic procedures to determine, for example, how to interpret a capability such as health in their concrete societal context.[77] Those with democratic commitments will probably prefer Sen's approach. An additional reason, however, is the great variety of circumstances in which policies oriented around human capabilities need to be implemented. Even if one starts with a general list, one needs democratic procedures to decide on the concrete forms the capabilities should take and the tradeoffs that might have to be made as multiple capabilities are developed. An important addition to this approach comes from philosophers Jonathan Wolff and Avner De-Shalit. They argue that, beyond *levels* of functioning, security also matters: individuals need to know they have *secure access* to the relevant resources and institutions that enable their functionings.[78]

In any journey toward an important goal it is vital to have reliable indicators of the progress being made along the way, and this will certainly be true of the efforts to reach the functions that the economic system and specific parts within it are meant to serve. Therefore, the questions will stay with us of what to measure and how to make sure that measurements do not distort social practices. But this risk can be mitigated if there are also other forms of communication, beyond the numbers: feedback mechanisms, surveys among users, or indirect measurements that are not susceptible to human distortion.[79] There are numerous ideas for going "beyond GDP," to get at a more nuanced and holistic picture (whether GDP grows or not will then be quite inessential).[80] There is currently renewed political interest and a mushrooming of new proposals.[81] But this trend is not as new as it may seem. The World Bank has already used the Human Development Index, which is based on the capability approach, since 1990, as a way of getting a better grasp on where different countries stand and what measures really work.[82]

Moreover, digital data collection and analysis allows for all kinds of scoreboards to be used on specific issues—for example, the consumption of beef versus legumes, or the number of kilowatt hours of electricity provided by solar panels.[83] It makes it also much easier to measure traffic flows and thus to determine the need for better infrastructures for non-emitting or low-emitting forms of mobility. Some commentators believe that the era of "big data" will make decentralized decision-making and markets completely superfluous.[84] Even if one does not share this view, one can agree that big data allows for a much more nuanced picture in the evaluation of both public policies and private economic endeavors. Democratic societies thereby get various tools for moving their economic system toward the desired functions. We are, thus, in a much better position than R. H. Tawney was in 1921 for democratically designing an economy that serves the functions we want it to serve.

Greening the Economy by Democratizing It

When discussing postgrowth with those who have previously believed in economic growth, one still hears skepticism about the compatibility of postgrowth with democracy. Some defenders of growth see it as a kind of untamable force, or as tamable only by giving up basic liberties.[85] Others see the search for newness, the fascination with knowledge and insight, and the desire to change things, as deeply rooted in human nature. Still others, with a darker view of human nature, focus more on that inner voice that warns people they must not be overtaken by others, which, in their view, means that competitiveness and the drive to outcompete others are not peculiar to this or that society, but universal features of mankind.[86]

In response, it should be emphasized, first, that human curiosity and the desire for change would not be suppressed in a postgrowth world. They would continue, hopefully, to fuel the development of more efficient (yes—here is a call for efficiency!) uses of natural resources, new medicines, or better social techniques for coordinating human behavior. To return to John Stuart Mill's vision: he held that in a "stationary state" there would be "as much scope as ever for all kinds of mental culture, and moral and social progress; as much room for improving the Art of Living, and much more likelihood of its being improved" as in the growth-fixated society of his own day.[87]

As to the human striving for "more," we need to ask what it really is a striving for. Adam Smith observed long ago that, ultimately, what people seek is the recognition of their peers: "it is the vanity, not the ease or the pleasure" that motivates them to work hard.[88] Philosophers from Hegel onward have taken on this idea of a human need for recognition, with many seeing it as a deeply rooted driver of human behavior.[89] But different societies put the premiums of recognition on different features and behaviors, whether certain bodily features, success at certain artisanal practices, or the possession of certain kinds of goods.

Arguably, it is the combination of competitiveness and inequality, discussed in the last chapter, that gave this struggle the specific shape it has taken in Western societies, interlacing it with economic growth. Because most of our basic material needs are fulfilled, we compete for the positional features of things: for their *better* versions, which make us stand out among others.[90] Yet, as Fred Hirsch memorably put it: "If everyone stands on tiptoe, no one sees better."[91] If our societies were structured in more horizontal, less vertical ways, then the struggle for recognition might take on rather different forms, and be channeled into quite different directions—and put less pressure on planetary boundaries, but also on human energies.

For these reasons, a democratic redirection of human energies in ways that go beyond GDP growth should not be regarded as impossible. In fact, a greener and more social economy could be one that would improve the quality of life for large parts of the population—so the question is rather, *what is holding us back?* And this is, again, a question about democratic politics and its ability to assert its primacy over the economy. For among the forces that stand in the way of change there is certainly the inertia of large, complex systems in which change in one area is difficult without change in other areas. But then, there are also the very concrete financial interests of specific individuals and organizations—first and foremost the fossil fuel industry, but also many industries that are closely interconnected with it. For them, the transformation brings undeniable losses. In many cases, they have fought for their interests on the political *hinterbühne*, through lobbying or by influencing the reporting on climate change, for example.[92] More and more, such behavior gets called out by climate activists, bringing the conflicts to the fore.

In an ideal world, democratic governments would simply join forces and impose measures on all industries that make them switch to sustainable business models—and they would find ways of retraining, and offering new jobs to, their workers. In the world we live in, this process is more difficult, so we need more creative ways of putting pressures on these industries—for example, by taking them to court.[93] A pessimist might think that the only chance to break the power of the fossil industries would be to buy them out in the same way in which slave traders were bought out when slave trade was abolished in Great Britain in the eighteenth century—not because this would be just (which it obviously isn't) but because it is the only way for achieving a greater good.[94] But hopefully, such desperate steps will not be needed. Public opinion is shifting, and quickly.⁹⁵ The more the legitimacy of making profits at the costs of the environment erodes, the less powerful players can demand compensation for having to change course.

In fact, making our economic systems more democratic is likely to be the best bet for a quick and successful green transition, because it can unleash the energies of the citizenry as a whole. While we certainly need basic research and certain public infrastructure changes, a large part of the transitions will have to come through the *rolling out* of innovations on a large scale. This will require governments to set the right frame, but it will also require local initiatives to have enough wiggle room to implement new solutions on the spot. Well-designed markets can allow for this, but so can institutional space for, say, neighborhood initiatives to use the excess heat from a data center to warm the water of the local swimming pool.⁹⁶ Citizens, whether as founders of social enterprises or as participants in local associations, need to have real scope of agency—and this means that the economic system must not be dominated by large players.

Citizens need to learn about successful models that have worked elsewhere (and, ideally, also about failures, so that others can avoid repeating them).⁹⁷ Historians of the Enlightenment and of the Industrial Revolution have emphasized how important the development of an infrastructure of knowledge—including postal services, academic journals, and so on—was for the interactions between different scientists, but also between scientists and practitioners, and thereby for the dissemination of innovation.⁹⁸ Today, we have an even better infrastructure of knowledge: the internet, despite all its problems, is a wonderful tool for engaging in inquiry and learning from each other. It can connect those who experiment with new solutions and speed up the process of change.

To take a concrete example of such "greening" from below: European farmers who reintroduce older species of legumes have started a network to exchange experiences about planting strategies, and to find buyers, such as food-producing companies who are willing to experiment with new products. This helps marketize plant-based proteins that enable consumers to cut down their CO2 emissions.[99] This is just one of countless initiatives that have developed, in the most unexpected places, connecting individuals who want to make a difference. The more such dynamics can be unleashed, the better they can fuel the transition toward an economic system that does not follow a blind imperative of growth but is in line with planetary boundaries and democratic values.

Such a green transition is possible—and individuals need to see the concrete steps that empower them to help bring it about. Social norms need to change, but so do hardwired infrastructures. This will not be possible without engagement on a broad front. At the same time, it will only work if individuals feel that they are not being treated unfairly in the process: that they can have a say, and that their basic interests are protected. The next chapter outlines a concrete proposal that, together with other measures, could recreate such a sense of optimism and possibility, and enable individuals to take on the environmental and democratic responsibility of greening the economic system: work-time reduction and the encouragement of civic work. For it will be hard to stabilize democracy if we do not allow citizens to dedicate to it more of what may be the most valuable resource in a human life: time.

5

TIME FOR DEMOCRACY

If John Maynard Keynes had been right, our lives would look very different. In 1930, he wrote the famous essay "Economic Possibilities for our Grandchildren." It predicts a massive reduction of working hours: the necessities of life would be produced within some hours per week per person. Except for a few individuals with "intense, unsatisfied purposiveness who will blindly pursue wealth," everyone would be able to return to a quieter and happier life. "We shall once more value ends above means and prefer the good to the useful," Keynes wrote.[1] But he was also slightly worried: wouldn't this lead people into an existential crisis, a "general 'nervous breakdown'"? Humanity would first have to learn to live with so much leisure.

Keynes could not have been more wrong. For many individuals and families, overwork and exhaustion are the rule. Advice to seek "work-life balance" can seem downright mocking to those who are forced, by sheer economic necessity, to work extremely long hours. To be sure, the sense of "not having enough time" has a subjective element, and some people might simply not dare to admit having time, because this might suggest that they are not that important.[2]

But for many individuals, especially among less privileged groups, the shortage of time is real. The situation is particularly dire in the United States: as early as 1992, economist Juliet Schor diagnosed "a profound structural crisis of time."[3] Since the 1970s, European countries have cashed out productivity gains in the form of shorter working hours and more vacation days, and also more generous leave policies for caretakers.[4] And yet, many individuals, especially parents of young children, are deeply exhausted.[5] But it is much worse in the United States: there, full-time employment means an average of forty-seven hours per week, around ten hours more than in most European countries.[6] Part-time options are scarcer, and for many, they are simply not affordable.[7]

One might be tempted to call working hours a matter of choice: some people want more money and work longer hours, while others opt for more leisure and therefore decide to live on smaller budgets. But this perspective overlooks the fact that labor markets, unlike many other markets, contain an element of force, at least in societies lacking unconditional welfare systems. In these societies, unless you are independently rich, you *have* to work to avoid destitution. And depending on the costs of living, and the rights people have vis-à-vis their employers, their choice about how many hours to work can be very limited. Add to that work time their hours spent commuting, performing household chores, and caring for children or other dependents, and it is no surprise that many individuals are exhausted. In one survey of parents in the United States, none of the responding mothers, and only five percent of the fathers, indicated that they "often" had time to spare.[8] Single parents carry the heaviest burden: the category of single mothers is among the most time-poor of all demographic groups across many societies.[9]

It should thus not come as a surprise that working time has become an issue again—not only in popular discourse and in a steady flow of advice books, but also in political philosophy. Julie Rose, for example, makes a powerful argument for understanding the distribution of free time as a matter of justice.[10] Free time is a crucial resource: without it, many other freedoms cannot be realized. Moreover, she argues, individuals need to have *coordinated* free time—that is, free time together with others, which is crucial for the freedom of assembly or for practicing the freedom of religion, which typically involves joint rituals. If paid work, together with care work and necessary daily chores, eats up too many hours, such freedoms end up being nothing but empty words.

This chapter approaches the question of working time from the perspective of democracy, and shows how doing so leads to more radical conclusions about the distribution of time. Time matters for democracy: if individuals have no time for it, we cannot expect them to be good democratic citizens. Lack of time has very concrete implications for how our democracies function. It is, for example, a big part of the explanation for why there are so few politicians from working-class backgrounds; as political scientist Nicholas Carnes has emphasized, running for office entails time commitments that people of modest means find very difficult to make.[11] Of course, this is also a matter of financial resources; sufficiencies of money and time are often intertwined. And yet, it is worth looking at our societies specifically through the lens of *time politics*—not only because time distribution has very concrete implications for all members of society, but also because money does not *always* buy time, or not the right type of time.

This will be the starting point of the next section: sketching the history of the struggle for time, and arguing that it needs to be a collective one. Working time is not a matter of individual choice, but of politics. Then the discussion will move to the question of care time, and the need to allow time for all socially necessary work, not just for work that is rewarded by markets. Reclaiming time for democracy goes beyond this call, however: it also means asking how time can be made available for people to engage in public activities and civic tasks. Tocqueville, when traveling to the United States in the nineteenth century from his native France, was impressed by the fact that Americans were active in all kinds of associations, creating high amounts of social capital.[12] But as Robert Putnam and other sociologists have argued, this kind of social capital is currently at a low point in the United States.[13] While the underlying causes are complex, time politics is one of the main levers that democratic societies can move to return to a better balance between time spent in private jobs and time spent in public activities. In the current situation, the general implementation of a four-day workweek, combined with incentives for civic engagement, could be a decisive step forward to strengthen democracy.

The Struggle for Time

Probably there have been struggles over working time as long as there have been working relations, in whatever form, between employers and employees. In many traditional societies, however, religious observances created a rhythm of work and rest with certain days being free from toil.[14] It was in the nineteenth century, when work took place more and more in the mines and factories of the Industrial Age, that the fight for work time broke out as one of the central struggles of the workers' movement.[15] The idea was to establish maximum working hours for adults and especially for children, who regularly worked under dire circumstances. Karl Marx, in his mature writings, analyzed the length of the working day as one of the key mechanisms of capitalist exploitation.[16] He noted that there is a certain amount of work time needed to produce all that is socially necessary, and that, for workers to perform it, they must be paid wages sufficient to sustain themselves and their families. But the value of every additional minute they work accrues to the capitalists—which is why the latter will always try to extend working time. The minutiae of this argument depend on Marx's "labor theory of value"—the idea that economic value is ultimately based on nothing but working time—and we must acknowledge that this theory is notoriously contested.[17] But the basic logic of working-time struggles does not depend on it. When labor unions started to form, setting limits on working hours was one of their core demands, and in short order, their efforts crystallized into a general call for an eight-hour workday.[18]

Even today, unions affect working time. A 2005 study of working hours across Western economies found a strong negative correlation between the share of workers covered by collective bargaining and the hours worked.[19] The authors argue that, because unions have incentives to maintain jobs for their members, they reliably, in crises, fight for reduced working hours rather than job losses.[20] From the perspective of free-market thinking, this may seem an inefficient distortion of the free play of market forces. But the authors, economists themselves, also consider another possibility: Might working-time regulations and union policies, as they exist in many European countries, "help solve a coordination problem?"[21] Maybe workers in the United States would also value more free time to spend it with their families and friends. Currently, two-parent, full-time-working families from middle-class backgrounds spend 135 hours on paid and unpaid work per week.[22] They might prefer the shorter weekly hours and longer vacations that European countries offer to most employees. In highly individualized labor markets, however, jobs with shorter hours may be impossible to find. For companies, it pays to have fewer workers with long hours, rather than distribute the work across more people, as it saves them per-person costs such as training or benefits; this is why overwork must also be expected in high-paying jobs.[23]

There are indeed good reasons for understanding working time as a collective and political problem, not as a matter of individual choice. There are advantages to coordinating working time and sharing social norms about when and how much to work. It can feel very strange to sit idly in a café on a Tuesday morning when everyone seems busily at work. But social norms play a role beyond this strange feeling: if most members of society work long hours, then the expectations about standards of living (and hence the hours needed to earn enough money) shift upward.[24] If one person decides to work less, her additional leisure hours will be lonely—and for many individuals, the point of having more free time is precisely to spend it together with others. Economists describe this as a "social multiplier" that increases the value of leisure time taken together.[25]

An additional argument for why working time is a collective issue stems from the difficulty of equating time with money. Often, time and money are imperfect substitutes; caring for one's children, for example, is work that many people want to do, at least in part, themselves rather than hire others to do.[26] But reducing working hours often comes with costs beyond the proportionate reduction of wages. The phenomenon of the "part-time penalty" is well established: those working part-time lose out on promotions and other opportunities such as attractive project assignments.[27]

Time poverty also limits the ability to make good choices, especially in societies in which most products and services need to be acquired in markets.[28] Making good choices in markets takes time. It can be fun to shop for products that one sees as expression of one's personality, such as clothes. But when it comes to challenges such as finding the right mortgage or buying health insurance—choices that are consequential for one's life in the long run—making decisions can be a burden: one wants to make them with care, ensuring that one does not overlook any important details and that one has understood all pros and cons. This takes time, and it also helps if one has advisors, in the form of paid professionals or experienced friends or family members with whom to talk things through. But time-poor individuals often lack all these things: the time and energy to think through decisions, and support from social networks, because their friends and family members are likely to be also time-poor.

This means that time-poor individuals are likely to make more decisions that are based on insufficient information, and maybe even on insufficient consideration of what they themselves really want—thinking about that also requires time, which, say, a single mother who is juggling several jobs hardly has.[29] For more privileged individuals, this is different: they benefit from the opportunity to choose from a wide variety of offers. Maybe this is one of the underlying reasons for why there is often so little sympathy for the plight of disadvantaged individuals: their situation is described as having made "bad choices," but no questions are asked about the *conditions* under which these choices had to be made.[30] Time poverty is one of the conditions that work against individuals' abilities to lead lives they can truly call their own. It also limits the time they can spend on politics, such as writing letters to representatives, which in turn means that their concerns receive less attention.[31] And as Maxine Eichner argues, time poverty in families, especially in those who are also materially poor, also means that many children cannot develop their full potential.[32]

Therefore, time and time poverty need to be considered political issues. But it is not only equality of opportunity that suffers: arguably, even more is at stake for democracy. Before developing this argument, let me first turn to time for care work.

Reclaiming Time to Care

Making time for care work is difficult to square with the logic of capitalism. Capitalism rewards activities that carry a market value. Care work in families does not do that; therefore, capitalism does not reward it, it might be thought. This is not wrong, but even capitalism needs workers to be well-fed and rested for the next working day, and in the longer term, there also need to be new cohorts of workers to replace those who retire. In the 1970s, some feminists provocatively requested "wages for housework" to make this basic point: the "productive" work of (typically male) workers presupposes the "reproductive" work of (typically female) workers in families.[33] "Reproductive work" was for a long time the work of women, at least in the overwhelming number of heterosexual households in which women, from the late nineteenth century onward, took up the role of "homemaker." Even today, homework is done to a greater degree by women than by men, in the "second shift," as Arlie Hochschild has memorably called it, after they get home from their paid jobs.[34] Why, then, these feminists asked, does their work go unrewarded, given that capitalism structurally depends on it?

Nowadays, this demand may seem strangely out of time, and maybe even dangerous. Wouldn't it cement a role for women that many of them have not chosen, and that, in capitalist societies, will never come with the same power and recognition as paid work? Moreover, today, being a stay-at-home-parent has become a luxury; many families require two incomes to pay the bills. And yet, the question of who takes care of the kids (and the elderly, the sick, and so on) has, in many countries, remained unresolved.[35] Or rather, it has been pushed onto individual families, instead of being addressed as a societal question. Whereas some countries in Europe—especially the Scandinavian ones—offer various forms of public support for childcare and facilitate work-time reductions for parents, many Anglophone countries do very little. The results are worrying: for example, children in the United States are below the average of rich countries on many counts, from academic achievements to mental health.[36] Surveys in the United States also indicate that parents are less happy than non-parents, in contrast to the situation in other countries.[37] The US Surgeon General recently called out the pressures on working parents, and the consequences for their mental health and well-being, as a public health crisis.[38]

Unregulated capitalism is not friendly to families, even though it structurally relies on the work that takes place within them. From a societal perspective, care work in families is at least as important for keeping things up and running as many forms of paid work—it is truly "essential work."[39] But "essential work" is not what capitalism rewards, at least as long as sufficient numbers of people are willing—or feel morally obliged—to engage in it without pay. Parents who have jobs outside the home often need to rely on others for childcare, typically less privileged women, who might even have to leave their own children behind, in the countries they migrated from.[40] Forms of feminism that call for full integration of women into the capitalist economy, without addressing the question of care work, have rightly been criticized.[41] It is important that women can access positions of prestige and power, but this leaves unanswered many questions about the *other* tasks, in care work, that are currently passed on to less privileged women, often along racialized lines.

This is an issue for democratic societies: How can they make their economic systems friendlier to parents and other caretakers, and thereby—given historical path-dependencies—also more gender just? There is no shortage of proposals, and many of them have been tried and tested in countries that have decided to consider care work a public issue. While not everything is perfect in those countries, there is much that other countries can learn from. Limits on working hours, paid vacation time, a right to part-time work and to returning to full-time work, public support for childcare—none of this is rocket science.[42] It is, rather, a question of political power: Can the citizens who would benefit from such policies make their voices heard, and can their concerns outweigh the short-term economic interests of employers or other groups?

In addition to such "pro-family" policies, as Eichner calls them, let me suggest that "care" is a broader concept and thus "time to care" also means more than "time for family work."[43] *Care* can be understood both as "caring for" someone and as "caring about" something, and it can take on many different forms. It can mean taking care of the social life in a neighborhood, caring for local biodiversity, or caring about the historical heritage of a community.[44] What these things have in common is that they are about objects or social relations that individuals find valuable, and that matter for social life. And while some of them may be idiosyncratic hobbies that matter only to small groups, many have a positive effect on others, making their days brighter and their lives richer.

But capitalism, at least in its pure form, can see only the forms of care for which people are willing to pay. It overlooks the many positive effects that unpaid care can have on society, even in the workplace itself. As work is more and more narrowly supervised, categorized, and "made efficient," there is also less space for caring about those with whom we spend most of our days, as coworkers.

There is a story—maybe *no è vero, è ben trovato*—about a team in a company in which there was one employee whose tasks were a little unclear to his colleagues. He seemed to spend a lot of time drinking coffee with others, without producing much measurable output. So, when a new manager came in and the financial situation deteriorated, it was this employee who was fired first. Quickly, the other team members felt that things were not going so smoothly anymore. Nobody organized birthday presents or social gatherings. Conflicts broke out between colleagues who lacked someone to vent with when their work was not going well. The communication between people became more difficult because no one invited them to see things from the perspective of the other person. After some time, it dawned upon them that it was the "unproductive" colleague who was missing. His role, while not formally defined, had been crucial for keeping up the functionality of the team, oiling the social wheels and thus making everyone else's work more productive.

This story often haunts me when I think about work under capitalism and the scarcity of time it creates for so many people.[45] Both in workplaces and in society as a whole, how many people have been driven away from roles as supporters of others, as mediators who resolved conflicts, as caretakers not only of specific individuals but also of groups and organizations? And how does our lack of time play into this development? If people feel that society "does not care" about them, who is it, specifically, who no longer has time for them? Some might say that capitalism has made all of us more egoistic and has pitted us against each other.[46] But maybe it is at least as important that it simply does not leave us enough time to care for each other and for the things we value. Should we then be surprised that the political atmosphere in many countries is so tense? If we no longer take the time to care for each other and for the things that make our lives richer, it can feel as if one's fellow citizens can only ever be one's competitors. This is not the ground on which a democratic culture can flourish.

Reclaiming Time for Democracy

Recent discussions about working hours have led to concrete proposals for new policies. The most prominent examples have been experiments with a four-day workweek, such as the six-month trial that sixty-one employers in the UK conducted in 2022, designed and monitored by a coalition of NGOs, advocacy groups, and researchers.[47] Other such trials had shown promise earlier—for example, in Iceland's public service sector, where carefully managed experiments were staged between 2014 and 2019.[48] The goal was to maintain levels of service provision without overworking employees in the fewer hours they spent working. In most cases, this goal was achieved, and employees reported feeling less stressed and depleted as they gained more time for family, friends, hobbies, and exercise (and were thus able to bring more energy and focus to their work); others in their lives benefited as well, including the grandparents of children whose parents worked fewer hours.[49] After these experiments, the shorter workweek was widely implemented in Iceland, and as of 2021, roughly 86 percent of the workforce had gained the right to work fewer hours.[50]

The 2022 UK experiment was equally successful. Participating companies were free to make their own choices as to how to reduce working hours, with some having everyone take the same day off and others providing for staggered days off or distributing the time reduction in other ways.[51] Employees jointly developed ideas for saving time, then working time was reduced, without salary reductions, from thirty-eight to thirty-four hours on average.[52] The surveys and interviews that accompanied the experiment showed positive results overall: no dips in revenues or other negative effects on companies, and many improvements for employees, including reduced stress and lower burnout rates.[53] Interestingly, more than half of the participants also indicated that their own perception of being able to do a good job went up.[54] Ninety percent of the participants wanted to continue to work in this way.[55]

These results are very promising, even though one should not overgeneralize from them: the companies that participated in this experiment did so on a voluntary basis, and they are probably active in fields in which a working-time reduction without a loss of productivity is a real possibility.[56] This may not work everywhere; in many areas, reducing working time while maintaining the same level of productivity or service provision *will* require hiring more people. But this does not mean that a four-day workweek would not be a good idea—it just means that it might cost more money, and that there might be resistance from some employers. But by keeping the format of the working-time reduction flexible, and by involving the employees in the discussion about how to save time, it might nonetheless be possible to find creative ways of reducing the overall workload.

Some theorists also approach the question from an environmental perspective: Could lower working hours also mean a more climate-friendly lifestyle? People would commute less, and depending on what happens to their incomes they might also consume fewer climate-unfriendly products and services.[57] But they might also engage in *more* CO2-intense activities, such as flying across the country to see friends (at least if the price for CO2 emissions stays the same).[58] What environmental effects to expect is likely to depend on many other contextual factors as well.[59] So working-time reduction must not be understood as a magic bullet that would solve all our social and environmental problems. Rather, it is a way of sharing the gains from increased productivity with employees, allowing them to lead more self-determined lives.[60]

And yet—is this all that we should want? What is missing from many current discussions about working time is the question of how much time citizens actually have *for democracy*.[61] Given how deprived of leisure time many individuals are, it is no surprise that they would spend additional free time mostly on family or hobbies.[62] But in a democratic society, individuals—at least those who wish to do so—should have time for work, family, *and* an active role in democratic life. To be sure, those engaging in reproductive work are already making an incredibly important contribution to society, which, in an ideally just society, would be treated on a par with productive work.[63] But even for them, a democratic society should create opportunities to engage in civic activities if they wish so, maybe in creative combinations of children's activities and public work.

We need to reclaim time both for our private lives and for democratic engagement—not in the form of mandatory enforcement, to be sure, but by way of creating opportunities and providing incentives and resources.[64] This can take on different forms, allowing individuals to design their own lives around different activities: not everyone has to do every form of work in every year of their life, but there should be enough opportunities for all of them spread over one's life.[65] Some researchers speak of "breathing" working lives, in the sense that the institutional framework should create space for phases of more or less intense engagement in paid work, and opportunities to take time off paid work, perhaps to volunteer for public causes.[66]

Why would such "public" time be a good thing for democracies? First, there are many tasks that markets do not reward but that are still extremely valuable for societies. Markets typically undervalue public goods, whether on the local, regional, or national level. Other tasks, such as acts of mutual help in neighborhoods, are difficult to measure, making it hard for market prices to form. In some such cases (for example, security) public provision, and hence also public employment, are the best answer, for independent reasons.[67] But in many cases, it is extremely valuable if citizens themselves can get engaged. They have the local knowledge that is necessary to understand what a community really needs and how policies can be implemented on the ground, and they can build ties of solidarity with their neighbors along the way.

A helpful concept for undergirding this argument is that of the "commons": resources that are held in common by a community, whether it is a local neighborhood or an association that pursues some shared purpose.[68] While such commons can be run by professionals if all individuals pay a contribution, governing them together avoids bureaucratization and top-heavy structures, and allows individuals to participate in running things that matter to them. This can happen more effectively if people with diverse skills participate in their governance (rather than homogeneous groups of retired people, as is currently often the case). And while the commons can be immaterial or material, a type that is currently in particular need of care and good governance is the environmental commons: local habitats of rare species, or green spaces that allow locals to connect to nature.

Some readers, especially those familiar with UK politics, might start to feel uncomfortable here. The proposal may sound similar to the idea of "big society" that conservative prime minister David Cameron once propagated: to engage civil society and NGOs in the provision of services that had previously been provided by the state.[69] To be sure, it corrected the infamous statement by an earlier UK prime minister, Margaret Thatcher, that "there is no such thing as society."[70] Yet Cameron's idea was rightly criticized. It contributed to the further retreat of the state from its core tasks and was thus a thinly disguised form of neoliberalism.[71] My answer to this worry is threefold. First, one central way in which individuals can contribute to society is in collective organizations, such as unions or NGOs, which all need volunteers in local chapters and in various committees. Their role is not to take over government functions, but to fulfil other roles, including pressuring public institutions or protecting the rights of their members *against* state institutions or other actors. Strengthening such organizations, and thereby their *collective* impact on politics and society, is quite different from the individualistic picture of engagement— whether it is through volunteering or charitable giving—that prevails among conservatives. It is based on a view of human beings as social beings who, *together*, can do much more than just fill the gaps of an underfunded welfare state. They can also bring about political change, which, in many areas, is urgently needed.

Second, this is *not* a proposal to reduce government spending. Rather, if working time were mandatorily reduced with wages remaining the same, it would be a way of making *employers* contribute to the public good, by giving employees more temporal resources to do so.[72] And third, the best way to organize such activities in practice is probably some form of collaboration—adapted to local circumstances and the tasks at hand—between civil servants, especially those with specific forms of expertise, and citizens. The latter would bring in new forms of knowledge: experiential knowledge, but also knowledge from their day jobs.[73]

An extremely interesting approach, in this context, is that of "democratic professionalism," as developed by political scientist Albert Dzur.[74] It starts from the observation that there seems to be a tension between democratic equality and the authority of professionals. This is what critics of professionalism have long held, thereby contributing to the hollowing out of many public institutions in which professionalism traditionally had its home.[75] A realistic view of the historical reality of professionalism shows that professionals, including doctors, have indeed often acted in ways that are difficult to reconcile with a democratic ethos—that is, as indisputable authorities whose expertise gives them a higher status than those of other citizens.

And yet, Dzur argues, professionalism can also be understood and practiced in a democratic way—and as such, it can be an important resource for enabling the involvement of citizens. This requires that professionals act as facilitators of "task sharing" and "lay involvement" in areas such as education, the administration of justice, or civic journalism. If citizens and professionals work together, they can build trust and engage in mutual learning processes.[76] This is not just a theoretical utopia—it is a model that already exists in various places, even though it may not always come under this label. Within the profession of academia, it takes on the form of "citizen science," with citizens becoming engaged as collaborators of professional researchers, whether by collecting environmental data or by co-shaping the research agenda for certain diseases through patient advocacy.[77] While such collaborations can raise tricky ethical questions, they can also, if run well, be a way of bringing a wider set of perspectives into a social system such as academia that has, historically, often closed itself off—and thereby making it better not only in terms of serving society, but also in terms of its own core task of knowledge generation. Such a model can also be applied to many other areas of public life, but it takes some creativity and the willingness to try out new things.[78] And without sufficient temporal resources, good ideas and promising projects all too often die a quick death.

The approach of "public work" brings together many of these points.[79] Harry Boyte, one of its proponents, understands citizens as "co-creators of the world."[80] This emphasizes the role of self-organized projects in which individuals "solve common problems and create things, material or symbolic, of lasting civic value."[81] This can take place on different levels and with regard to very different tasks, but always with an eye to what it means to share a life with others. "Today it is as if people decorate their own apartments and attend to their own issues while the building collapses," Boyte writes.[82] The quote is reminiscent of a claim made already much earlier by John Kenneth Galbraith, about the imbalance between public and private investments: many Americans drive expensive private cars over public roads full of potholes.[83]

There is also a second line of argument for why making time, in people's lives, for such civic activities is a good idea for democracy, and maybe even essential for its long-term stability. The question here is where, in their daily lives, citizens have opportunities for acquiring democratic skills, habits, and ways of thinking, and for relating to each other in ways that embody the principles of equal moral worth and equal voice. Part of the answer, as argued in earlier chapters, needs to be rethinking markets and employment relations from a democratic perspective. But economic relations as we know them are at a huge distance from this ideal. And even if improvements were made, economic relations will likely retain some degree of instrumentality. It is, therefore, a good strategy to also think about *other* social spaces in which individuals can experience democratic principles in action.

For Tocqueville, the French aristocrat who visited the United States in the nineteenth century, one of its most noteworthy features was the way in which Americans got together in various associations, in which their democratic ethos and their willingness to defend the constitution were nourished. "In no country in the world has the principle of association been more successfully used or applied to a greater multitude of objects than in America," he wrote.[84] In associations that are democratically run, individuals experience, on a small scale, how democratic deliberation and decision-making work. This also includes developing an understanding of how hard it can be to reach fair compromises in the face of material or ideological conflict—an understanding that could, hopefully, also improve citizens' understanding of "Politics with a capital p," on the national and even international level.

Interacting with others as equals provides citizens with opportunities to learn from each other, to appreciate why others hold certain positions, and to question things they took for granted. They can come to see that their own views are not the only possible ones, and where others come from in developing theirs. This can help them to learn to respect others—as one should, among democratic citizens—but also to acquire practical skills of conflict management. In practical contexts, one often needs to find compromises even if one does not agree on everything and accepts some things only while gnashing one's teeth. But if things go well, the teeth-gnashing is distributed evenly over time, and individuals learn that they can do things together even across deep ideological divides.

At the moment, associational life, with all its opportunities for democracy, is at a low point. The sociologist Robert Putnam has gathered a plethora of data about the social and cultural changes in the United States since the postwar years.[85] He finds that many indicators for social cohesion have a characteristic inverted U-shape that peaks somewhere in the 1950s or 1960s, and this also holds for associational life.[86] There was a wave of associational activity between 1870 and 1920, when many membership organizations, such as the Scouts or the Rotary Clubs, were founded.[87] National chapter-based associations grew in the first half of the twentieth century (with a dip in the 1930s because of the economic crisis) and peaked in the post-WWII years.[88] Since then, their memberships have been in decline. The same holds for many other forms of associational life and individuals' engagement in it. For example, between 1973 and 1994, "the number of men and women who took any leadership role in any local organization—from "old-fashioned" fraternal organizations to New Age encounter groups—was cut in half."[89] In the mid-1970s, the average American adult attended roughly one club meeting a month; this number has declined massively, with two-thirds of Americans not attending any meetings by the mid-2000s.[90]

Of course, the processes underlying these figures are complex, and Putnam goes to great length to unravel their different economic and cultural layers, including their complex interrelations with the fight for racial and gender justice (it is decidedly *not* a nostalgic account that wants to go back to some imaginary past). He discusses the new individualism of the 1960s, with its emphasis on individual development and the rejection of conventionalism.[91] While endorsing values such as freedom and individuality, he ends up calling for a rebalancing between individuality and community.[92] But of course, one cannot simply "bring about" such a cultural shift. What *can* be done is to create opportunities for people to engage in shared activities—and time is a key resource that can allow them to do so.

But how, then, one might ask, does this align with the previous argument, which focused more on the practical work of providing certain goods, such as local public goods? Wouldn't *all* forms of associational life have the positive effects that individuals get to know others and learn democratic skills, at least all that are internally diverse and democratic? Up to a point, I agree—in associational life, let many flowers blossom! And yet, we should appreciate that the activities described above—which involve shared, socially useful, activities, often on a local level—have something specific to offer. If individuals gather along lines of identity (for example, as "the businesspeople" of a region), they are less likely to encounter individuals with different backgrounds and different views. The same holds, admittedly, if local activities take place in highly segregated neighborhoods. But this is something one can work against—for example, by carving out projects in ways that include different types of neighborhoods.

What also matters to this argument is that there is a special kind of magic in doing something together, as opposed to simply being at something together. Probably everyone who has ever been at a large social event has experienced the awkwardness of feeling obliged to make conversation with people they barely know. It is much easier to engage in social interactions around meaningful tasks to do. Maybe this is why, at extended family gatherings, relatives seem compelled to move to the kitchen and prepare food together. The discomfiture of being together without working on something together is worse in places where the political landscape is highly polarized, and a misunderstood comment is likelier to trigger an aggressive reaction. Robert Talisse has recently argued that too much talk of politics in everyday life comes at a price: by always foregrounding political identities, it can deepen the gulf between people, closing down their opportunities to get to know each other in different roles.[93] To sidestep this obstacle, he suggests spending more time interacting with others in shared activities such as singing in choirs or cleaning up parks together.[94]

This is excellent advice, but there is also a caveat: if structures of income and working time allow only privileged individuals to engage in such mutual endeavors, they might only reinforce existing lines of exclusion. We need time politics allowing *everyone* to participate in such activities (and as long as incomes are as unequal as they are today, we might also need a "participation income" for volunteers).[95] When these activities are too loosely organized, however, it might well happen that only like-minded individuals flock together. Empirical research shows that, at the moment, most cross-partisan conversations in American life take place either at the workplace or in school boards.[96] These spaces bring together people who would otherwise hardly have the intention to meet. Workplaces are also more racially integrated than many voluntary associations.[97] But with the fissuring of many workplaces discussed earlier, new separations were introduced, and these have reduced the opportunities for individuals in different types of jobs to interact. Local projects of the kind described in the first argument above offer such a possibility: they tend to be sufficiently small-scale to allow for direct interaction between people from different backgrounds.[98]

This bridges to a third argument, that making time for public work gives society the flexibility it needs to respond to the urgent demands that arise at different points in history. The core idea here is that the divide between market work and public work cannot be set once and for all. In a time of crisis—for example, with the onset of war or in the wake of natural disaster—priorities shift from normal times. Different kinds of tasks have to be done. In some periods, it is enough to set up a good framework of rules by which markets and voluntary activities can deliver what is needed. But the exigencies of other periods may also, or instead, require public work—and at such times, it is very helpful if, through structures and associations already in place, people have built trust in each other, and professional and lay people have learned to collaborate effectively. These are investments that enable quick adaptations in emergencies and solutions to challenges at hand.

A recent event making the case for such investment was the influx of Ukrainian refugees into German cities following Russia's 2022 attack on Ukraine. Suddenly, there were thousands of women and children who needed to be housed, fed, and cared for, first and foremost in Berlin—a city whose public administration is infamous, however, for its dysfunctionality.[99] Not everything went smoothly in the provision for these refugees, but insofar as it did work, it was to a great extent due to civil society efforts—the work of thousands of citizens in all kinds of associations. Thanks to Germany's relatively generous holiday provisions, people could take paid time off from their jobs to work as volunteers—and given the country's relatively short, legally limited working hours, many also pitched in after their workdays were done. The same happened in thousands of other cities and towns across Europe. In a time of crisis, lots of people found ways to get engaged in forms of public work, helping to address a humanitarian challenge that would hardly have been met by the public administrations on their own, let alone by market forces.[100]

This emergency was addressed, within a relatively short time period, through the collaboration of public services, civil society organizations, and citizens in various volunteering roles. But there can also be challenges that require societies to make more fundamental shifts: when it is not enough that the rules are set, but when the very functioning of these rules, and the complex interactions between all the different players, need to be reevaluated and society as a whole needs to change course. In such situations, forms of public work, and engagement by volunteers and civic associations, are all the more needed.

We can draw here an (admittedly imperfect) analogy from the history of science. Thomas Kuhn famously described periods in which "normal science" happens within an established paradigm: people do experiments or analyze data to better explain certain phenomena within a framework of shared assumptions. But from time to time, he observed, researchers realize that the current paradigm does not allow for some observed phenomenon at hand and a new one is needed to understand what is going on.[101] Times of paradigm change are more turbulent and conflict-ridden. And yet it is only within the new paradigm that research can progress. In somewhat similar ways, the socioeconomic life of our societies may sometimes require phases in which what counted as "normal" is reevaluated and priorities are readjusted. In such phases, new and creative forms of collaboration are needed. If a society has a tradition of civic work, this is an extremely valuable resource it can draw on in such situations. If it does not, such times might be good moments to start one.

Climate change, biodiversity loss, and other current environmental problems require a paradigm shift—a transformation toward an ecologically and socially sustainable system that allows all individuals to lead flourishing lives without violating the planetary boundaries. Some commentators even draw parallels to a wartime economy.[102] These historical parallels may be problematic, and certainly wartimes should not be glorified. But it is true that our societies need to change course, fast. And this can take place better if we combine market-based work with new forms of public work, for which citizens are given more free time.

There is a nagging question, however, that some might have about the politics of time suggested here. Why think that people would take up democratic projects instead of just doing whatever they want, in ways that are as individualistic as ever, maybe just watching Netflix?[103] And wouldn't we even see a multiplication of offers, by private companies, trying to benefit from people's newly won free time with all kinds of digital entertainments? Now, ideally, citizens should have *both* time to engage in public work *and* time to watch Netflix. But it is not utopian to hope that opportunities for democratic work would be taken up—not by everyone, but by considerable numbers of people.

For one thing, many people feel the need to make a meaningful contribution to society. Psychological research has shown in many ways that "purpose" is a key motivator for work.[104] Even though the term has been captured, for that very reason, by the corporate world, many jobs offer limited opportunities to serve a genuine purpose. Democratic projects could become an additional source of meaning and agency for individuals. The community and solidarity experienced in civic work teams could develop a real pull, comparable to the one that sports teams have always exerted. If social norms develop that make a few hours of democratic work per week normal, then this could also help nudge people along.

Individuals' willingness to volunteer is likely to depend, however, on a sense that they are being treated fairly. Individuals who get an unfair deal in their work life may not be easily convinced that they should do even more for society. But many people share the intuition that if one receives the resources necessary for a good life from society, one should also contribute to ensure such a life for others. This basic sense of reciprocity might be the most important motivator for public work, but only if (or, more hopefully, once) individuals are being treated fairly in their working lives and in their overall bundle of opportunities.[105] Therefore, time politics and opportunities for democratic work need to go hand in hand with other socioeconomic reforms, as discussed in earlier chapters, that lift everyone out of poverty, reduce inequality, and improve equality of opportunity.

How could such time politics be implemented? Under the current conditions, the policy proposal to shorten the workweek, while keeping pay at the same level (or better, increasing pay, for independent reasons) is one of the most promising policy proposals.[106] For the sake of coordination, to facilitate public work, it would probably make most sense to have one day per week that is conventionally marked for civic activities. Introducing such a day could also offer a way of making corporations contribute more to the public good than they currently do (without even having to mention the word "taxes").

An additional strategy is to provide individuals with opportunities to take time off paid work in the form of a paid sabbatical—currently a privilege in certain highly-paid jobs, but a principle that could be applied more broadly.[107] Take one phenomenon mentioned earlier: the lack of time among working class people to run for office, because they cannot afford to leave their jobs behind for some months. Why not change the rules such that individuals who run for political office—for example, with a commitment from a party that nominates them as candidate—have a right to get paid leave? "Then just *anyone* could run for office," I have heard people say in reaction, in a slightly worried and potentially outraged tone. But that is exactly the point: in a democracy anyone can, in principle, run for office—and there should be mechanisms, mostly within political parties, to advance the most capable candidates. Right now, however, one has to have access to massive financial resources (or many online followers) to do this. And *that* is certainly not the right selection criterion.

If societies build the infrastructures for such temporary shifts in individuals' activities, they become more flexible, both on the individual and on the societal level. They allow individuals to realize combinations of paid work and other activities that can be flexibly adapted to the different circumstances of their life courses. In addition to the possibility of taking paid time off for care work, they can, in some periods, work less because they want to do more civic work, or because they want to retrain for a different kind of job, or because they want to run for political office.[108] On a societal level, such strategies also increase flexibility: in times of crises or far-reaching transformations, they allow a society to draw on different types of work, organized in different kinds of social networks. And who knows—maybe in the future, the balance between market-based and civic work could shift even more toward the latter, all while individuals keep enough free time for care work and leisure.

The time seems ripe for taking serious political steps in this direction—and not only for the "overworked American."[109] It is just as important for the citizens of other democratic countries. The social-ecological transformation will require many different sets of skills, in many different combinations. If citizens get a chance to get engaged, we can unleash social dynamics that solve problems, while they also bring together individuals who would otherwise never have encountered each other, and thereby rebuild social capital and trust.[110] We should not miss this opportunity just because capitalism eats up too many of our hours. Building on this argument, the next, final chapter asks how such changes could be brought about in the here and now.

6

REPAIRING DEMOCRACY ON THE OPEN SEA

In 2021, in the middle of the Covid-19 lockdowns, a group of students invited a Marxist filmmaker, another philosopher, and me to a webinar about the future of work. We quickly found common ground: we agreed that many current forms of work are deeply undemocratic, exploitative, and not in line with basic values of human decency. Where we disagreed was on a question the students pressed us to answer: How to bring about change? The Marxist filmmaker shrugged his shoulders with a sad smile. For him, true change could come only with revolution, a complete overthrow of capitalist power relations. The other two of us argued against this view, holding that the current system is deeply unjust but does still allow for change from within—in steps that seem small but can add up to bigger progress—with the aim of turning the whole system ultimately into something different, something better.

How is change possible in the current situation? This is a question that many citizens, and especially young people, ask themselves. It is clear that many problems currently afflicting the economic, political, and other realms cannot be fixed by adapting a few legal subclauses here and there. If our institutional systems were living bodies, the diagnosis might well be multiple organ dysfunction syndrome. And it is the multiplication of crises that keeps us caught in the status quo. The education system fails to empower individuals; the economic system makes them work too many hours, so they cannot fight for their rights; the legal system also does not offer sufficient opportunities to have those fights; and changes in these systems (and so many others) are not forthcoming because the political system has been captured by big money. And so on, and so on. How, then, can true change happen?

This chapter argues that we should not give up hope of genuinely changing our economic practices.[1] We need not wait for some big system shift (and sit idle until it happens) but can start in the here and now. To the credit of the Marxist filmmaker, it was evident that idle waiting was not his attitude. He kept making his critical movies, portraying the misery and dehumanization that many working-class individuals experience, and thereby moving large numbers of individuals to think harder about the current social conditions.

To be democratic, social change needs to have broad support. Protest, of the disruptive kind, plays a crucial role in building this. But maybe most important is that social norms and expectations change on a broad scale, and with them, power relations and ultimately laws. This chapter will make the case for a democratic form of change, in part by drawing on the work of Anthony Kwame Appiah, who has analyzed how earlier "moral revolutions" in human history brought about shifts in what counted as "honorable." This kind of change is what we need today to bring our economic systems back in line with democratic values. We certainly also need political reforms to democratize democracy—addressing the outsized role of money in politics, for example, and the untransparent practices of many lobby groups. (As noted in the Introduction, the details cannot be spelled out here because they will be country-specific.) But political reform often stands in a chicken-and-egg relation with change in the economic system. The more progress is made on *both* fronts, the more mutually reinforcing the different reforms can be in defending and strengthening democracy against onslaughts like those of recent decades.

We need to unlearn the myths about the economic system that have been so detrimental to democratic values, such as the myth that efficiency is an ultimate value, or the myth that the economic game is all about "winning." We need a positive vision of a democratic economy as a collaborative system, in which different jobs complement each another and everyone has equal standing as a citizen. Arguably, it has been the lack of a positive vision that has stymied many protest movements in the last few years. After a brief discussion of how arguments for reform can be put forward in practice, in the non-ideal circumstances in which many of us work, this chapter will offer a final set of proposals for how the possibility of democratic change, building on the power of the many, can become a reality.

Social Change, Democratic Style

If someone were to design a society from scratch, according to democratic principles, it would look radically different from the societies we currently live in. Philosophers like to do this: John Rawls's famous theory of justice, for example, invites us to imagine what principles of justice we would endorse from behind a "veil of ignorance," not knowing what role we would have in society.[2] This is an extremely productive intellectual exercise, and it has sparked intense discussions about how to think about the principles, metrics, and applications of justice. But it can also distract attention from the rather different task that we have *as citizens,* who cannot build a new society from scratch and must work from within existing institutions.

Even in times when there is a radical break in the political and economic system of a society, the human beings that make up that society remain the same. If we believe in the equal worth of all humans, then we need to make social change *with* these people, not against them. One of the strongest arguments in favor of an evolutionary approach is that it allows for social learning processes in which *all* members of society, or at least broad majorities, can come to understand and appreciate the reasons behind changes, thereby creating legitimacy and acceptance.[3] Moreover, such learning processes can help societies find out what really works in practice to advance the objectives that can, in the abstract, be agreed on. This positive dynamic of social learning and improvement is essential to realizing a more sustainable and democratic economic system.[4]

This argument also inherently rejects another approach that is sometimes suggested, especially to prevent the worst forms of climate change: a technocratic, top-down approach in which "experts" take the lead. At first glance, this may appear a very different way of thinking about social change, at least if one assumes that the experts are among those currently recognized as such, and thus probably not quite the same people as potential leaders of revolutions. And yet, from a democratic perspective, the two approaches lead to parallel questions: how would "the masses" be convinced to follow those in the lead? How much democratic legitimacy would these approaches have? And how large is the risk of sliding into undemocratic territory if people do not like what the experts, or the leaders of the revolution, ask them to do? This is not a rejection of expertise—but the question needs to be how to integrate expertise into democratic decision-making processes, not how to replace the latter by the former.

There is an insight from the philosophy of science that nicely captures this evolutionary approach to social change: the metaphor of Neurath's Boat. It harks back to the ancient Ship of Theseus paradox, which invites us to ponder whether a ship of which every piece has been at one point or another removed and replaced remains the same vessel.[5] Similarly, Austrian philosopher Otto Neurath used the image of a ship being constantly repaired and improved in localized ways during a voyage to make a point about human knowledge acquisition: it always involves destruction and replacement of what has been in place but, while eventually all may be overhauled, the scope of each change is limited and the older, established knowledge continues to provide stability through the disruption. As he put it:

> We are like sailors who on the open sea must reconstruct their ship but are never able to start afresh from the bottom. Where a beam is taken away a new one must at once be put there, and for this the rest of the ship is used as support. In this way, by using the old beams and driftwood the ship can be shaped entirely anew, but only by gradual reconstruction.[6]

The same holds, arguably, for renewing the institutions and social practices of societies. We cannot replace every element at once, but we can replace them step by step, and should focus hardest on the most rotten ones endangering the whole construction. The aim remains the ambitious one of arriving at a better overall system.

The original story of the Ship of Theseus was about an effort to maintain what had existed in the past as truly as possible. This provided the thought experiment of whether an object retains its identity if, while keeping its form, it sheds every bit of its original material. Neurath's metaphor is about the process of building something new and different. The ship he envisions is altered in both material and form quite substantially over time, just as human knowledge has been transformed across history by old understandings being put to rest one after another. This also holds for social change, in which some long-standing institutions and practices should be abolished once and for all. Often, it takes many small actions to reach the tipping points at which this can happen.[7]

This approach has one big open flank, however: the risk that incremental objectives breed complacency, or lead to rotten compromises with the powers that be, causing progressive momentum to flag. When steps are too halting, they become indistinguishable from greenwashing, artwashing, and all the other hollow forms of advocacy touted by the corporate world and other powerful players in recent decades. What is genuine progress and what is mere cosmetics is a question of structural change, not of good intentions. After all, those employees who work in Corporate Social Responsibility offices probably share many views of the protestors at the company gates. But if all they get to do is distribute a bit of money to local environmental initiatives, and they have no say on operational changes that could reduce their corporations' CO2 footprints, their impact will not amount to much.

A good way to evaluate changes and the structural role they might play is to analyze the extent to which they would contribute to power shifts. Would a proposed change make a real difference to who can decide about what, and who has power over whom? Power can shift along many different dimensions, discursive, financial, attentional, and so on.[8] Classic Marxist theory assumes that ultimately, to bring about real progress, property relations must change. This remains an important point of attention today, given the high priority of tackling inequalities in wealth and the economic power disparities that go along with it. But there are also other forms of power with the potential to shift social relations—for example, legal power that determines what property owners are allowed to do with their possessions, and discursive power that shifts what is sayable in public, and hence what individuals or organizations dare to do. Mere words, however—such as public declarations about *responsibility* and *purpose*—are not enough. Strong governance structures and checks and balances are needed to create accountability and to ensure real action.

The need to shift power away from those with economic and other forms of capital, back to the democratic citizenry, permeates all policy areas. It is not surprising, therefore, that proposals for redressing this imbalance have been put forward by many scholars (in addition to proposals for reducing material inequality directly, as discussed earlier). Some, inspired by ancient Athens, suggest forms of citizen involvement via lotteries. This would mean an end to candidates running for election and needing large financial means to fund their campaigns—and would therefore upend a system that overwhelmingly favors rich, white, male, and academically educated office-seekers. Instead, "lottocratic" representation would bring individuals from all walks of life into power.[9] Experiments in many countries have been promising in the sense that the discussions of lottocratic assemblies were constructive and yielded nuanced political proposals—but they have been a massive disappointment when it comes to real change, as the political establishments in these countries have done almost nothing to implement the suggestions developed by these assemblies.[10] Without a commitment from those currently in power to take a new format seriously, it remains an academic exercise. At worst, such experiments can even distract attention from other strategies aimed at increasing the share of non-white, non-male, and working-class representatives in existing political structures.

Others have proposed ways to strengthen the power of the working class directly. For example, an additional chamber of representatives elected exclusively by members of the working class could be added to a parliament.[11] Or, taking inspiration from ancient Rome, other "plebeian" institutions could be added to the current system.[12] Such institutions can be designed to close gaps in the political representations of certain groups as they exist in many countries. Advocates of the natural environment—representing the interests of fragile areas, for example, and at-risk species—could also be added to decision-making processes, as environmentalists suggest.[13]

Not all of these would have to be permanent solutions (although some, such as those for the natural environment, probably should be). In the longer run, one hopes, it may be possible to reduce inequalities along various lines, and to adapt the selection mechanisms for policymakers, such that all political bodies naturally represent all parts of society. But given the current challenges, and the urgency of environmental problems, short-term strategies are needed for redressing the existing power imbalances. Detailing the exact form that policies should take is probably less important than ensuring they have real power, with a clear mandate to make decisions and have them implemented.

Changing Norms, Unlearning Myths

To understand how broadly shared social change can take place, it is instructive to look at historical campaigns that brought about changes we today take for granted, such as the reform of various social practices that put individuals at risk of disfigurement or death. The philosopher Anthony Kwame Appiah has analyzed various examples of "moral revolutions," such as the one that ended dueling in Europe and the abolition of the British slave trade.[14] He shows that a key factor in all these social movements was a change in norms regarding what counted as "honorable" in a society (hence the title of his book, *The Honor Code*). Dueling, or trading in slaves, had long been seen as something that normal, decent people did. Behavior shifted when a practice began to be seen as dishonorable: when one's participation in it brought raised eyebrows rather than applause.[15]

This approach emphasizes the importance of social recognition for human behavior—given that, for all of us as social creatures, our desire for enhanced standing among our peers does indeed influence how we behave.[16] Insofar as that is true for a culture, changing the narrative of what counts as "honorable" is one of the most powerful ways to change society—but it is a lever that can only be shifted if large numbers of people join in.[17] With regard to climate change and our behavior as consumers, such a shift has already begun: a few years ago, the Swedish invented the term *flygskam,* flight shame, to describe the pang of guilt that someone concerned with climate change has when engaging in unnecessary travel by air. Increasingly, it is becoming seen as less than honorable to jump on a jet without a convincing argument that the purpose of the journey justifies the environmental harm.[18] In many social circles flyers now feel compelled to explain themselves, and employers, including many companies and universities, have changed their travel policies to discourage flying unless it is strictly necessary. One might object that this is still an individualized rather than a structural approach—the latter would involve lobbying for, say, new high-speed railway lines and research on green fuels. But these are not mutually exclusive alternatives. On the contrary, individual and structural approaches typically complement each other, with structural change following when the views of a critical mass of people have shifted to regard a behavior as objectionable.

We urgently need such shifts of what counts as normal, in the economic system and with regard to climate change. For the former, there are three fields, in particular, where a change in what counts as "honorable" can support behavioral and institutional change. First, we need to unlearn the myth that "increasing efficiency" is a sufficient justification for whatever economic decisions one takes. As argued earlier, efficiency cannot be an ultimate value, and it all too often serves to hide practices of domination and exploitation. We cannot assume that someone saying "efficiency" is automatically referring to socially beneficial processes or outcomes. Instead, we need to demand an account of how exactly value is being created: Does efficiency create opportunities for some at the cost of others, within or beyond the borders of one's country, or does it produce genuinely mutually beneficial, fairly distributed gains? Sometimes the latter cannot be achieved—for example, if the demand for certain products declines and jobs cannot be defended—but even then, we should not be content with claims about what the most "efficient" solution is. We should demand justifications for how the different values and interests at stake are being balanced. It will certainly not always be possible to find answers that satisfy everyone, but it would still be an important step forward if values and interests could be openly discussed and negotiated. If corporations in particular could no longer hide behind claims of "efficiency," and if there were more public attention to their practices, the fear of reputational damage might also contribute to shifting corporate behavior on a large scale. And this could be the first step toward a transformation into worker-run, publicly accountable organizations in which meaningful, nonextractive work takes place.

The second myth is about property. There was a period in Western history in which strengthening the private property of "normal" people—peasants, small artisans, small traders, and their families—was a crucial mechanism for them to protect themselves against the power of feudal overlords, or the rapacious and arbitrary taxation that religious or worldly authorities imposed on them. This is why thinkers such as Adam Smith welcomed stronger property rights for all members of society; the hope was that such rights would lead to a flourishing economy.[19] But today's circumstances are very different: we live in complex economic systems in which a one-sided focus on property rights has contributed to extreme inequalities of income and wealth. These are polarizations that, as argued in Chapter 3, threaten democracy.

One can grant that every individual should have the right to own a certain minimum of *personal* property. But the forms of private property that threaten democracy are not of that kind. They concern abstract rights in shares, land, and real estate that have no direct use value for their owners, and are often organized in long chains of intermediation in the financial sector, such as pension funds that own shares of companies that own buildings, and so on.[20] And yet these property rights come with the right to control things, and the right to extract profits. And they can amass to huge fortunes that put their owners into a separate universe, out of touch with the lived realities of normal people.[21] Democratic societies can and should prevent this through taxation, but also by organizing their economies differently from the start, so that such huge fortunes are never, ever amassed. It is a myth that all firms need to be privately owned, with the kinds of extractive property arrangements that we currently see. Other forms of ownership, whether public or cooperative, are also possible.[22] We need to shake off the myth that they would *per se* be illegitimate or suspicious, and instead find the right governance structures for them to serve the public good and to protect the rights and dignity of all their stakeholders.

The third myth we need to unlearn is that the economy is a game that is all about winning and losing, and that "winners" have rights to larger shares of the pie than others. This is often a thinly veiled form of social Darwinism, resting on the misguided assumption that those who win are somehow better moral beings. A completely unrealistic account of individual achievement—mixing up a misguided understanding of meritocracy with wrong ideas about markets—seems to spring from the highly unequal social contexts in which such achievements take place.[23]

This nonsensical myth needs to be replaced by the insight that our economy is based on the complementarity of different tasks, and also to a great extent on the technologies, technical and social, that we have inherited from past generations and that we all benefit from, for free.[24] While some limited, well-regulated forms of competition can have their purpose—or simply arise out of freedoms that individuals are granted, such as free choice of occupation—most of the rhetoric of "winning" and "outcompeting others" and "getting to the top" is quite misleading. Instead of everyone's vying to get to the top, they should be trying to find their places in networks of interlocking tasks and roles, such that all can make meaningful contributions and the social purpose of the economic system can be fulfilled on a basis of fairness and reciprocity. And the power of collaboration is also what is needed in the realm of civil society, to rebuild the kinds of associations and organizations that can help deepen democracy and achieve real "power by the people."[25]

"All well and good," a skeptic might say, "but have you tried discussing this with my boss?" It's a fair challenge to ask how such ideas could be carried into those concrete workplaces where the decisions that make up "the economy" are being made. In such contexts, the counterargument to any "green" or "social" proposal is often not that something is wrong with it—in many workplaces, the discursive battle about the importance of protecting the environment has been won.[26] Rather, the objection raised is that there is no money. The pressure to cover costs is something that many organizations, whether private or public, have to live with, at least in the short term. And yet, in many organizations, there is at least some wiggle room to decide, for example, not to source materials from suppliers that use sweatshop labor.

It can be difficult to speak out about values in contexts where the only goal seen as legitimate is efficiency. One interesting approach in business ethics starts precisely from the fact that we need to learn to talk about values in business contexts.[27] It focuses on the concrete social situations and attempts to prepare individuals for "giving voice to values"—speaking up when moral questions are on the table but are not framed as such.[28] This is a skill that one can learn, and it feels less odd the more one gets used to it. In prior research on ethics in organizations, another point stood out in my conversations with practitioners who had dared to speak truth to power. They told me about the networks of like-minded individuals they relied on to discuss such issues and to prepare difficult conversations.[29] We are social animals when it comes to moral progress, as well, and when carrying values into social spheres where doing so has, in the past, often been frowned upon, we need to find allies.

The more the public discourse shifts into this direction, the easier it becomes for individuals inside organizations to make another type of argument. Without even having to enter difficult conversations about values, they can point to reputational risks. Even an organization that has no interest whatsoever in moral values usually has an interest in its public "license to operate."[30] Raising the fear of scandal can be an effective strategy that can be used even in contexts in which counterarguments from costs weigh heavily. In a time when information makes it way very easily to the public, and social media campaigns can do real harm to the reputation of an organization (to its "brand value," which can be one of its most valuable assets), such arguments can persuade decision-makers.

There is certainly no one-size-fits-all recipe for bringing these discussions into organizations—a lot depends on context, and no amount of theory can replace the practical wisdom needed to navigate specific settings. Those who have more security and other privileges are better positioned to initiate these difficult conversations than the most precarious members of organization, and therefore also have greater responsibility to do so. We should harbor no illusions that this will be easy. But it is a task that must be taken up, by as many people as possible, if we want to change the course of our economic system, together with other forms of protest and organizing. On the positive side, it is a task that can counter self-doubts and worries about the meaningfulness of one's work.[31] Many different types of jobs gain meaning when ecological and social values are carried into them in ways large and small. And in the cases in which one's efforts lead to nothing, the words of Samuel Beckett apply: "No matter. Try again. Fail again. Fail better."[32]

The Power of the Many

How can the vision of a society in which more and more people join the fight for a more just and greener economy become a reality? Answering this question by adducing policy proposals will inevitably invite the charge of running into an infinite regress (for what are the conditions for *these* policy proposals to succeed?) or a vicious circle (are certain reforms the precondition for unleashing positive social dynamics while such dynamics are needed to push for these reforms?). This comes with the territory of complex social relations in which everything depends on everything else, or so it seems. And yet, we can identify certain key levers that seem more likely than others to allow for crucial steps forward. Previous chapters have argued that we need to ban extractive markets and rein in corporate power, strengthen workers' rights, and massively reduce inequality. Moreover, working-time reduction and incentives for civic works can be an important lever in today's situation, especially for the United States, with its inhumanely high working hours.

Another lever has to do with economic insecurity and the fears it creates. R. H. Tawney, the British socialist quoted in an earlier chapter, wrote about this decades ago, and apart from the assumptions about heterosexual couples, his words still ring true today: "Of all emotions the most degrading and the least compatible with freedom is fear. The brutal fact is that, as far as the mass of mankind are concerned, it is by fear, rather than by hope, that the economic system is normally kept running—fear of unemployment, fear of losing a house, fear of losing savings, fear of being compelled to take children away from school, fear of what one's wife will say when these pleasant events all happen together."[33] After several decades of neoliberal hegemony, the deregulation of labor markets has increased the risk of unemployment.[34] Meanwhile, the declining quality of many public schools has made the issue of school (and college!) fees an issue again for many families. Increasingly frequent environmental hazards, such as floods or wildfires, create additional risks.[35] The need to pay out of pocket for health care adds to the financial insecurity that many families experience.[36] It is a problem that a public health service, or a reform of the health insurance system, could address. And an expansion of the welfare state could reduce the fear of unemployment. It does not have to be an unconditional basic income—a tool that many activists currently favor—or the job guarantee discussed earlier. But in any case, it needs to be a strong safety net that takes the sting out of the fear of job loss and creates a basic sense of economic security.

This matters profoundly for people's ability to take action, for reasons that stem from basic human psychology. Fear and insecurity can make it almost impossible to pay attention to anything other than the immediate pressures one experiences, such as the bills that need to be paid. Researchers in psychology call this phenomenon the "scarcity mindset": our mind goes into tunnel vision, fading out everything that is not of the greatest urgency, so that we can focus on the immediate threat.[37] And all too often, questions about social change lie outside of the tunnel. If that happens, only full-time activists have time to fight for social progress, while everyone else is just busy surviving. We should not be surprised if this creates tensions and resentments between individuals and groups whose values might, in fact, largely overlap.

The sociologist Michèle Lamont also argues for the need for cultural change, to overcome the omnipresent fear of failing and falling in neoliberal societies.[38] She sees the constant pressure to perfect oneself and to get to the topic as one of the causes of the mental health crisis among young people. Instead of a cultural script about moving ever upward on the income and consumption scales, we need a broader understanding of different kinds of worth, and new social narratives anchored not in competitiveness or stigmatization but in equality and collaboration. A democratization of the economy would provide such a new narrative—one about the equal moral value of each individual, but also about the necessary contributions that different kinds of work make. The prevalence of rag-to-riches narratives and the stigmatization of the poor, especially the non-white poor, that Lamont decries would find far less support in an economic system centered on democratic values.

Here is another practical suggestion—and while it may sound like a concession to "the right," it is one that can and should also be endorsed by "the left" (for whatever these labels are still worth). In a nutshell, it is this: do not overburden small initiatives with paperwork. In many Western democracies, people trying to get useful things done—whether they are individuals working to start social businesses, or small NGOs eligible for public subsidies, or neighborhood projects formalizing into more enduring associations—are confronted with an enormous tangle of red tape. This creates an unlevel playing field: large, existing players with experienced legal departments and tax advisors can deal with these hurdles, whereas newcomers struggle and may be discouraged before they even begin.

This is not a matter of what rules are in place and how strict they are (many areas, from environmental regulation to occupational safety, require strict rules). It is instead a matter of how clear those rules are, how intuitive the forms are to complete, and how easy or difficult it is to get advice or feedback in progress. Providing such services is costly, and this may be where readers from "the right" start to lose interest in the idea. But it is an investment in public infrastructure that can in turn facilitate private engagement. Without competent and responsive public services, small players are often defeated by a Kafkaesque bureaucracy, while established players or more privileged individuals have the means to hire others to hack through the bureaucratic thicket. Democratic societies should provide public services for the whole society, not just for those who can pay legal or administrative advisors.

Fighting for workers' rights, the reduction of inequality, and time for democracy, taking fear out of the economic system, reducing bureaucratic hurdles for individuals and small players to start something new—all these changes represent powerful levers for moving toward a more democratic and sustainable economy. They would facilitate more experimentation, on a small scale, to discover and develop solutions that work in practice—in the language of activists, "prefiguring" changes that could be brought about at much larger scale. Scholars have long been interested in such projects, and rightly so: they can teach us valuable lessons about what is or is not a viable approach, and why. The *Real Utopias* project, for example, has collected analyses of such experiments, while the *Participedia* project collects accounts of participatory experiments that aim at strengthening democracy, and the *Environmental Justice Atlas* maps cases of environmental conflict and resistance against environmental harm, creating awareness of the global struggle for environmental justice.[39] The more we can learn from what has already been tried, the better the next generation of experiments can be, and the more social technologies can be developed and refined, to the point where they can be implemented on a broad scale.

Within this field of experimentation, there is a particular need for more thinking, research, and experimentation on at least two questions. The first concerns the division of labor between centralized and decentralized mechanisms. It is clear that many aspects of the green transformation, such as the shift toward fossil-fuel-free transportation, will require a complex interplay between decentralized and centralized changes. Investments in electric grids and electric charging points will need at least public steering, if not public provision. But should we continue to think in centralized terms of "public infrastructures," or should we consider the possibility that energy could also be provided in a more decentralized way? This is one of the eternal questions of our interconnected world: What needs to happen on a local level, what on a national or even a global level, and how can the different levels be connected in a productive way?

The second question concerns accountability mechanisms beyond markets. We have learned the hard way that markets often fail to keep their promise of creating accountability of the right kind. But it is not always clear what better alternatives we have. How can we prevent large organizations from abusing their power by, for example, lowering the quality of services they are supposed to deliver, or demanding unfairly high prices from consumers? How, for example, can the leadership of a hospital be held to account? Who should sit at the table at which committee meetings, with what forms of expertise and speaking for which interests? And how different should these structures be from the accountability structures of, say, a company that produces electric buses? And last but not least, one of the most difficult questions from a research perspective: How do formal governance structures hang together with *informal* social structures, with all their interpersonal and cultural dimensions that are so difficult to grasp by abstract, theoretical concepts?[40]

The better we can answer these questions, the better we can design the institutional frameworks of our economy, and the better we can adjust the line between public and private institutions and assign the right territories to markets, state provision, and civil society. We should also remember, however, that no institutional framework will ever be perfect: circumstances change, and institutions have a tendency to decline. From time to time, they need reform and repair simply because, over the years, the mechanisms that hold them together are likely to weaken.[41] But the more we understand different institutional solutions, the better equipped we are to try out new approaches and replace the rotten planks of our democratic ship with better ones.

Such a world will not be paradise. It will still be inhabited by human beings, with all their large and small sorrows, quirks, conflicts, and love and hate stories. It will, moreover, remain a world in which individuals with widely diverging ideas of the good life need to find ways to come to agreements. But they need to apply the values they *do* agree on—what John Rawls famously called the "overlapping consensus"—not only to the political realm, but also to the economy, which will undoubtedly raise new controversies about what exactly these values mean in practice. There will be new conflicts, debates in parliaments and in other political bodies, and court cases. And yet, there is no reason to think that such a world would be impossible.

My hope is that we can create a system that is more caring, that makes space for diversity and vulnerability, and that replaces the power games and bitter rivalries that we currently see, at so many levels, with collaborative practices. For ultimately, if life had played out a bit differently, we might have ended up in the position of that other person that we, just now, resent or despise so much. We are all bodily creatures, and as such immensely vulnerable, physiologically and psychologically, and depend on larger ecosystems that we need to protect for future generations. Human life would be impossible without collaboration and care from others, especially at the beginning and the end of life, but not only then.[42] This shared vulnerability, but also the possibility of joining forces, is one of the rationales for democracy. It is time to apply its principles to the economic system, as well.

After the fall of the Iron Curtain, there was a sense of triumph in the democracies of Western Europe and the United States, epitomized in the famous pronouncement by political scientist Francis Fukuyama that the "end of history" had been reached.[43] Capitalism and democracy, instead of a planned economy and dictatorship—that was the model that all countries were now supposed to implement. Of course, in retrospect, the naivete of this statement is evident, but it probably reflects what many at the time thought. For those of us who grew up in these years, however, it also created a strange feeling of emptiness, which can probably best be described as a lack of mission. If left barely anything for us to do, other than carry on with what our forefathers had built—which seemed an exceedingly boring life task. Nothing of world-historical importance would happen after 1989, after all!

This could not have been more wrong. History keeps moving, and preventing it from undermining all that has already been achieved with regard to democracy and human rights has turned out to be far from a trivial matter. It has also become much clearer, thanks also to the work of social scientists crunching large data sets, that it is not enough to have rights be formally equal if the aim is to create true equality among individuals from different backgrounds and with different demographic features. "Black Lives Matter" and "MeToo" have been some of the most vocal movements that have called out the continuing racism and sexism that prevails in many parts of society. Movements against ableism and other forms of discrimination have been less visible but their concerns are just as justified. Democratic societies cannot understand themselves as having reached the pinnacle of history if so much work remains to be done!

This book has been about the many ways in which the economic system is similarly unfinished business, as far as the tasks of democracy are concerned. To move toward ways of fulfilling our needs while staying within the planetary boundaries, without externalizing costs or harms to others, and making such a system work fairly for everyone—this is an enormous task. We have lots of building blocks in front of us: different types of rights, different institutional solutions, different ways of coordinating economic activities. But we need to put them together in new ways. We have communication technologies that offer fantastic opportunities to learn from each other, but we need to give individuals the space to use them for good. We need to fight the power of those who resist these changes, but also the power of our own habits and lazy ways of thinking. It's not going to be easy. But no one can say that our generation, and those following us, do not have a mission to fulfill.

Notes

Introduction

1. I focus on Western societies, lacking in-depth familiarity with other political and economic systems around the world. Some arguments may apply to other countries, but more work would be needed to reflect on their specific situations.
2. On the United States, see Anne Case and Angus Deaton, *Deaths of Despair and the Future of Capitalism* (Princeton: Princeton University Press, 2020). For UK data, see Danny Dorling, "The Biggest Story in the UK Is Not Brexit. It's Life Expectancy," *The Correspondent*, December 16, 2019, https://thecorrespondent.com/177/the-biggest-story-in-the-uk-is-not-brexit-its-life-expectancy/197470651092-d2e0df85.
3. See, for example, Thomas Piketty, *Capital in the Twenty-First Century* (Cambridge, MA: Harvard University Press, 2014); Robert B. Reich, *The System: Who Rigged It, How We Fix It* (New York: Penguin Books, 2021); Matthew Desmond, *Poverty, by America* (New York: Crown, 2023).
4. Elizabeth Popp Berman, *Thinking Like an Economist: How Efficiency Replaced Equality in U.S. Public Policy* (Princeton: Princeton University Press, 2022).
5. See, for example, Thomas Christiano, *The Constitution of Equality: Democratic Authority and Its Limits* (Oxford: Oxford University Press, 2008).

6. See also Samuel Bowles and Herbert Gintis, *Democracy and Capitalism: Property, Community, and the Contradictions of Modern Social Thought* (New York: Basic Books, 1986), esp. chap. 2.
7. Sheri Berman, *The Primacy of Politics: Social Democracy and the Making of Europe's Twentieth Century* (Cambridge: Cambridge University Press, 2012).
8. John Dewey, "Creative Democracy: The Task before Us," in *John Dewey and the Promise of America* (Columbus: American Education Press, 1939), 12–17.
9. See, for example, David Harvey, *A Brief History of Neoliberalism* (Oxford: Oxford University Press, 2005); Wendy Brown, *Undoing the Demos: Neoliberalism's Stealth Revolution* (New York: Zone Books, 2015); Thomas Biebricher, *The Political Theory of Neoliberalism* (Stanford: Stanford University Press, 2019).
10. On the history of neoliberalism see, for example, Angus Burgin, *The Great Persuasion: Reinventing Free Markets since the Depression* (Cambridge, MA: Harvard University Press, 2012); Lawrence B. Glickman, *Free Enterprise: An American History* (New Haven, CT: Yale University Press, 2019); Naomi Oreskes and Erik M. Conway, *The Big Myth: How American Business Taught Us to Loathe Government and Love the Free Market* (New York: Bloomsbury, 2023).
11. Other accounts of the current crisis of democracy focus (more) on changes in public communication (e.g., through social media) or cultural factors (including racist insider-outsider dynamics). While I do not want to deny the role of these dimensions, I take the relation between the economic and the political system to be an additional (and maybe the most central) factor.
12. Mark Blyth, *Austerity: The History of a Dangerous Idea* (New York: Oxford University Press, 2013).
13. See, for example, Joseph E. Stiglitz, "Inequality and Economic Growth," *Political Quarterly* 86, no.1 (2016): 134–155; Piketty, *Capital in the Twenty-First Century*.
14. See, for example, Jason W. Moore, ed., *Anthropocene or Capitalocene? Nature, History, and the Crisis of Capitalism* (Oakland, CA: PM Press, 2016).
15. One example is "doughnut economics." Kate Raworth, *Doughnut Economics: Seven Ways to Think Like a Twenty-First-Century Economist* (London: Penguin, 2017). Another is the "well-being economy" concept.

See "What Is a Wellbeing Economy," Wellbeing Economy Alliance website, https://weall.org/what-is-wellbeing-economyhttps://weall.org/what-is-wellbeing-economy.
16. This is the argument behind the calls to democratize work in approaches of participatory democracy. See, for example, Carole Pateman, *Participation and Democratic Theory* (Cambridge: Cambridge University Press, 1970). This issue is discussed in Chapter 2.
17. On democratizing the economy, see, for example, Nadia Johanisova and Stephan Wolf, "Economic Democracy: A Path for the Future?" *Futures* 44, no. 6 (2012): 562–570. In the recent Anglophone discussion, positions closely related to those presented here include Danielle Allen, *Justice by Means of Democracy* (Chicago: University of Chicago Press, 2023), which has a stronger focus on the political realm but covers the economy in chap. 6; Marjorie Kelly, with Ted Howard, *The Making of a Democratic Economy: Building Prosperity for the Many, Not Just the Few* (Oakland: Berrett-Koehler, 2019); Marjorie Kelly, *Wealth Supremacy: How the Extractive Economy and the Biased Rules of Capitalism Drive Today's Crises* (Oakland: Berrett-Koehler, 2023); Andrew Cumbers, *The Case for Economic Democracy* (Cambridge: Polity Press, 2020); David Schweickart, *After Capitalism*, 2nd ed. (Lanham, MD: Rowman & Littlefield, 2011).
18. Colin Crouch, *Post-Democracy* (Cambridge: Polity, 2004).
19. For a criticism, see Paul Krugman, "How Did Economists Get It So Wrong?" *New York Times*, September 2, 2009, SM36.
20. A challenge in writing about the influence of economic thinking on society is that the positions of academic economists are often far more nuanced than the watered-down versions of theories that inform public discourse and sometimes also policymaking. Certain ideas about human utility maximization, for example, can translate from being modeling assumptions to being worldviews that inform what Stuart Hall has called *practical ideologies*, "which make the conditions of life intelligible to the masses, and which exercise a practical and material force by organizing their actions." Stuart Hall, "Popular-Democratic vs Authoritarian Populism: Two Ways of Taking Democracy Seriously," in *Marxism and Democracy*, ed. Alan Hunt (London: Lawrence and Wishart, 1980), 157–185, at 173. See also Dani Rodrik, *Economic Rules: Why Economics Works, When It Fails, and How to Tell the Difference* (Oxford: Oxford University Press, 2015), especially at p. 170, on the

ways in which economists have often defended market values in public despite holding more differentiated views in academic debates. On the influence of economic models on management practices, see Sumantra Ghoshal, "Bad Management Theories Are Destroying Good Management Practices," *Academy of Management Learning and Education* 4, no. 1 (2005): 75–91.

21. See, for example, Anibal Quijano, "Coloniality of Power, Eurocentrism and Latin America," *Nepantla: Views from the South* 3 (2000): 533–580.
22. See, for example, Dewey, "Creative Democracy"; Jürgen Habermas, *The Theory of Communicative Action*, vol. 2, *Lifeworld and System: A Critique of Functionalist Reason* (Boston: Beacon Press, 1987); Axel Honneth, *The Struggle for Recognition: The Moral Grammar of Social Conflicts* (Cambridge: Polity, 1995); Elizabeth Anderson, "What Is the Point of Equality?" *Ethics* 109, no. 2 (1999): 287–337. Adam Smith and G. W. F. Hegel, I believe, also align with this tradition. Space here does not allow for a full defense of the claim, which is based on research for my doctoral dissertation and first book: Lisa Herzog, *Inventing the Market: Smith, Hegel, and Political Theory* (Oxford: Oxford University Press, 2013).
23. John Dalberg-Acton, "Letter to Bishop Mandell Creighton," April 5, 1887, in *Historical Essays and Studies*, ed. J. N. Figgis and R. V. Laurence (London: Macmillan, 1907), 503–508.
24. See, for example, Brishen Rogers, *Data and Democracy at Work: Advanced Information Technologies, Labor Law, and the New Working Class* (Cambridge, MA: MIT Press, 2023), 39.
25. It should thus not come as a surprise that fascist regimes have also used the language of "efficiency." See, for example, Johann Chapoutot, *Free to Obey: How the Nazis Invented Modern Management* (New York: Europa Compass, 2023).
26. Note that, in the history of economic thought, scarcity has been understood in rather different ways. See Frederik Albritton Jonsson and Carl Wennerlind, *Scarcity: A History from the Origins of Capitalism to the Climate Crisis* (Cambridge, MA: Harvard University Press, 2023).
27. See, for example, Andreu Mas-Colell, Michael D. Whinston, and Jerry R. Green, *Microeconomic Theory* (New York: Oxford University Press, 1995), 313.

28. "Kaldor-Hicks efficiency," *Oxford Reference*, https://www.oxfordreference.com/display/10.1093/oi/authority.20110803100028833#:~:text=Quick%20Reference,one%20is%20made%20worse%20off.
29. Michael Bennett, "The Choice of Efficiencies and the Necessity of Politics," *Critical Review of International Social and Political Philosophy* 26, no. 6 (2023): 877–896.
30. See Coral Davenport, "You've Never Heard of Him, but He's Remaking the Pollution Fight," *New York Times*, May 28, 2023, for an example of current reevaluation questions in US politics.
31. Julian Le Grand, "Justice Versus Efficiency: The Elusive Trade-Off,' *Ethics* 100, no. 3 (1990): 554–568. .
32. Le Grand, "Justice Versus Efficiency," 566.
33. An example is "true cost accounting." See, for example, Ian Fitzpatrick, Richard Young, and Robert Barbour, *The Hidden Cost of UK Food* (Bristol: Sustainable Food Trust, 2017).
34. See, for example, Joshua Cohen, "Money, Politics, Democratic Equality," in *Philosophy, Politics, Democracy: Selected Essays* (Cambridge, MA: Harvard University Press, 2009), 268–301. Chapter 3 of this book explores the topic further.
35. Nancy Fraser, *Cannibal Capitalism: How Our System Is Devouring Democracy, Care, and the Planet—and What We Can Do About It* (London: Verso Books, 2022).
36. See, for example, Michael C. Munger and Mario Villarreal-Diaz, "The Road to Crony Capitalism," *Independent Review* 23, no. 3 (2019): 331–344.
37. See, for example, Oreskes and Conway, *The Big Myth*.
38. See also Bowles and Gintis, *Democracy and Capitalism*, chap. 5.
39. Joseph A. Schumpeter, *Capitalism, Socialism and Democracy* (London and New York: Routledge 1976 [1942]), chaps. 21–22, esp. pp. 228–236.
40. Joseph A. Schumpeter, "Der Unternehmer in der Volkswirtschaft von heute," in *Strukturwandlungen der Deutschen Volkswirtschaft*, ed. Bernhard Harms (Berlin: Hobbing, 1929), 303–326.
41. See Anthony Downs, *An Economic Theory of Democracy* (New York: Harper and Bros., 1957).
42. For an overview, see Christian List, "Social Choice Theory," *Stanford Encyclopedia of Philosophy* (Winter 2022 edition), ed. Edward N. Zalta and Uri Nodelman, https://plato.stanford.edu/archives/win2022/entries/social-choice/.

43. Jason Brennan, *Against Democracy* (Princeton: Princeton University Press, 2017). For an insightful critique, see Thomas Christiano, "Review of Brennan's *Against Democracy,*" *Notre Dame Philosophical Reviews*, May 19, 2017, https://ndpr.nd.edu/reviews/against-democracy/.
44. See, for example, Brennan, *Against Democracy*.
45. See also Lisa Herzog, *Citizen Knowledge: Markets, Experts, and the Infrastructure of Democracy* (New York: Oxford University Press, 2023), chap. 6.
46. For another view, see Robert B. Talisse, *Overdoing Democracy: Why We Must Put Politics in Its Place* (New York: Oxford University Press, 2019), chaps. 1–4. The title is slightly misleading, for Talisse does not argue against democracy but rather holds that certain democratic values (e.g., civic solidarity) get crowded out if others (e.g., party competition) are overemphasized. This point will be taken up in Chapter 5.
47. Jürgen Habermas, *Moral Consciousness and Communicative Action* (Cambridge, MA: MIT Press, 1990), 159.
48. John S. Dryzek, "The Forum, the System, and the Polity: Three Varieties of Democratic Theory," *Political Theory* 45, no. 5 (2017): 610–636, at 611.
49. See, for example, Carole Pateman, "Participatory Democracy Revisited," *Perspectives on Politics* 10, no. 1 (2012): 7–19.
50. For a similar view, see Jane Mansbridge et al., "A Systemic Approach to Deliberative Democracy," in *Deliberative Systems: Deliberative Democracy at the Large Scale,* ed. John Parkinson and Jane Mansbridge (Cambridge: Cambridge University Press, 2012), 1–26.
51. Cohen, "Money, Politics, Democratic Equality."
52. See, for example, Nicholas Carnes, *White-Collar Government: The Hidden Role of Class in Economic Policy-Making* (Chicago: University of Chicago Press, 2013).
53. This is a danger that is visible in, for example, Paul Collier and John Kay, *Greed Is Dead: Politics after Individualism* (London: Penguin, 2020).
54. John Rawls, "The Idea of an Overlapping Consensus," *Oxford Journal of Legal Studies* 7 no. 1 (1987): 1–25; see also Rawls, *Political Liberalism* (New York: Columbia University Press, 1993).
55. Rosa Luxemburg, "Die Freiheit der Andersdenkenden," in *Zur russischen Revolution,* ed. Paul Levi (Berlin: Dietz, 1990 [1918]), 150–158.
56. On the emancipatory versus libertarian notion of freedom (and its historical role in US domestic and global politics), see Aziz Rana, "A Different Freedom," *Boston Review,* December 12, 2023.

57. This coheres with a view expressed in Daron Acemoglou and James A. Robin, *Why Nations Fail: The Origins of Power, Prosperity, and Poverty* (New York: Crown, 2012), 50–57. The argument there is that cultural differences cannot explain differences in poverty and wealth between nations; it stands independently of the book's broader claims, some of which have been heavily criticized.
58. The Me Too movement united people fighting against sexual harassment, while the Black Lives Matter movement opposed police violence and discrimination against African Americans. Of course, these are only two prominent social justice movements among many.
59. On campaign reform in the United States, see, for example, Bruce Ackerman and Ian Ayres, *Voting with Dollars: A New Paradigm for Campaign Finance* (New Haven: Yale University Press, 2002).
60. See Herzog, *Citizen Knowledge*.
61. For discussions and proposals see, for example, Lisa Herzog, ed., *Just Financial Markets? Finance in a Just Society* (Oxford: Oxford University Press); Kelly, *Wealth Supremacy*, 165–180; Schweickart, *After Capitalism*, 61–66; Raworth, *Doughnut Economics*, 233–237.
62. See, for example, Schweickart, *After Capitalism*, 85–87.
63. For diagnostic approaches, see, for example, Piketty, *Capital in the Twenty-First Century*; Harvey, *A Brief History of Neoliberalism*; Oreskes and Conway, *The Big Myth*.
64. This approach roughly follows Sen's "non-ideal" approach. See Amartya Sen, "What Do We Want from a Theory of Justice?" *Journal of Philosophy* 103, no. 5 (2006): 215–238.

1. Markets, Corporations, and Their Alliance against Democracy

1. John Tomasi, *Free Market Fairness* (Princeton: Princeton University Press, 2012), 66, 78, 81.
2. Karl Marx and Friedrich Engels, "The Communist Manifesto," in Karl Marx and Friedrich Engels, *Selected Works*, vol. 1, trans. Samuel Moore (Moscow: Progress Publishers, 1969 [1888]), 98–137, 16.
3. James Heartfield, *The 'Death of the Subject' Explained* (Charleston: Book Surge, 2006), 173.
4. Of course, money is also a social construct—for reasons of space, I cannot discuss this topic. See, for example, Christine A. Desan, "The Constitutional Approach to Money: Monetary Design and the Production

of the Modern World," in *Money Talks: Essays in Honor of Viviana Zelizer,* ed. Nina Bandelj, Frederick F. Wherry, and Viviana A. Zelizer (Princeton: Princeton University Press, 2017), 109–130.

5. Adam Smith, *An Inquiry into the Nature and Causes of the Wealth of Nations,* ed. R. H. Campbell and A. S. Skinner, textual editor W. B. Todd (Oxford: Clarendon Press, 1976 [1776]), book I, chap. V–XI.

6. This is the message of the general equilibrium model, which is included in numerous economics textbooks. See, for example, Gregory N. Mankiw, *Principles of Economics,* 8th ed. (Boston: Cengage Learning, 2018); Paul A. Samuelson and William D. Nordhaus, *Economics,* 19th ed. (New York: McGraw-Hill, 2010).

7. This point was made in particular by the "Austrian School" of economics. See, for example, Friedrich August von Hayek, "The Use of Knowledge in Society," *American Economic Review* 35, no. 4 (1945): 519–530; Ludwig von Mises, *Economic Calculation in the Socialist Commonwealth* (Auburn, AL: Mises Institute, 1990 [1920]).

8. For example, in the "darknet." See Andreas Diekmann, Ben Jann, Wojtek Przepiorka, and Stefan Wehrli, "Reputation Formation and the Evolution of Cooperation in Anonymous Online Markets," *American Sociological Review* 79, no. 1 (2014): 65–85.

9. Liam B. Murphy and Thomas Nagel, *The Myth of Ownership: Taxes and Justice* (New York: Oxford University Press, 2002).

10. See, for example, John Rawls, *Justice as Fairness: A Restatement,* ed. Erin Kelly (Cambridge, MA: Belknap Press of Harvard University Press, 2001), 138. For a discussion, see, for example, Tilo Wesche, "The Concept of Property in Rawls's Property-Owning Democracy," *Analyse & Kritik* 1 (2013): 99–111.

11. See, for example, A. M. Honoré, "Ownership," in *Oxford Essays in Jurisprudence,* ed. A. G. Guest (Oxford: Oxford University Press, 1961), 107–147.

12. Lisa Herzog, "Was bedeutet es, 'Märkte einzubetten'? Eine Taxonomie,' *Zeitschrift für praktische Philosophie* 3, no. 1 (2016): 13–52.

13. See, for example, Thomas Hajduk and Christoph Schank, "The Model of the Honorable Merchant: Bridging Compliance and Integrity?" in *Handbook of Virtue Ethics in Business and Management,* ed. Alejo José G. Sison, Gregory R. Beabout, and Ignacio Ferrero (Dordrecht: Springer, 2017), 987–994.

14. This has been theorized in Gary S. Becker, *The Economics of Discrimination* (Chicago: University of Chicago Press, 1957).

15. Neil Fligstein, "Markets as Politics: A Political-Cultural Approach to Market Institutions," *American Sociological Review* 6, no. 4 (1996): 656–673, 670.
16. Tomasi, *Free Market Fairness*, 66.
17. Recent accounts of exploitation are of different types. For a liberal account, see Mark R. Reiff, *Exploitation and Economic Justice in the Liberal Capitalist State* (New York: Oxford University Press, 2013). For a Marxist account, see Nicholas Vrousalis, *Exploitation as Domination* (Oxford: Oxford University Press, 2023). Many existing forms of exploitation can be captured by these and other accounts (of which Vrousalis provides an overview in chap. 1). Another form of exploitation that happens *behind* market transactions is the way in which capitalist firms rely on *unpaid* labor, such as in families, without contributing to its financial liability, as feminist thinkers have pointed out. See, for example, Nancy Fraser, "Contradictions of Capital and Care," *New Left Review* 100 (2016): 99–117. On the racialization of such work, see, for example, Diamond Ashiagbor, "Race and Colonialism in the Construction of Labour Markets and Precarity," *Industrial Law Journal* 50, no. 4 (2021): 506–531.
18. Similarly, see Stuart White, *The Civic Minimum: On the Rights and Obligations of Economic Citizenship* (Oxford: Oxford University Press, 2003), 46. White speaks of "abusive exchanges" that violate individuals' key interests.
19. See Maristella Svampa, *Neo-Extractivism in Latin America: Socio-Environmental Conflicts, the Territorial Turn, and New Political Narratives* (Cambridge: Cambridge University Press, 2019). Other important contributions can be found in Permanent Working Group on Alternatives to Development, *Beyond Development: Alternative Visions from Latin America*, ed. M. Lang and D. Mokrani (Amsterdam: Transnational Institute and Rosa Luxemburg Foundation, 2013). For a feminist perspective, see Veronica Gago, *Feminist International: How to Change Everything* (London: Verso, 2020), esp. chaps. 3 and 4.
20. See Svampa, *Neo-Extractivism*, 6–7.
21. See, for example, Thomas Philippon, *The Great Reversal: How America Gave Up on Free Markets* (Cambridge, MA: Harvard University Press, 2019), 20–21; Brian Kogelmann, "Public Choice and Political Equality," in *Wealth and Power: Philosophical Perspectives*, ed. Michael Bennett, Huub Brouwer, and Rutger Claassen (New York: Routledge, 2022), 67–84, at 71–73.

22. See, for example, Tim Hubbard and James Love, "We're Patently Going Mad," *The Guardian*, March 4, 2004; Peter Drahos and John Braithwaite, *Information Feudalism: Who Owns the Knowledge Economy* (New York: Taylor & Francis, 2002); James Boyle, *The Public Domain: Enclosing the Commons of the Mind* (New Haven: Yale University Press, 2008).
23. See, for example, Sendhil Mullainathan and Eldar Shafir, *Scarcity* (New York: Penguin, 2013), chap. 5; Lisa Herzog, "What Could Be Wrong with a Mortgage? Private Debt Markets from a Perspective of Structural Justice," *Journal of Political Philosophy* 25, no. 4 (2017): 411–434.
24. See, for example, Margaret M. Blair and Lynn A. Stout, "A Team Production Theory of Corporate Law," *Virginia Law Review* 85, no. 2 (1999): 247–328; David Ciepley, "Beyond Public and Private: Toward a Political Theory of the Corporation," *American Political Science Review* 107, no. 1 (2013): 139–158.
25. See, for example, Jacob T. Levy, *Rationalism, Pluralism, and Freedom* (New York: Oxford University Press, 2014).
26. Ciepley, "Beyond Public and Private."
27. Ronald H. Coase, "The Nature of the Firm," *Economica* 4, no. 16 (1937): 386–405.
28. Of course, capital concentrated in the hands of individuals also creates risks of one-sided power, as I also discuss in Chapter 2.
29. Milton Friedman, "The Social Responsibility of Business Is to Increase Its Profits," *New York Times*, September 13, 1970, 17. On the principal agent approach applied to firms, see Michael C. Jensen and William H. Meckling, "Theory of the Firm: Managerial Behavior, Agency Costs and Ownership Structure," *Journal of Financial Economics* 3, no. 4 (1976): 305–360.
30. See, for example, historically, E. Merrick Dodd, "For Whom Are Corporate Managers Trustees?" *Harvard Law Review* 45, no. 7 (1932): 1145–1163.
31. Joel Bakan, *The Corporation: The Pathological Pursuit of Profit and Power* (London: Constable, 2004).
32. For a history of the concept, see Laurenz Volkmann, *Homo oeconomicus, Studien zur Modellierung eines neuen Menschenbildes in der englischen Literatur vom Mittelalter bis zum 18. Jahrhundert* (Heidelberg: Universitätsverlag Winter, 2003).
33. See, for example, Amartya K. Sen, "Rational Fools: A Critique of the Behavioral Foundations of Economic Theory," *Philosophy & Public*

Affairs 6, no. 4 (1977): 317–344; on human work motivation see, as an overview, Daniel H. Pink, *Drive: The Surprising Truth About What Motivates Us* (New York: Riverhead Books, 2009).

34. Jürgen Habermas, *The Theory of Communicative Action*, 2 vols. (Boston: Beacon Press, 1987).
35. This point has also been acknowledged from a libertarian perspective. See, for example, Michael C. Munger and Mario Villarreal-Diaz, "The Road to Crony Capitalism," *Independent Review* 23, no. 2 (2019): 331–344. They describe this as a form of "crony capitalism" that arises as soon as it becomes more profitable for companies not to develop useful products but to "use the power of the state to extract resources from others or to protect those existing products from competition" (p. 340). Their view is too pessimistic, however, about the ability of democracies to resist. On lobbying, from a philosophical perspective, see Phil Parvin, "Hidden in Plain Sight: How Lobby Organisations Undermine Democracy," in Bennett, Brouwer, and Claassen, *Wealth and Power*, 229–251. For the development in the United States, see, for example, Robert B. Reich, *Saving Capitalism: For the Many, Not the Few* (New York: Alfred A. Knopf, 2015); and Robert B. Reich, *The System: Who Rigged It, How We Fix It* (New York: Vintage, 2021).
36. Mancur Olson Jr., *The Logic of Collective Action: Public Goods and the Theory of Groups* (Cambridge, MA: Harvard University Press, 1965).
37. Smith, *The Wealth of Nations*, I.X.I.26.
38. See, for example, Naomi Oreskes and Eric Conway, *Merchants of Doubt: How a Handful of Scientists Obscured the Truth on Issues from Tobacco Smoke to Global Warming* (London: Bloomsbury, 2010).
39. For a historical account, see Bas van Bavel, *The Invisible Hand? How Market Economies Have Emerged and Declined Since AD 500* (Oxford: Oxford University Press, 2016). For a systematic perspective, see Rutger Claassen and Lisa Herzog, "Making Power Explicit: Why Liberal Egalitarians Should Take (Economic) Power Seriously," *Social Theory and Practice* 47, no. 2 (2021): 221–246.
40. Muhammad Azizul Islam, Pamela Abbott, Shamima Haque, and Fiona Gooch, "Impact of Global Clothing Retailers' Unfair Practices on Bangladeshi Suppliers during Covid-19," Centre for Global Development, University of Aberdeen Business School, January 2023, https://www.abdn.ac.uk/business/documents/Impact_of_Global_Clothing_Retailers_Unfair_Practices_on_Bangladeshi_Suppliers_During_COVID-19.pdf.

41. See also Luigi Zingales, "Towards a Political Theory of the Firm," *Journal of Economic Perspectives* 31, no. 3 (2017): 113–130, who speaks of a "Medici vicious circle." For a discussion, see Philippon, *The Great Reversal*, 202–203.
42. Van Bavel, *The Invisible Hand?*
43. See Jeffrey Fynn-Paul, review of Van Bavel, *Invisible Hand? Low Countries Historical Review* 133 (2018): 45–49. For other critical discussions, see Jonathan Barth, "Review: The History, Essence, and Future of Global Capitalism," *Journal of World History* 29, no. 2 (2018): 284–295; Bart Lambert, review of Van Bavel, *Invisible Hand? English Historical Review* 133, no. 565 (2018): 1564–1566.
44. Margaret Jane Radin, *Boilerplate: The Fine Print, Vanishing Rights, and the Rule of Law* (Princeton: Princeton University Press, 2012).
45. Philippon, *The Great Reversal*.
46. In Europe, by contrast, there is a transnational competition authority, which is more independent. See Philippon, *The Great Reversal*, Part II.
47. On the negative effects of monopolization on innovation, see Heather Boushey, *Unbound: How Inequality Constricts Our Economy and What We Can Do about It* (Cambridge, MA: Harvard University Press, 2019), 122–126.
48. On how monopolistic tendencies in markets for agriculture and social media hinder innovation, see Zephyr Teachout, *Break 'Em Up: Recovering Our Freedom from Big Ag, Big Tech, and Big Money* (New York: All Points Books, 2020), chap. 1.
49. Philippon, *The Great Reversal*, 23, 239.
50. Smith, *The Wealth of Nations*, I. II.II.
51. See, for example, "Climate Change 2023: Synthesis Report," Intergovernmental Panel on Climate Change (IPCC), 2023, https://www.ipcc.ch/report/ar6/syr/.
52. The Yellow Vest Protests in France have become a symbol of this challenge. See, for example, Colin Kinniburgh, "Climate Politics after the Yellow Vests," *Dissent,* Spring 2019, https://www.dissentmagazine.org/article/the-yellow-vests-uncertain-future. It is a topic that is covered here in Chapter 4.
53. Jason Hickel, *Less Is More: How Degrowth Will Save the World* (London: Penguin, 2021), 192. More generally, see Zak Cope, *The Wealth of (Some) Nations: Imperialism and the Mechanics of Value Transfer* (London: Pluto Press, 2019).

54. Stefan Lessenich, *Neben uns die Sintflut: Die Externalisierungsgesellschaft und ihr Preis* (Berlin: Hanser Berlin, 2016).
55. For a constitutional law perspective, see Rosalind Dixon, "Fair Market Constitutionalism: From Neo-liberal to Democratic Liberal Economic Governance," *Oxford Journal of Legal Studies* 43, no. 2 (2023): 221–248. Note, however, that arguments here deviate somewhat from Dixon's "democratic liberal" model.
56. See also Lisa Herzog, *Citizen Knowledge: Markets, Experts, and the Infrastructure of Democracy* (New York: Oxford University Press, 2023), chap. 7.
57. On protecting individuals against "market vulnerability," see also White, *The Civic Minimum*, 44–45.
58. Georg A. Akerlof and Robert J. Shiller, *Phishing for Phools: The Economics of Manipulation and Deception* (Princeton: Princeton University Press, 2015).
59. Aristotle, *Nicomachean Ethics*, ed. and trans. Robert C. Bartlett and Susan D. Collins (Chicago: University of Chicago Press, 2012), VII.2–11.
60. David Laibson, "Golden Eggs and Hyperbolic Discounting," *Quarterly Journal of Economics* 112, no. 2 (1997): 443–477.
61. Daniel Kahneman, *Thinking, Fast and Slow* (New York: Farrar, Straus and Giroux, 2013).
62. This is a mandatory rule for online shops (with certain exceptions) in the European Union. See "Guarantees and Returns," a page of the EU's "Your Europe" website: https://europa.eu/youreurope/citizens/consumers/shopping/guarantees-returns/index_en.htm.
63. See, for example, N. Gregory Mankiw, *Principles of Economics*, 8th ed. (Boston: Cengage Learning, 2018), chap. 7.
64. For an early formulation, see John C. Harsanyi, "On the Rationality Postulates Underlying the Theory of Cooperative Games," *Journal of Conflict Resolution* 5, no. 2 (1961): 179–196, at 180. For experiments in different cultural contexts, see Joseph Henrich, Robert Boyd, Samuel Bowles, Colin Camerer, Ernst Fehr, Herbert Gintis, and Richard McElreath, "In Search of Homo Economicus: Behavioral Experiments in 15 Small-Scale Societies," *Economics and Social Behavior* 9, no. 1 (2001): 73–78. Interestingly, in more interdependent societies, the percentages offered and accepted in an initial round of play are higher than in small-scale societies.

65. For another view, proposing that policymakers should disaggregate which groups in society would benefit from growth, see Boushey, *Unbound*, 201–204.
66. This holds, for example, for many presentations of the general equilibrium model (e.g., Mankiw, *Principles of Economics,* chap. 4).
67. Here one touches on the debate about "limits of markets" or "commodification." See, for example, Margaret J. Radin, *Contested Commodities* (Cambridge, MA: Harvard University Press, 1996); Elizabeth Anderson, *Values in Ethics and Economics* (Cambridge, MA: Harvard University Press, 1992); Debra Satz, *Why Some Things Should Not Be for Sale: The Moral Limits of Markets* (Oxford: Oxford University Press, 2010); Michael J. Sandel, *What Money Can't Buy: The Moral Limits of Markets* (New York: Farrar Straus Giroux, 2012).
68. See also Anderson, *Values in Ethics and Economics,* chap. 1 and 3.
69. Karl Polanyi, *The Great Transformation* (Boston: Beacon Press, 1944), 57; for a discussion see also Frank Cunningham, "Market Economies and Market Societies," *Journal of Social Philosophy* 36, no. 2 (2005): 129–142.
70. For example, Wendy Brown, *Undoing the Demos: Neoliberalism's Stealth Revolution* (New York: Zone Books, 2015).
71. Waheed Hussain, "Pitting People Against Each Other," *Philosophy & Public Affairs* 48, no. 1 (2020): 79–113.
72. See, for example, Alain de Botton, *Status Anxiety* (London: Vintage, 2005).
73. See also the discussions in Chapters 4 and 5.
74. Friedrich August von Hayek, *Law, Legislation and Liberty,* vol. 2, *The Mirage of Social Justice* (Chicago: University of Chicago Press, 1978), 76.
75. This is also how I read G. W. F. Hegel's account of markets. See Lisa Herzog, *Inventing the Market: Smith, Hegel, and Political Theory* (Oxford: Oxford University Press, 2013), chap. 3.
76. This has been emphasized in particular by so-called ordoliberals. See, for example, Franz Böhm, *Wettbewerb und Monopolkampf: Eine Untersuchung zur Frage des wirtschaftlichen Kampfrechts und zur Frage der rechtlichen Struktur der geltenden Wirtschaftsordnung* (Berlin: Carl Heymann, 1933). See also Thomas Biebricher, Werner Bonefeld, and Peter Nedergaard, eds., *The Oxford Handbook of Ordoliberalism* (Oxford: Oxford University Press, 2022).

77. Polanyi, *The Great Transformation*, chap. 4.
78. See, for example, Maxine Eichner, *The Free-Market Family: How the Market Crushed the American Dream (and How It Can Be Restored)* (New York: Oxford University Press, 2020).
79. This topic is covered in Chapter 5.
80. Albert O. Hirschman, *Exit, Voice, and Loyalty: Responses to Decline in Firms, Organizations, and States* (Cambridge, MA: Harvard University Press, 1970).

2. Workers

1. See, for example, Daniel T. Rodgers, *The Work Ethic in Industrial America, 1850–1920* (Chicago: University of Chicago Press, 2014).
2. See, for example, Jonathan Lord, "Quiet Quitting Is a New Name for an Old Method of Industrial Action," *The Conversation*, 9 September 2022, https://theconversation.com/quiet-quitting-is-a-new-name-for-an-old-method-of-industrial-action-189752.
3. See, for example, Anna Scheyett, "Editorial: Quiet Quitting," *Social Work* 68, no. 1 (2023): 5–7.
4. See also Ruth Dukes and Wolfgang Streeck, *Democracy at Work: Contract, Status and Post-Industrial Justice* (Cambridge: Polity, 2023).
5. See also Axel Honneth, *Der arbeitende Souverän* (Berlin: Suhrkamp, 2023).
6. See the references in Chapter 5 for data on work time.
7. This view deviates from those who hope or fear that artificial intelligences and robots will soon take over most jobs. While we can certainly expect changes with regard to many tasks, allowing work-time reductions, the history of technological innovations provides reasons to think that the "end of work" is not on the horizon.
8. Oliver Decker and Elmar Brähler, *Autoritäre Dynamiken: Alte Ressentiments—neue Radikalität* (Gießen: Psychosozial-Verlag, 2020).
9. David Weil, *The Fissured Workplace: Why Work Became So Bad for So Many and What Can Be Done to Improve It* (Cambridge, MA: Harvard University Press, 2014).
10. Anca Gheaus and Lisa Herzog, "The Goods of Work (Other than Money!)," *Journal of Social Philosophy* 47, no. 1 (2016): 70–89.
11. Ronald H. Coase, "The Nature of the Firm," *Economica* 4, no. 16 (1937): 386–405.

12. Kathi Weeks, *The Problem with Work. Feminism, Marxism, Antiwork Politics, and Postwork Imaginaries* (Durham, NC: Duke University Press, 2011), 2.
13. Arthur O. Lovejoy, *The Great Chain of Being: A Study of the History of an Idea* (Cambridge, MA: Harvard University Press, 1971).
14. See also Aaron Dignan, *Brave New Work: Are You Ready to Reinvent Your Organization?* (London: Penguin, 2019).
15. Andrew Cumbers, *The Case for Economic Democracy* (Cambridge: Polity, 2020), 46.
16. In the Marxist tradition, this topic has been discussed as one dimension of "alienation." See, for example, Rahel Jaeggi, *Alienation* (New York: Columbia University Press, 2016).
17. Samuel Bowles and Herbert Gintis, "Power and Wealth in a Competitive Capitalist Economy," *Philosophy & Public Affairs* 21, no. 4 (1992): 324–353, at 335–337.
18. Truman F. Bewley, *Why Wages Don't Fall during a Recession* (Cambridge, MA: Harvard University Press, 2002); see also Weil, *The Fissured Workplace*, 81–83.
19. See, for example, Elizabeth Anderson, *Private Government: How Employers Rule Our Lives and Why We Don't Talk about It* (Princeton: Princeton University Press, 2017); xix.
20. In retail settings, people use the term "clopening" for the inconsiderate scheduling that has one working the closing shift one day and the opening shift the next. See, for example, Jodi Kantor, "Starbucks to Revise Policies to End Irregular Schedules for Its 130,000 Baristas," *New York Times,* August 15, 2014, A11.
21. Iris Marion Young, "Five Faces of Oppression," in *Justice and the Politics of Difference* (Princeton: Princeton University Press, 2009), 39–65, at 56–58.
22. Weil, *Fissured Workplace*.
23. Weil, *Fissured Workplace*, 120.
24. The relationship between fairness perceptions and work behavior have been explored in the organizational justice literature. See, for example, Jerald Greenberg, "Organizational Justice: Yesterday, Today, and Tomorrow," *Journal of Management* 16, no. 2 (1990): 399–432.
25. Weil, *Fissured Workplace*, 120.
26. Weil, *Fissured Workplace*, for example, 130.

27. For a detailed ethnographic study, see, for example, Mary L. Gray and Siddharth Suri, *Ghost Work: How to Stop Silicon Valley from Building a New Global Underclass* (New York: Harcourt, 2019).
28. See, for example, Valeria Pulignano, Stefania Marino, Mathew Johnson, Markieta Domecka, and Me-Linh Riemann, "'Digital Tournaments': The Colonization of Freelancers' 'Free' Time and Unpaid Labour in the Online Platform Economy," *Cambridge Journal of Economics* 48, no. 1 (2024): 133–150; see also Phil Jones and James Muldoon, "Rise and Grind: Microwork and Hustle Culture in the UK," Autonomy Research, June 25, 2022, 29, https://autonomy.work/wp-content/uploads/2022/06/riseandgrind11.pdf.
29. Jones and Muldoon, "Rise and Grind," 7; this study is based on a survey of 1,189 workers on the online platforms Clickworker, Prolific, and Amazon Mechanical Turk, complemented by seventeen in-depth, online interviews.
30. Fabian Stephany, Otto Kässi, Uma Rani, and Vili Lehdonvirta, "Online Labour Index 2020: New Ways to Measure the World's Remote Freelancing Market," *Big Data & Society* 8, no. 2 (2021).
31. "Seven Ways Platform Workers Are Fighting Back," Trades Union Congress (TUC), London, November 5, 2021, https://www.tuc.org.uk/research-analysis/reports/seven-ways-platform-workers-are-fighting-back, 5.
32. Monica Anderson, Colleen McClain, Michelle Faverio, and Risa Gelles-Watnick, "The State of Gig Work in 2021," Pew Research Center, December 8, 2021, https://www.pewresearch.org/internet/2021/12/08/the-state-of-gig-work-in-2021/.
33. Jones and Muldoon, "Rise and Grind," 14, 24.
34. Jones and Muldoon, "Rise and Grind," 14.
35. Jones and Muldoon, "Rise and Grind," 18, 23.
36. The notion of black box, in this context, is from Frank Pasquale, *The Black Box Society: The Secret Algorithms That Control Money and Information* (Cambridge, MA: Harvard University Press, 2016).
37. For example, Jones and Muldoon, "Rise and Grind," 37–39.
38. Trebor Scholz, "Platform Cooperativism: Challenging the Corporate Sharing Economy," Rosa Luxemburg Stiftung, New York, January 2016, https://rosalux.nyc/wp-content/uploads/2020/11/RLS-NYC_platformcoop.pdf.

39. Paul Apostolidis, *The Fight For Time: Migrant Day Laborers and the Politics of Precarity* (Oxford: Oxford University Press, 2018).
40. "More Than 60 Per Cent of the World's Employed Population Are in the Informal Economy," press release, International Labour Organization (ILO), Geneva, April 30, 2018, https://www.ilo.org/resource/news/more-60-cent-worlds-employed-population-are-informal-economy.
41. See, for example, Stuart White, *The Civic Minimum: On the Rights and Obligations of Economic Citizenship* (Oxford: Oxford University Press, 2003), chap. 3. An exception arguably holds for individuals who are not given a fair chance to participate in society; see, for example, Tommie Shelby, "Justice, Work, and the Ghetto Poor," *Law & Ethics of Human Rights* 6, no. 1 (2012): 70–96.
42. Some theorists frame this issue as one about "meaningful" work and connect it to the democratization of work; see notably Ruth Yeoman, *Meaningful Work and Workplace Democracy: A Philosophy of Work and a Politics of Meaningfulness* (London: Palgrave Macmillan, 2014).
43. Herman Melville, "Bartleby, the Scrivener: A Story of Wall Street" (Project Gutenberg, 2004 [1853]).
44. This also raises questions about the normative desirability, from a democratic perspective, of wealth that is so great that it allows capable individuals to not work at all. Problems of inequality, more generally speaking, are explored in Chapter 3.
45. Adam Smith, *An Inquiry into the Nature and Causes of the Wealth of Nations*, 2 vols., ed. R. H. Campbell and A. S. Skinner, textual ed. W. B. Todd (Oxford: Clarendon Press, 1976 [1776]), I.X.I.
46. See, for example, David H. Autor and David Dorn, "The Growth of Low-Skill Service Jobs and the Polarization of the US Labor Market," *American Economic Review* 103, no. 5 (2013): 1553–1597.
47. Rev. Dr. Martin Luther King Jr., *All Labor Has Dignity* (Boston: Beacon Press, 1963/2011), 172, quoted in Adelle Blackett, "Work in Dignity," in *Democratize Work: The Case for Reorganizing the Economy*, ed. Isabelle Ferreras, Julie Battilan, and Dominique Méda (Chicago: University of Chicago Press, 2022), 67.
48. See, for example, Samuel Arnold, "The Difference Principle at Work," *Journal of Political Philosophy* 20, no. 1 (2012): 94–118, 110.
49. Adam Smith, *The Wealth of Nations*, V.I.III.II.50–51.
50. Émile Durkheim, *The Division of Labor in Society*, tr. George Simpson (Glencoe, IL: Free Press, 1933 [1893]).

51. For a discussion, see Lisa Herzog, "Durkheim on Social Justice: The Argument from "Organic Solidarity," *American Political Science Review* 112, no. 1 (2018): 112–124.
52. Weil, *Fissured Workplace*, 22.
53. Weil *Fissured Workplace*, chaps. 8–12.
54. Cynthia Estlund, *Working Together: How Workplace Bonds Strengthen a Diverse Democracy* (New York: Oxford University Press, 2003).
55. Diana C. Mutz and Jeffrey J. Mondak, "The Workplace as a Context for Cross-Cutting Political Discourse," *Journal of Politics* 68, no. 1 (2006): 140–155.
56. See, for example, Arindrajit Dube, "Impact of Minimum Wages: Review of the International Evidence," report prepared for Her Majesty's Treasury (UK), November 4, 2019, https://assets.publishing.service.gov.uk/media/5dc0312940f0b637a03ffa96/impacts_of_minimum_wages_review_of_the_international_evidence_Arindrajit_Dube_web.pdf.
57. I thank Frauke Schmode for fruitful discussions of this topic.
58. Joseph Fishkin, *Bottlenecks: A New Theory of Equal Opportunity* (New York: Oxford University Press, 2014).
59. A sad exception to this claim is that life expectancy has recently gone down for certain demographic groups in certain countries; for example in the United States. See Anne Case and Angus Deaton, *Deaths of Despair and the Future of Capitalism* (Princeton: Princeton University Press, 2020).
60. See the "Educational Leave and Part-Time Education" page of the Austrian government website at https://www.oesterreich.gv.at/themen/arbeit_und_pension/bildungskarenz_und_bildungsteilzeit.html.
61. Pavlina R. Tcherneva, *The Case for a Job Guarantee* (Cambridge: Polity, 2020).
62. See, for example, for Austria, Maximilian Kasy and Lukas Lehner, "Employing the Unemployed of Marienthal: Evaluation of a Guaranteed Job Program," Munich, CESifo Working Paper No. 10394, April 2023. For an overview, see also Olivier De Schutter, "The Employment Guarantee as a Tool to Fight against Poverty: Report of the Special Rapporteur On Extreme Poverty and Human Rights," *United Nations General Assembly, Human Rights Council*, Fifty-third session, June 19–July 14, 2023.
63. Lisa Herzog, *Inventing the Market: Smith, Hegel, and Political Theory* (Oxford: Oxford University Press, 2013), chap. 4.
64. The classic text making this argument is Carole Pateman, *Participation and Democratic Theory* (Cambridge: Cambridge University Press,

1970), chaps. 3–4. Contemporary empirical research has found a positive relation between workplace democracy and workers' political participation. See John W. Budd, J. Ryan Lamare, and Andrew R. Timming, "Learning About Democracy at Work: Cross-National Evidence on Individual Employee Voice Influencing Political Participation in Civil Society," *ILR Review* 71, no. 4 (2018): 956–985; Andrew Timming and Juliette Summers, "Is Workplace Democracy Associated with Wider Pro-democracy Affect? A Structural Equation Model," *Economic and Industrial Democracy* 41, no. 3 (2020): 709–726, quoted in Tom Christiano, "Why Does Worker Participation Matter? Three Considerations in Favour of Worker Participation in Corporate Governance," in *Wealth and Power: Philosophical Perspectives,* ed. Michael Bennett, Huub Brouwer, and Rutger Claassen (New York: Routledge, 2023), 127–144, at 140.

65. For an overview, see Robert Frega, Lisa Herzog, and Christian Neuhäuser, "Workplace Democracy: The Recent Debate," *Philosophy Compass* 14, no. 4 (2019): e12574. For an intervention in the US context, see Anderson, *Private Government;* see also Isabelle Ferreras, Julie Battilan, and Dominique Méda, eds., *Democratize Work: The Case for Reorganizing the Economy* (Chicago: University of Chicago Press, 2022). On workplace democracy as a key element in a broader program of transformation see David Schweickart, *After Capitalism,* 2nd ed. (Lanham, MD: Rowman & Littlefield, 2011). For my own reasons to endorse workplace democracy, see Lisa Herzog, *Reclaiming the System: Moral Responsibility, Divided Labor, and the Role of Organizations in Society* (Oxford: Oxford University Press, 2018), chaps. 9 and 10.

66. Piketty notes that stock market values are lower in Germany, which he explains as a matter of companies being less fully under the control of shareholders. Thomas Piketty, *Capital in the Twenty-First Century* (Cambridge, MA: Harvard University Press, 2014), 145–146.

67. See also, from an economic (!) perspective, Jean Tirole, "Corporate Governance," *Econometrica* 69, no. 1 (2001): 1–35; Michael Magill, Martine Quinzii, and Jean-Charles Rochet, "A Theory of the Stakeholder Corporation," *Econometrica* 83, no. 5 (2015): 1685–1725.

68. See similarly—and also for additional arguments that support workplace democracy—Christiano, "Why Does Worker Participation Matter?" 127–128, 141. Christiano argues that we need a toolkit of instruments because different instruments will work in different circumstances.

69. Felix Gerlsbeck and Lisa Herzog, "The Epistemic Potentials of Workplace Democracy," *Review of Social Economy* 78, no. 3 (2020): 307–330.
70. On challenges of knowledge management within organizations see Herzog, *Reclaiming the System*, chap. 6.
71. This is contrary to earlier predictions about the impossibility of codetermination. See, for example, Michael Jensen and William Meckling, "Rights and Production Functions: An Application to Labor-Managed Firms and Codetermination," *Journal of Business* 52, no. 4 (1979), 469–506.
72. Erling Barth, Alex Bryson, and Harald Dale-Olsen, "Union Density Effects on Productivity and Wages," *Economic Journal* 130, no. 631 (2020): 1898–1936.
73. See, for example, Sara LaFuente, "Dual Majorities for Firm Governments," in Ferreras, Battilan, and Méda, *Democratize Work*, 73–78, at 73–76.
74. See the meta-study led by Christine Unterrainer, "Organizational and Psychological Features of Successful Democratic Enterprises: A Systematic Review of Qualitative Research," *Frontiers in Psychology* 13 (2022), 947559. See also Fathi Fakhfakh, Virginie Pérotin, and Monica Gago, "Productivity, Capital, and Labor in Labor-Managed and Conventional Firms: An Investigation on French Data," *Industrial and Labor Relations Review* 65, no. 4 (2012): 847–879. On cooperatives as a model of "good work," see Marjorie Kelly and Ted Howard, *The Making of a Democratic Economy: Building Prosperity for the Many, Not Just the Few* (Oakland: Berrett-Koehler, 2019), chaps. 5 and 6.
75. John Stuart Mill, *Principles of Political Economy*, in *Principles of Political Economy and Chapters on Socialism*, ed. J. Riley (Oxford: Oxford University Press, 1994 [1871]), II.1.
76. Samuel Bowles and Herbert Gintis, "A Political and Economic Case for the Democratic Enterprise," *Economics and Philosophy* 9 (1993): 75–100, at 95–96.
77. This quote is from Jack Welch. See, for example, Steve Denning, "Why Can't We End Short-Termism?" *Forbes*, July 22, 2014.
78. Soumyajit Mazumder and Alan D. Yan, "What Do Americans Want from (Private) Government? Experimental Evidence Demonstrates That Americans Want Workplace Democracy," *American Political Science Review* 118, no. 2 (2024): 1020–1036.

79. See, for example, Luke Savage, "If America Had Fair Laws, 60 Million Workers Would Join a Union Tomorrow," *Jacobin,* January 21, 2023, https://jacobin.com/2023/01/unions-fair-labor-laws-america-economic-policy-institute.
80. See, for example, Mark R. Reiff, *In the Name of Liberty: The Case for Universal Unionization* (Cambridge: Cambridge University Press, 2020). On the role of unions for fighting inequality see also Tom Malleson, *Against Inequality: The Practical and Ethical Case for Abolishing the Superrich* (New York: Oxford University Press, 2023), 33.
81. Isabelle Ferreras, "From the Politically Impossible to the Politically Inevitable: Taking Action," in Ferreras, Battilan, and Méda, *Democratize Work,* 23–46, at 30–32; Sharon Block and Benjamin Sachs, "Clean Slate for Worker Power: Building a Just Economy and Democracy," Labor and Worklife Program, Harvard Law School, January 23, 2020, 38–39, https://clje.law.harvard.edu/app/uploads/2020/01/Clean-Slate-for-Worker-Power.pdf.
82. For background, see Natalie Videbæk Munkholm, "Board Level Employee Representation in Europe: An Overview," Directorate General for Employment, Social Affairs and Inclusion, European Commission, March 2018, https://eu.eventscloud.com/file_uploads/e0bd9a01e363e66c18f92cf50aa88485_Munkholm_Final_EN.pdf.
83. Isabelle Ferreras, *Firms as Political Entities: Saving Democracy through Economic Bicameralism* (Cambridge: Cambridge University Press, 2017).
84. On stakeholders other than workers, see also Jeff Moriarty, "Participation in the Workplace: Are Employees Special?" *Journal of Business Ethics* 92 (2001): 373–384.
85. Michael Bennett and Rutger Claassen, "The Corporate Social Assessment: Making Public Purpose Pay," *Review of Social Economy* 82, no. 1 (2024): 147–175.
86. See, for example, Detlef Gerst, Thomas Hardwig, Martin Kuhlmann, and Michael Schumann, "Group Work in the German Automobile Industry: The Case of Mercedes-Benz," in *Teamwork in the Automobile Industry: Radical Change or Passing Fashion?* ed. Jean-Pierre Durand, Paul Stewart, and Juan-José Castillo (Basingstoke: Macmillan, 1999), 366–394.
87. A key thinker in this movement is Frithjof Bergmann. See, for example, his *New Work, New Culture: Work We Want and a Culture That Strengthens Us* (Alresford: John Hunt, 2019).

88. Andreas Boes, Tobias Kämpf, Thomas Lühr, and Alexander Ziegler, "Agilität als Chance für einen neuen Anlauf zum demokratischen Unternehmen?" *Berliner Journal für Soziologie* 28 (2018): 181–208.
89. An instructive read on the insufficiency of technology is Erin L. Kelly and Phyllis Moen, *Overload: How Good Jobs Went Bad and What We Can Do about It* (Princeton: Princeton University Press, 2020). As Kelly and Moen showed in a field experiment in a tech firm, more democratic forms of workplace organization can work very well, with great improvements for workers' health and well-being, but are not immune to a new board fearing productivity losses and having the power to reverse them.
90. See, for example, Simon Pek, Sébastien Mena, and Brent Lyons, "The Role of Deliberative Mini-Publics in Improving the Deliberative Capacity of Multi-Stakeholder Initiatives," *Business Ethics Quarterly* 33, no. 1 (2023): 102–145.
91. Wolfgang G. Weber, Christine Unterrainer, and Thomas Höge, "Psychological Research on Organisational Democracy: A Meta-Analysis of Individual, Organisational, and Societal Outcomes," *Applied Psychology: An International Review* 69, no. 3 (2020): 1009–1071.
92. See, for example, Inigo Gonzalez-Ricoy, "Ownership and Control Rights in Democratic Firms: A Republican Approach," *Review of Social Economy* 78, no. 3 (2020): 411–430.
93. See also Cumbers, *The Case for Economic Democracy*, 86–95.
94. Tcherneva, *The Case for a Job Guarantee*. Similar advantages can come from an unconditional basic income; for reasons of space I here cannot discuss their comparative strengths and weaknesses in detail. I take it that a job guarantee in combination with generous social insurance (but which need not be unconditional) is a more promising approach, overall, than an unconditional basic income.
95. Robert Scholz and Sigurt Vitols, "Board-Level Codetermination: A Driving Force for Corporate Social Responsibility in German Companies?" *European Journal of Industrial Relations* 25, no. 3 (2019): 233–246.
96. Many other steps have to do with changes within the political system—for example, making regulatory bodies more independent—which are not discussed in this book for reasons of space.
97. For a practical report on how such processes can take place, see Joana Breidenbach and Bettina Rollow, *New Work Needs Inner Work* (München: Franz Vahlen, 2019).

3. Inequality

1. See, for example, Thomas Piketty and Emmanuel Saez, "Income Inequality in the United States, 1913–1998," *Quarterly Journal of Economics* 118, no. 1 (2003): 1–39. A good overview of numerous studies can be found in Heather Boushey, *Unbound: How Inequality Constricts Our Economy and What We Can Do about It* (Cambridge, MA: Harvard University Press, 2019).
2. See, for example, Alessio Terzi, *Growth for Good: Reshaping Capitalism to Save Humanity from Climate Catastrophe* (Cambridge, MA: Harvard University Press, 2022), 3.
3. Juliana Menasce Horowitz, Ruth Igielnik, and Rakesh Kochhar, "Trends in Income and Wealth Inequality," report, Pew Research Center, January 9, 2020, https://www.pewresearch.org/social-trends/2020/01/09/trends-in-income-and-wealth-inequality/.
4. See, for example, Gaby Hinsliff, "Why Inheritance Is the Dirty Secret of the Middle Classes, Harder to Talk about Than Sex," *Guardian*, December 3, 2022. On the situation in France, see Christophe Guilluy, *Twilight of the Elites: Prosperity, the Periphery, and the Future of France* (New Haven: Yale University Press, 2019), chap. 1. Space here does not allow for full discussion of housing inequality.
5. Kate Pickett and Richard Wilkinson, *The Spirit Level: Why More Equal Societies Almost Always Do Better* (London: Allen Lane, 2009). Some of Pickett and Wilkinson's empirical claims have been questioned, but arguments here do not rely on those.
6. This is a topic further discussed in Chapter 1.
7. For a recent overview, see Liam Shields, "Sufficientarianism," *Philosophy Compass* 15, no. 11 (2020): e12704, 1–10.
8. Jonathan Wolff and Avner de-Shalit, *Disadvantage* (Oxford: Oxford University Press, 2007).
9. For a recent call to end poverty, including concrete policy proposals, see Matthew Desmond, *Poverty, By America* (New York: Crown, 2023).
10. The relation between wealth inequality and economic mobility of the next generation has been called the "Great Gatsby curve." See, for example, Terzi, *Growth for Good*, 3–4. On economic mobility in the United States, see, Ray Chetty, David Grusky, Maximilian Hell, Nathaniel Hendren, Robert Manduca, and Jimmy Narang, "The Fading American Dream: Trends in Absolute Income Mobility since 1940," *Science* 356, no. 6336 (2017): 398–406.

11. Adam Smith, *An Inquiry into the Nature and Causes of the Wealth of Nations*, 2 vols., ed. R. H. Campbell and A. S. Skinner, textual ed. W. B. Todd (Oxford: Clarendon Press, 1976 [1776]), V.II.II.IV.3.
12. Albena Azmanova, *Capitalism on Edge: How Fighting Precarity Can Achieve Radical Change Without Crisis or Utopia* (New York: Columbia University Press, 2020).
13. Azmanova, *Capitalism on Edge*, chap. 5.
14. See, for example, Fact Sheet, press release, summarizing "Economic Well-Being of U.S. Households in 2022," Federal Reserve System, Washington, DC, May 2023, https://www.federalreserve.gov/newsevents/pressreleases/files/other20230522a1.pdf. Only 63 percent of those surveyed said they would have "cash or its equivalent" available to cover a $400 emergency.
15. See, for example, Anne Case and Angus Deaton, *Deaths of Despair and the Future of Capitalism* (Princeton: Princeton University Press, 2020), 205.
16. See also Jennifer Nedelsky and Tom Malleson, *Part-Time for All: A Care Manifesto* (New York: Oxford University Press, 2023), 213–216.
17. N. Gregory Mankiw, "Spreading the Wealth Around: Reflections Inspired by Joe the Plumber," *Eastern Economic Journal* 36 (2010): 285–298, 36.
18. Mankiw, "Spreading the Wealth Around," 36.
19. N. Gregory Mankiw, "Defending the One Percent," *Journal of Economic Perspectives* 27, no. 3 (2013): 21–34, at 30–31. For an alternative view, see Josh Bivens and Lawrence Mishel, "The Pay of Corporate Executives and Financial Professionals as Evidence of Rents in Top 1% Incomes," *Journal of Economic Perspectives* 27, no. 3 (2013): 57–78. In fact, in a later blogpost, Mankiw showed self-doubts about deservedness based on genetic differences. See N. Gregory Mankiw, "On Just Desert," *Greg Mankiw's Blog*, April 26, 2006, https://gregmankiw.blogspot.com/2006/04/on-just-deserts.html.
20. For an overview, see Fred Feldman and Brad Skow, "Desert," *Stanford Encyclopedia of Philosophy* (Winter 2020 Edition), ed. Edward N. Zalta, https://plato.stanford.edu/archives/win2020/entries/desert/.
21. Joel Feinberg, "Justice and Personal Desert," in *Nomos VI: Justice*, ed. Carl J. Friedrich and John W. Chapman (New York: Atherton Press, 1963), 69–97.
22. See, for example, Huub Brouwer, "Automation, Desert, and the Case for Capital Grants," in *Wealth and Power: Philosophical Perspectives*,

ed. Michael Bennett, Huub Brouwer, and Rutger Claassen (New York: Routledge, 2022), 295–313, 300–302.

23. See also Brouwer, "Automation, Desert, and the Case for Capital Grants," 306.

24. See, for example, Stuart White, *The Civic Minimum: On the Rights and Obligations of Economic Citizenship* (Oxford: Oxford University Press, 2003), chap. 3, for a discussion of what fair equality of opportunity would require.

25. See, for example, Brouwer, "Automation, Desert, and the Case for Capital Grants," 302; David Miller, *Principles of Social Justice* (Cambridge, MA: Harvard University Press, 1999), esp. chap. 7.

26. See also Tom Malleson, *Against Inequality: The Practical and Ethical Case for Abolishing the Superrich* (New York: Oxford University Press, 2023). Malleson compares meritocracy (in a morally loaded sense) to ableism, in the sense that it "ranks people in a social hierarchy on the basis of characteristics that are arbitrary from a moral point of view" (167).

27. See Christopher Hill, "Desert and the Moral Arbitrariness of the Natural Lottery," *Philosophical Forum* 16 (1985): 207–222. See similarly John Rawls, *A Theory of Justice* (Cambridge, MA: Belknap Press of Harvard University Press, 1971), 15.

28. On the phenomenon of "superstar" wages, see Sherwin Rosen, "The Economics of Superstars," *American Economic Review* 71, no. 5 (1981): 845–858. For a more recent (and empirically undergirded) perspective, see Ulrike Malmendier and Geoffrey Tate, "Superstar CEOs," *Quarterly Journal of Economics* 124, no. 4 (2009): 1593–1638.

29. See also Joseph Heath, "On the Very Idea of a Just Wage," *Erasmus Journal for Philosophy and Economics* 11, no. 2 (2018): 1–33.

30. For a discussion of why market prices cannot measure social contribution, see also Markus Furendal, "Defining the Duty to Contribute: Against the Market Solution," *European Journal of Political Theory* 18, no. 4 (2019): 469–488. Chapter 5 of this book also discusses the role of reproductive work for productive work.

31. Heath, "On the Very Idea of a Just Wage," 12.

32. Nancy Folbre, "Just Deserts? Earnings Inequality and Bargaining Power in the U.S. Economy," Washington Center for Equitable Growth, October 4, 2016, https://equitablegrowth.org/working-papers/earnings-inequality-and-bargaining-power/.

33. This topic is further explored in Chapter 2. See also Malleson, *Against Inequality*, 157.
34. This is part of the "gender pay gap," the causes of which are an ongoing topic of research. For a recent overview for the United States, see Rakesh Kochhar, "The Enduring Grip of the Gender Pay Gap," Pew Research Center, March 1, 2023, https://www.pewresearch.org/social-trends/2023/03/01/the-enduring-grip-of-the-gender-pay-gap/.
35. Heath, "On the Very Idea of a Just Wage," 15.
36. Malleson, *Against Inequality*, 147.
37. Lisa Herzog, Katrin Sold, and Bénédicte Zimmermann, "Essential Work: A Category in the Making?" in *Shifting Categories of Work: Unsettling the Ways We Think about Jobs, Labor, and Activities*, ed. Lisa Herzog and Bénédicte Zimmermann (London: Routledge, 2022), 252–264.
38. For example, Brouwer, "Automation, Desert, and the Case for Capital Grants."
39. Rawls here used the notion of "legitimate expectations." Rawls, *A Theory of Justice*, 310–315.
40. See also recently Ingrid Robeyns, *Limitarianism: The Case Against Extreme Wealth* (London: Allen Lane, 2024).
41. On the need to distinguish among various spheres based on their different distributive logics, see also Michael Walzer, *Spheres of Justice: A Defense of Pluralism and Equality* (New York: Basic Books, 1983).
42. Martin Gilens and Benjamin Page, "Testing Theories of American Politics: Elites, Interest Groups, and Average Citizens," *Perspectives on Politics* 12, no. 3 (2014): 564–581. See also Martin Gilens, *Affluence and Influence: Economic Inequality and Political Power in America* (Princeton: Princeton University Press, 2014).
43. The problem is particularly great in the United States, where campaign contributions are about fifty times higher than in most parts of Europe. Thomas Philippon, *The Great Reversal: How America Gave Up on Free Markets* (Cambridge, MA: Harvard University Press, 2019), 193. Philippon (in chap. 10) summarizes various strands of research on this issue.
44. See, for example, Julia Cagé, *The Price of Democracy: How Money Shapes Politics and What to Do About It* (Cambridge, MA: Harvard University Press, 2020), 44–50. See also Kay Lehman Schlozman, Henry E. Brady, and Sidney Verba, *Unequal and Unrepresented* (Princeton: Princeton University Press, 2018), 212–214.

45. Having no time often means that those citizens cannot hold their representatives to account. See, for example, Thomas Christiano, "Why Does Worker Participation Matter? Three Considerations in Favour of Worker Participation in Corporate Governance," in Bennett, Brouwer, and Claassen, *Wealth and Power*, 127–144, at 139.
46. This is a general result from the research on the social determinants of health. See, for example, Michael Marmot, *The Status Syndrome: How Social Standing Affects Our Health and Longevity* (New York: Owl Books, 2004).
47. Nicholas Carnes, *The Cash Ceiling: Why Only the Rich Run for Office—And What We Can Do About It* (Princeton: Princeton University Press, 2018).
48. Pierre Bourdieu, "The Forms of Capital," *Handbook of Theory and Research for the Sociology of Education*, ed. J. Richardson (New York: Greenwood, 1986), 241–258.
49. See also Phil Parvin, "Hidden in Plain Sight: How Lobby Organisations Undermine Democracy," in Bennett, Brouwer, and Claassen, *Wealth and Power*, 229–251, at 242–248.
50. For general discussions, see Emma Saunders-Hastings, *Private Virtues, Public Vices: Philanthropy and Democratic Equality* (Chicago: University of Chicago Press, 2022); Theodore M. Lechterman, *The Tyranny of Generosity: Why Philanthropy Corrupts Our Politics and How We Can Fix It* (Oxford: Oxford University Press, 2022).
51. Michael Bennett, Huub Brouwer, and Rutger Claassen, "Introduction: The Wealth-Power Nexus," in Bennett, Brouwer, and Claassen, *Wealth and Power*, 1–22. The Walton Family Foundation represents just 0.04 percent of the family's net worth (at 1).
52. Robert R. Reich, *Just Giving: Why Philanthropy Is Failing Democracy and How It Can Do Better* (Princeton: Princeton University Press, 2018), esp. chap. 4.
53. On this combination, see Emma Saunders-Hastings, "Economic Power and Democratic Forbearance: The Case of Corporate Social Responsibility and Philanthropy," in Bennett, Brouwer, and Claassen, *Wealth and Power*, 186–205, 187.
54. Reich, *Just Giving*, 1–7 and chap. 4.
55. See also Sanders-Hastings, "Economic Power and Democratic Forbearance."
56. On the clustering of disadvantage, see also Wolff and de-Shalit, *Disadvantage*, chap. 5.

57. Pierre Bourdieu, *Outline of a Theory of Practice* (Cambridge: Cambridge University Press, 1977); and Bourdieu, *Distinction: A Social Critique of the Judgment of Taste* (Cambridge, MA: Harvard University Press, 1984).
58. For example, Jennifer Morton, *Moving Up without Losing Your Way: The Ethical Costs of Upward Mobility* (Princeton: Princeton University Press, 2019).
59. Maria J. Kefalas and Patrick J. Carr, *Hollowing Out the Middle: The Rural Brain Drain and What It Means for America* (New York: Beacon Press, 2010), for example, at 48.
60. Elizabeth Anderson, "What Is the Point of Equality?" *Ethics* 109, no. 2 (1999): 287–337, at 313.
61. Fred Hirsch, *Social Limits to Growth* (London: Routledge & Kegan Paul, 1977).
62. See the classic Thorstein Veblen, *The Theory of the Leisure Class* (Oxford: Oxford University Press, [1918] 2007). On the necessity to consider relative positions even if one understands poverty in absolute ways, see Amartya Sen, "Poor, Relatively Speaking," *Oxford Economic Papers* 35 (1983): 153–169.
63. See also Michèle Lamont, "From 'Having' to 'Being': Self-Worth and the Current Crisis of American Society," *British Journal of Sociology* 70, no. 3 (2019): 660–707, 665.
64. Robert H. Frank, "Positional Externalities Cause Large and Preventable Welfare Losses," *American Economic Review* 95, no. 2 (2005): 137–141.
65. Alain de Botton, *Status Anxiety* (London: Vintage, 2005).
66. For another view, see also Waheed Hussain, "Pitting People Against Each Other," *Philosophy & Public Affairs* 48, no. 1 (2020): 79–113.
67. The topic is covered in Chapter 5 of this book.
68. See, for example, Boushey, *Unbound,* 92–101 and 110–113; Malleson, *Against Inequality,* chap. 1–3, on taxation (also refuting the claim that it would harm growth).
69. See, for example, Anthony B. Atkinson, *Inequality: What Can Be Done?* (Cambridge, MA: Harvard University Press, 2015), esp. chap. 6, taking up a proposal by Bruce Ackerman and Anne Alstott, *The Stakeholder Society* (New Haven: Yale University Press, 1999).
70. See, for example, Jedediah Purdy, *This Land Is Our Land: The Struggle for a New Commonwealth* (Princeton: Princeton University Press, 2019), xxv.

71. Purdy, *This Land Is Our Land,* 103–107.
72. Elizabeth Anderson, "Fair Opportunity in Education: A Democratic Equality Perspective," *Ethics* 117, no. 4 (2007): 595–622.
73. The term was coined by Jacob S. Hacker, "The Institutional Foundations of Middle-Class Democracy," *Policy Network* 6, no. 5 (2011): 33–37. See also Kate Raworth, *Doughnut Economics: Seven Ways to Think Like a Twenty-First-Century Economist* (London: Penguin, 2017), chap. 5.
74. Liam Murphy and Thomas Nagel, *The Myth of Ownership: Taxes and Justice* (New York: Oxford University Press, 2002).
75. See, for example, Daniel Kahneman, Jack L. Knetsch, and Richard H. Thaler, "Experimental Tests on the Endowment Effect and the Coase Theorem," *Journal of Political Economy* 98, no. 6 (1990): 1325–1348.
76. For one such proposal, see Boushey, *Unbound,* 198–203.
77. For a discussion of empirical data about inequality and productivity, and for ways to support low-income families, see Boushey, *Unbound,* chaps. 1 and 2.
78. See also "Raj Chetty on 'The Lost Einsteins,'" Brookings Institution, presentation recorded January 11, 2018, https://www.brookings.edu/events/raj-chetty-on-the-lost-einsteins/.
79. See, for example, Ross Levine and Yona Rubinstein, "Smart and Illicit: Who Becomes an Entrepreneur and Do They Earn More?" NBER Working Paper No. 19276, August 2013, rev. September 2015.
80. Mihaly Csíkszentmihályi, *Flow: The Psychology of Optimal Experience* (New York: Harper, 1990).
81. Nobel Prize Foundation, Press Release, 2021, https://www.nobelprize.org/prizes/economic-sciences/2021/press-release/. On the earlier critique, see Boushey, *Unbound,* 9–10.
82. On the importance of gaining self-esteem from equal citizen status rather than from relative status on an income scale, see Pablo Gilabert, "Self-Esteem and Competition," *Philosophy and Social Criticism* 49, no. 6 (2023): 711–742.
83. This distinguishes my view from communitarian visions. See, for example, Paul Collier and John Kay, *Greed Is Dead: Politics After Individualism* (London: Penguin, 2020).
84. Giacomo Corneo, *Is Capitalism Obsolete? A Journey through Alternative Economic Systems* (Cambridge, MA: Harvard University Press, 2017), 254–259.

4. From Growth to Functions

1. "Personal square," by Studio 212 Fahrenheit. See "Kunstwerken met gepaste afstand in het Noorderplantsoen," *Kunstpuntgroningen,* July 3, 2020, https://www.kunstpuntgroningen.nl/pers/kunstwerken-met-gepaste-afstand-in-het-noorderplantsoen/.
2. For the latter point, see Alessio Terzi, *Growth for Good: Reshaping Capitalism to Save Humanity from Climate Catastrophe* (Cambridge, MA: Harvard University Press, 2022). For a history (and endorsement) of GDP, see Diane Coyle, *GDP: A Brief but Affectionate History* (Princeton: Princeton University Press, 2014).
3. Critical voices among philosophers include John Stuart Mill and John Rawls. For a discussion, see Julie Rose, "On the Value of Economic Growth," *Politics, Philosophy and Economics* 19, no. 2 (2020): 128–153.
4. John Stuart Mill, *Principles of Political Economy and Chapters on Socialism,* ed. J. Riley (Oxford: Oxford University Press, 1994 [1871]), 126–129. For discussions, see Rose, "On the Value of Economic Growth," 130; Fredrik Albritton Jonsson and Carl Wennerlind, *Scarcity: A History from the Origins of Capitalism to the Climate Crisis* (Cambridge, MA: Harvard University Press, 2023), 117–120.
5. Readers might be reminded of the so-called Easterlin paradox according to which, beyond a certain point, more income does not make individuals happier. Richard A. Easterlin, "Does Economic Growth Improve the Human Lot? Some Empirical Evidence," in *Nations and Households in Economic Growth: Essays in Honor of Moses Abramovitz,* eds. P. A. David and M. W. Reder (New York: Academic Press, 1974), 89–125. However, some more recent empirical studies claim that there is no satiation point for happiness. See, for example, Betsey Stevenson and Justin Wolfers, "Economic Growth and Subjective Well-Being: Reassessing the Easterlin Paradox," NBER Working Paper No. 14282, August 2008. Empirical research is ongoing, with inconsistent results. For discussions see Rose, "On the Value of Economic Growth," 7–8; Brian Kogelmann, "We Must Always Pursue Economic Growth," *Utilitas,* 34, no. 4 (2022): 478–492, at 480–481. Arguments in this book do not rely on this research, because they do not depend on claims about subjective happiness.
6. Isabelle Cassiers and Kevin Maréchal, "The Economy in a Post-Growth Era: What Project and What Philosophy?" in *Post-growth Economics*

and Society: Exploring the Paths of a Social and Ecological Transition, eds. Isabelle Cassiers, Kevin Maréchal, and Dominique Méda (London: Routledge, 2018), 1–12, at 2 (emphasis in the original). See, similarly, Jason Hickel, *Less Is More: How Degrowth Will Save The World* (London: Penguin, 2021). Hickel makes explicit that "degrowth is not about reducing GDP. It is about reducing the material and energy throughput" (204).

7. See, for example, Terzi, *Growth for Good*, 57.
8. David Ciepley, *Liberalism in the Shadow of Totalitarianism* (Cambridge, MA: Harvard University Press, 2007).
9. Johan Rockström et al., "A Safe Operating Space For Humanity," *Nature* 461, no. 7263 (2009): 472–475; Will Steffen et al., "Planetary Boundaries: Guiding Human Development on a Changing Planet," *Science* 347, no. 6223 (2015), 1259855.
10. Kate Raworth cites research on the enormous impact that fossil fuels had on the growth path of the Western world in the last two centuries. Kate Raworth, *Doughnut Economics: Seven Ways to Think Like a Twenty-First-Century Economist* (London: Penguin, 2017), pos. 4010–4019. Also see Robert U. Ayres and Benjamin Warr, *The Economic Growth Engine* (Cheltenham: Edward Elgar, 2009).
11. See, for example, Thomas Piketty, *Capital in the Twenty-First Century* (Cambridge, MA: Harvard University Press, 2014).
12. See, for example, Łukasz Rachel and Lawrence H. Summers, "On Secular Stagnation in the Industrialized World," *Brookings Papers on Economic Activity* (Spring 2019): 1–76; Robert J. Gordon, "The Demise of US Economic Growth: Restatement, Rebuttals and Reflections," NBER Working Paper no. 19895, February 2014.
13. Herman E. Daly, *From Economic Growth to a Steady-State Economy* (Cheltenham: Edward Elgar, 2014).
14. Hickel, *Less Is More*; Tim Jackson, *Prosperity Without Growth: Economics for a Finite Planet* (London: Earthscan/Routledge, 2009); Tim Jackson, *Post Growth: Life after Capitalism* (Cambridge: Polity, 2021). These well-known authors build on earlier work by many, including scholars of feminist and heterodox economics and indigenous approaches. See also Hickel, *Less Is More*, 31. For a useful review of the more recent literature, see, for example, Anja Eliasson and Erik Grönlund, "Degrowth—Characteristic Elements and Strategies," Presentation at the 27nd International Sustainable Development Research Society Conference,

Mid Sweden University, July 13–15, 2021, https://oxford-abstracts.s3.amazonaws.com/01bc6bab-d23b-4fc4-9b13-ff479f3f480a.pdf.
15. Terzi, *Growth for Good*, 208; Hickel, *Less Is More*, 203.
16. Terzi, *Growth for Good*, 28; Hickel, *Less Is More*, 187–194.
17. See, for the following, Philipp Lepenies, *The Power of a Single Number: A Political History of GDP* (New York: Columbia University Press, 2016). See also Coyle, *GDP*, chaps. 1–3; Mariana Mazzucato, *The Value of Everything: Making and Taking in the Global Economy* (London: Penguin, 2019), chap. 3.
18. Lepenies, *The Power of a Single Number*, chaps. 2–4.
19. Lepenies, *The Power of a Single Number*, 92.
20. Lepenies, *The Power of a Single Number*, 127–130.
21. See also Terzi, *Growth for Good*, 23.
22. Simon Kuznets, *National Product in Wartime* (New York: National Bureau of Economic Research, 1945), x, quoted in Lepenies, *The Power of a Single Number*, 88.
23. See, for example, Hickel, *Less Is More*, 167; Terzi, *Growth for Good*, 23–24.
24. See, for example, Lepenies, *The Power of a Single Number* 2; Hickel, *Less Is More*, 91–92.
25. This topic is explored in Chapter 1 of this book. See also Hickel, *Less Is More*, 91–92.
26. See, for example, Donald T. Campbell, "Assessing the Impact of Planned Social Change," Occasional Paper Series, Dartmouth College Public Affairs Center, 1976.
27. Cathy O'Neil, *Weapons of Math Destruction: How Big Data Increases Inequality and Threatens Democracy* (London: Penguin, 2015), chap. 3.
28. For an ethnography of the effects on universities, see Wendy Espeland, "Narrating Numbers," in *World of Indicators: The Making of Governmental Knowledge*, ed. Richard Rottenburg, Sally Merry, Sung-Joon Park, and Joanna Mugler (Cambridge: Cambridge University Press, 2015), 56–75.
29. O'Neil, *Weapons of Math Destruction*, 60.
30. This is suggested, for example, by the book title: Joseph E. Stiglitz, Amartya Sen, and Jean-Paul Fitoussi, *Mismeasuring Our Lives: Why GDP Doesn't Add Up* (New York: New Press, 2010).
31. Hickel, *Less Is More*, 96.
32. For example, Terzi, *Growth for Good*, chap. 3.

33. For example, Terzi, *Growth for Good*, 72–3.
34. This is a dictum often attributed to Peter Drucker, although its meaning (that much of the most important work of executives in organizations defies measurement) is sometimes misconstrued. Paul Zak, "Measurement Myopia," *Drucker Institute*, blog post, April 4, 2013, https://www.drucker.institute/thedx/measurement-myopia/.
35. Rockström et al., "A Safe Operating Space for Humanity;" Steffen et al., "Planetary Boundaries."
36. Terzi, *Growth for Good*, 155.
37. See, for example, Terzi, *Growth for Good*, 20–21; Hickel, *Less Is More*, 152–153. Chapter 3 of this book further explores the topic.
38. The distinction between price and value goes back to Immanuel Kant, *The Metaphysics of Morals* (Cambridge: Cambridge University Press, 2017 [1797]), §37.
39. See, for example, Hickel, *Less Is More*, chap. 6; see also Jennifer Nedelsky and Tom Malleson, *Part-Time for All: A Care Manifesto* (New York: Oxford University Press, 2023), 83–87.
40. Falling to a certain extent in this camp is Kogelmann, "We Must Always Pursue Economic Growth." Kogelmann assumes that critics of growth would want to actively *stop* growth by means that he describes as illegitimate.
41. Herman Daly, "Envisioning a Successful Steady State Economy," *Solutions Journal*, February 22, 2016, https://thesolutionsjournal.com/?p=1338.
42. Terzi, *Growth for Good*, 188–190.
43. Hickel, *Less Is More*, 207–217.
44. Terzi, *Growth for Good*, 183.
45. There are certainly some deeper systemic questions in the background. See, for example, Raworth, *Doughnut Economics*, chap. 7. Not discussed here, for reasons of space, are relations to the financial and monetary system, and the different positions the two camps hold. But many steps discussed by postgrowth proponents are possible even within the current system of banking. In other words, these steps can and should can happen *before* a transformation of the monetary system; for the latter there are independent reasons, but it does not seem to be on the horizon.
46. Terzi holds that "The model proposed here is definitely one that moves away from the neoliberal tenets, such as low taxation, embedded in the so-called Washington Consensus." Terzi, *Growth for Good*, 184.

47. Some critics of growth, to be sure, want to go beyond capitalism—but they differ as to what exactly this means. Those growth critics who are arguing for a strong primacy of politics would seem to be on firmer ground than those calling for the socialization of all means of production, which is not necessary for greening the economy. As noted, however, in the Introduction, arguing about "isms" is less interesting than debating actual measures taken to democratize the economy.
48. See also Terzi, *Growth for Good,* 41, 206.
49. For a list of possible measures, see, for example, Paul Hawken, ed., *Drawdown: The Most Comprehensive Plan Ever Proposed to Reverse Global Warming* (New York: Penguin, 2017).
50. Terzi argues that only capitalism can truly deliver on innovation. Terzi, *Growth for Good*, 39–40. Others insist that technological progress can also take place in a non-growing economy. See, for example, Rose, "On the Value of Economic Growth"; Hickel, *Less Is More,* 197–198.
51. In the United States, this happens in particular through the Inflation Reduction Act. See https://www.whitehouse.gov/cleanenergy/inflation-reduction-act-guidebook/.
52. See, for example, International Labor Organization, "What Is a Green Job?" April 13, 2016, https://www.ilo.org/global/topics/green-jobs/news/WCMS_220248/lang—en/index.htm.
53. See the website of the EU Emissions Trading System at https://climate.ec.europa.eu/eu-action/eu-emissions-trading-system-eu-ets_en.
54. Evidence of this claim is that, in 2023, a big conference called "Beyond Growth" was convened by members of the European Parliament and other organizations. See the program at https://www.beyond-growth-2023.eu/.
55. See, for example, Raworth, *Doughnut Economics;* Wellbeing Economics Alliance website at https://weall.org/.
56. This term was historically used for the pursuit of economic growth as policy goal. See Elizabeth Popp Berman, *Thinking Like an Economist: How Efficiency Replaced Equality in U.S. Public Policy* (Princeton: Princeton University Press, 2022), 33.
57. On new public infrastructures, see Kate Aronoff, Alyssa Battistoni, Daniel Aldana Cohen, and Thea Riofrancos, *A Planet to Win: Why We Need a Green New Deal* (London: Verso, 2019), 21–22.
58. For certain types of goods (for example, medical services) there are independent arguments against the use of markets. See, for example,

Angus Deaton, "How Misreading Adam Smith Helped Spawn Deaths of Despair," *Boston Review,* August 2, 2023.

59. A similar approach is suggested by Robert Skidelsky and Edward Skidelsky, *How Much Is Enough? Money and the Good Life* (London: Penguin, 2012). Those authors, however, rely on a relatively homogenous notion of "the good life." The notion used here, based on democratically determined functions, seems more appropriate for modern, pluralistic societies with a mix of values and lifestyles.

60. On "democratic steering" of the economy, see Danielle Allen, *Justice by Means of Democracy* (Chicago: University of Chicago Press, 2023), 182–186. See also Aronoff et al., *A Planet to Win,* 43–44.

61. R. H. Tawney, *The Acquisitive Society* (New York: Harcourt, Brace, 1921), 24.

62. Tawney, *Acquisitive Society,* 66, 81, 86. For a discussion, see Stuart White, *The Civic Minimum: On the Rights and Obligations of Economic Citizenship* (Oxford: Oxford University Press, 2003), 56.

63. Tawney, *Acquisitive Society,* 28–29.

64. Tawney, *Acquisitive Society,* 34.

65. Tawney, *Acquisitive Society,* 149–150.

66. Tawney, *Acquisitive Society,* for example, 96–97. See also Chapter 2 of this book.

67. For example, Terzi, *Growth for Good,* 56–57.

68. Daly, *From Economic Growth to a Steady-State Economy,* 15.

69. For another view, see Aronoff et al., *A Planet to Win,* 21.

70. Commentators often refer to the Yellow Vest protests in France as a negative example. For a discussion, see, for example, Colin Kinniburgh, "Climate Politics after the Yellow Vests," *Dissent,* Spring, 2019, https://www.dissentmagazine.org/article/the-yellow-vests-uncertain-future.

71. This is captured in the concept of a "just transition." See especially Dimitris Stevis and Romain Felli, "Global Labour Unions and Just Transition to a Green Economy," *International Environmental Agreements: Politics, Law and Economics* 15, no. 1 (2015): 29–43.

72. On how the "Keynes Accommodation" allowed for the growth of both profits and wages, see Samuel Bowles and Herbert Gintis, *Democracy and Capitalism: Property, Community, and the Contradictions of Modern Social Thought* (Abingdon: Routledge, 1986), 55–60.

73. See notably William A. Galston, *The New Challenge to Market Democracies: The Political and Social Costs of Economic Stagnation* (Washington,

DC: Brookings Institution Press, 2014); Benjamin M. Friedman, *The Moral Consequences of Economic Growth* (New York: Knopf, 2005).
74. Benjamin M. Friedman treats the Great Depression as the "great exception." Friedman, *The Moral Consequences of Economic Growth*, chap. 7.
75. See also Rose, "The Value of Economic Growth"; Aronoff et al., *A Planet to Win*.
76. Martha Nussbaum and Amartya Sen, eds., *The Quality of Life* (Oxford: Oxford University Press, 1993); Martha Nussbaum, *Women and Human Development: The Capabilities Approach* (Cambridge: Cambridge University Press, 2000); Amartya Sen, *Development as Freedom* (Oxford: Oxford University Press, 1999).
77. This is the response to the charge that there would be no way of dealing with dissent in a postgrowth society. On that charge, see, for example, Terzi, *Growth for Good*, 56–57.
78. Jonathan Wolff and Avner de-Shalit, *Disadvantage* (Oxford: Oxford University Press, 2007), esp. chap. 8.
79. An example was the measurement of virus load in wastewater during the Covid-19 pandemic, which circumvented questions about incorrect or incomplete reports by citizens.
80. On being "agnostic" about growth, see Raworth, *Doughnut Economics*, chap. 7. See also Jeroen C. J. M. van den Bergh, "Environment versus Growth: A Criticism of 'Degrowth' and a Plea for 'a-Growth,'" *Ecological Economics* 70, no. 5 (2011): 881–890.
81. See, for example, Kathrin Kühn, "Warum wir Wohland anders vermessen müssen," *Deutschlandfunk,* May 21, 2023, https://www.deutschland funk.de/bruttooekoinlandsprodukt-warum-wir-wohlstand-anders-ver messe`n-muessen-dlf-cabae024-100.html.
82. See the website of the Human Development Index at https://hdr.undp .org/data-center/human-development-index#/indicies/HDI.
83. Of course, this should happen in ways that guard individuals' privacy right—a requirement that is relatively easy to meet because many societally relevant issues require only aggregated, not individualized, data.
84. Leigh Phillips and Michal Rozworksi, *The People's Republic of Walmart: How the World's Biggest Corporations Are Laying the Foundation for Socialism* (London: Verso, 2019).
85. Kogelmann, "We Must Always Pursue Economic Growth."

86. This debate goes back at least to the eighteenth century, with Rousseau's charges of individuals "living only in the opinion of others." Jean-Jacques Rousseau, *The Discourses and Other Early Political Writings* (Cambridge: Cambridge University Press, 1997), 187.
87. Mill, *Principles of Political Economy*, 129.
88. Adam Smith, *The Theory of Moral Sentiments*, ed. D. D. Raphael and A. L. Macfie (Oxford: Clarendon Press, 1976 [1790]), 50.
89. See, notably, Axel Honneth, *The Struggle for Recognition* (Cambridge, MA: MIT Press, 1986); Nancy Fraser and Axel Honneth, *Redistribution or Recognition? A Political-Philosophical Exchange* (London: Verso, 2003).
90. See, for example, Alain de Botton, *Status Anxiety* (London: Hamish Hamilton, 2004).
91. Fred Hirsch, *The Social Limits to Growth* (Cambridge, MA: Harvard University Press, 1976), 5.
92. See, for example, John Cook, Geoffrey Supran, Stephan Lewandowsky, Naomi Oreskes, and Edward Maibach, "America Misled: How the Fossil Fuel Industry Deliberately Misled Americans About Climate Change," Center for Climate Change Communication, George Mason University, October 2019, https://www.climatechangecommunication.org/wp-content/uploads/2023/09/America_Misled.pdf.
93. Notably, consider the 2021 case against Royal Shell Dutch in the Netherlands. For a summary, see "Royal Dutch Shell Must Reduce CO_2 Emissions," De Rechtspraak, May 26, 2021, https://www.rechtspraak.nl/Organisatie-en-contact/Organisatie/Rechtbanken/Rechtbank-Den-Haag/Nieuws/Paginas/Royal-Dutch-Shell-must-reduce-CO2-emissions.aspx.
94. For background, see Kris Manjapra, "When Will Britain Face Up to Its Crimes Against Humanity?" *Guardian,* March 29, 2018.
95. See, for example, Alec Tyson and Brian Kennedy, "Two-Thirds of Americans Think Government Should Do More on Climate," Pew Research Center, June 23, 2020.
96. Zoe Kleinman, "Tiny Data Centre Used to Heat Public Swimming Pool," *BBC,* March 14, 2023.
97. Michal Shur-Ofry, "Access-to-Error," *Cardozo Arts & Entertainment Law Journal* 34 (2016): 357–400.
98. Joel Mokyr, *The Gifts of Athena: Historical Origins of the Knowledge Economy* (Princeton: Princeton University Press, 2002).
99. See the Leguminosen-Netzwerk website at https://www.legunet.de/.

5. Time for Democracy

1. John Maynard Keynes, "Economic Possibilities for Our Grandchildren," in *Essays in Persuasion* (New York: Norton, 1963 [1930]), 358–373. Visions of reduced work time were also shared by other historical thinkers such as William Godwin. See Fredrik Albritton Jonsson and Carl Wennerlind, *Scarcity: A History from the Origins of Capitalism to the Climate Crisis* (Cambridge, MA: Harvard University Press, 2023), 101. Important contemporary contributors include André Gorz, *Critique of Economic Reason* (London: Verso, 1989); Kathi Weeks, *The Problem with Work: Feminism, Marxism, Antiwork Politics, and Postwork Imaginaries* (Durham, NC: Duke University Press, 2011), chap. 4; Frigga Haugg, "The Four-In-One Perspective": A Manifesto for a More Just Life," *Socialism and Democracy* 23, no. 1 (2009): 119–123; Dominique Méda, *Travail, la revolution necessaire* (Paris: L'Aube, 2010); Jennifer Nedelsky and Tom Malleson, *Part-Time for All: A Care Manifesto* (New York: Oxford University Press, 2023).
2. See, for example, Erin Griffith, "Why Are Young People Pretending to Love Work?" *New York Times*, January 26, 2019.
3. Juliet Schor, *The Overworked American: The Unexpected Decline of Leisure* (New York: Basic Books, 1992).
4. Maxine Eichner, *The Free-Market Family: How the Market Crushed the American Dream (and How It Can Be Restored)* (New York: Oxford University Press, 2020), chap. 3; Alberto Alesina, Edward Glaeser and Bruce Sacerdote, "Work and Leisure in the United States and Europe: Why So Different?" *NBER Macroeonomics Annual* 20 (2005): 1–64.
5. See, for example, for the Netherlands, Marguerite van den Berg, *Werk is geen oplossing* (Amsterdam: Amsterdam University Press, 2021).
6. Eichner, *The Free-Market Family*, 45–46.
7. Eichner, *The Free-Market Family*, chap. 2.
8. Eicher, *The Free-Market Family*, 14, drawing on data from Brigid Schulte, *Overwhelmed: Work, Love, and Play When No One Has the Time* (New York: Sarah Crichton Books, 2014), 25.
9. Robert E. Goodin, "Temporal Justice," *Journal of Social Policy* 39, no. 1 (2010): 1–16, at 5–6.
10. Julie Rose, *Free Time* (Princeton: Princeton University Press, 2016).
11. Nicholas Carnes, *White-Collar Government: The Hidden Role of Class in Economic Policy-Making* (Chicago: University of Chicago Press,

2013). See also Nicholas Carnes, *The Cash Ceiling: Why Only the Rich Run For Office, and What We Can Do About It* (Princeton: Princeton University Press, 2018).
12. Alexis de Tocqueville, *Democracy in America*, 2 vols. (New York: Snova, 2019 [1863]). Of course, the society Tocqueville saw had deep flaws in other respects, mostly with regard to slavery, racism, and gender justice.
13. See Robert D. Putnam with Shaylyn Romney Garrett, *The Upswing: How We Came Together a Century Ago and How We Can Do It Again* (New York: Simon & Schuster, 2020).
14. A. J. Veal, "A Brief History of Work and Its Relationship to Leisure," in *Work and Leisure*, ed. John T. Haworth and A. J. Veal (London: Routledge, 2004), 15–33.
15. See, for example, Daniel T. Rodgers, *The Work Ethic in Industrial America, 1850–1920* (Chicago: University of Chicago Press, 2014), chap. 6.
16. Karl Marx, *Capital: A Critique of Political Economy,* Chicago: Charles H. Kerr, 1906 [1867]), vol. 1, chap. 7.
17. For a discussion, see, for example, Mark Blaug, *Economic Theory in Retrospect*, 5th ed. (Cambridge: Cambridge University Press, 1996), chap. 7.
18. See, for example, Robert Whaples, "Winning the Eight-Hour Day, 1909–1919," *Journal of Economic History* 50, no. 2 (1990): 393–406.
19. Alesina et al., "Work and Leisure," 20.
20. Alesina et al., "Work and Leisure," 24–25.
21. Alesina et al., "Work and Leisure," 5.
22. Eichner, *The Free-Market Family*, 14.
23. Schor, *The Overworked American*, chap. 3. Schor also sees consumer culture as a contributing factor (chap. 5). An additional factor might be the work ethic in Protestant countries. See Elizabeth Anderson, *Hijacked: How Neoliberalism Turned the Work Ethic against Workers and How Workers Can Take It Back* (Cambridge: Cambridge University Press, 2023).
24. Eichner, *The Free-Market Family*, chap. 3.
25. Alesina et al., "Work and Leisure," 5. See also Rose, *Free Time*, chap. 5.
26. Eichner, *The Free-Market Family*.
27. See, for example, Alan Manning and Barbara Petrongolo, "The Part-Time Pay Penalty for Women in Britain," *Economic Journal* 118, no. 526 (2005): 28–51; Síle O'Dorchai, Robert Plasman, and Francois Rycx,

"The Part-Time Wage Penalty in European Countries: How Large Is It for Men?" *International Journal of Manpower* 28, no. 7 (2007): 571–603.
28. The next paragraphs follow Lisa Herzog, "You're Free to Choose, But Do You Have Time to Choose? Structural Injustice and the Epistemic Burdens of Market Societies," *Hypatia* 39 (2024): 177–193.
29. For a testimonial, see Stephanie Land, *Maid: Hard Work, Low Pay, and a Mother's Will to Survive* (New York: Hachette, 2019).
30. On how liberalism overlooks the social construction of preferences, see Samuel Bowles and Herbert Gintis, *Democracy and Capitalism: Property, Community, and the Contradictions of Modern Social Thought* (Abingdon: Routledge, 1986), 21.
31. See, for example, Brian Kogelmann, "Public Choice and Political Equality," in *Wealth and Power: Philosophical Perspectives,* ed. Michael Bennett, Huub Brouwer, and Rutger Claassen (New York: Routledge, 2022), 67–84, 69.
32. Eichner, *The Free-Market Family,* Introduction, chaps. 5 and 6.
33. For discussions, see Stefania Barca, *Forces of Reproduction* (Cambridge: Cambridge University Press, 2020), 37–38; Weeks, *The Problem with Work,* 113–137; Katrina Forrester, "Feminist Demands and the Problem of Housework," *American Political Science Review* 116, no. 4 (2022): 1278–1292.
34. Arlie Hochschild with Anne Machung, *The Second Shift: Working Parents and the Revolution at Home* (New York: Viking, 1989).
35. See also Joan C. Tronto, *Caring Democracy: Markets, Equality, and Justice* (New York: New York University Press, 2013), 26.
36. Eichner, *The Free-Market Family,* chap. 1.
37. Jennifer Glass, Robin Simon, and Matthew Andersson, "Parenthood and Happiness: Effects of Work–Family Reconciliation Policies in 22 OECD Countries," *American Journal of Sociology* 122, no. 3 (2016): 886–929.
38. Office of the US Surgeon General, "Parents Under Pressure: The U.S. Surgeon General's Advisory on the Mental Health & Well-Being of Parents," Washington, 2024.
39. See, for example, Lisa Herzog, Katrin Sold, and Bénédicte Zimmermann, "Essential Work: A Category in the Making?" in *Shifting Categories of Work: Unsettling the Ways We Think about Jobs, Labor, and Activities,* eds. L. Herzog and B. Zimmermann (New York: Routledge, 2022), 252–264.

40. Arlie R. Hochschild, "Global Care Chains and Emotional Surplus Value," in *On the Edge: Living with Global Capitalism,* ed. Will Hutton and Anthony Giddens (London: Jonathan Cape, 2000), 130–146; Rhacel S. Parreñas, *Servants of Globalization: Women, Migration and Domestic Work* (Stanford: Stanford University Press, 2001).
41. See, for example, Nancy Fraser, "How Feminism Became Capitalism's Handmaiden—And How to Reclaim It," *Guardian,* October 14, 2013.
42. Eichner, *The Free-Market Family,* chap. 10. Jennifer Nedelsky and Tom Malleson suggest a more radical approach of "part time work for all"—that is, fewer hours of paid work and more hours of care work as the standard case for everyone. While I endorse the call for work-time reduction with regard to paid work, I am not convinced that universalized care work is necessary or desirable; care work not done for the right reasons can easily do more harm than good. Nedelsky and Malleson's strongest arguments stem from the need to end the devaluation of care work, and this is a goal I share. But I am more optimistic that this can happen in different ways, as is already the case in many European countries. The argument that societal decision-makers should have some experience of care (the case, that is, against the "care/policy divide") remains a strong one, but it does not require a *permanent* engagement in care work. Nedelsky and Malleson, *Part-Time for All,* 9–10, 94–98.
43. On the many meanings of care, see Tronto, *Caring Democracy,* ix–x and 18–20. On caring for the earth, see Nedelsky and Malleson, *Part-Time for All,* 83–91.
44. On a broad notion of care, see Kate Aronoff, Alyssa Battistoni, Daniel A. Cohen, and Thea Riofrancos, *A Planet to Win: Why We Need a Green New Deal* (London: Verso, 2019), 81–89.
45. See also Erin Kelly and Phyllis Moen, *Overload: How Good Jobs Went Bad and What We Can Do about It* (Princeton: Princeton University Press, 2020).
46. Waheed Hussain, "Pitting People Against Each Other," *Philosophy & Public Affairs* 48, no. 1 (2020): 79–113.
47. "The Results Are In: The UK's Four-Day Week Pilot," Autonomy Research, Hampshire, UK, February 2023, https://autonomy.work/wp-content/uploads/2023/02/The-results-are-in-The-UKs-four-day-week-pilot.pdf.
48. Guomundur D. Haraldsson and Jack Kellam, "Going Public: Iceland's Journey to a Shorter Working Week," Autonomy Research, Hampshire,

UK, June 2021, https://autonomy.work/wp-content/uploads/2021/06/ICELAND_4DW.pdf.
49. Haraldsson and Kellam, "Going Public," 34 (no overwork in compressed hours), 42–46 (positive effects on workers and their environment).
50. Haraldsson and Kellam, "Going Public," 53.
51. Autonomy Research, "Results Are In," 20–21.
52. Autonomy Research, "Results Are In," 32 (reduction); 54 (preparation period).
53. Autonomy Research, "Results Are In," 36–38.
54. Autonomy Research, "Results Are In," 42.
55. Autonomy Research, "Results Are In," 45.
56. One indication for that worry is that there was a high degree of highly educated employees. See Autonomy Research, "Results Are In," 20. About 68 percent of participating employees had at least an undergraduate degree.
57. Jason Hickel argues that reduced working hours would reduce energy consumption. Jason Hickel, *Less Is More: How Degrowth Will Save the World* (London: Penguin, 2021), 221–222.
58. See also Alessio Terzi, *Growth for Good: Reshaping Capitalism to Save Humanity from Climate Catastrophe* (Cambridge, MA: Harvard University Press, 2022), 55–56.
59. Empirical research finds different effects. See, for example, Martin Pullinger, "Working Time Reduction Policy in a Sustainable Economy: Criteria and Options for Its Design," *Ecological Economics* 103 (2014): 11–19; Giorgios Kallis, Michael Kalush, Hugh O'Flynn, Jack Rossiter, and Nicholas Ashford, "'Friday Off': Reducing Working Hours in Europe," *Sustainability* 5 (2013): 1545–1567. For a discussion of these and other studies, see Patrick Bottazzi, "Work and Social-Ecological Transitions: A Critical Review of Five Contrasting Approaches," *Sustainability* 11, no. 3852 (2019): 1–19, 5–6.
60. Juliet Schor also argues for more self-provisioning work, to decrease dependence on markets. I remain agnostic on this point—some individuals may like it, but it need not be for everyone. Juliet B. Schor, *Plenitude: The New Economics of True Wealth* (New York: Penguin, 2010).
61. Two noteworthy exceptions are Tronto, *Caring Democracy*, esp. x–xiv (with a focus on "caring with" between citizens and institutions); and Desiree Lim, "Domination and the (Instrumental) Case for Free Time,"

Law, Ethics and Philosophy 5 (2017): 74–90 (with a focus on the need for time for keeping power-wielders in check). For an opposing view—which argues for time-minimizing democratic politics, and therefore praises the advantages of voting over other forms of participation—see Kevin J. Elliot, *Democracy for Busy People* (Chicago: University of Chicago Press, 2023). I agree with Elliot that it is important to take the temporal dimension of democracy seriously, but go into the opposite direction of challenging the necessity of "busy-ness," rather than give up on more demanding approaches to democracy, because I take the latter, in which citizens have more opportunities for active participation, to be the best chance to keep democracy stable over time.

62. For the UK trial, see Autonomy Research, "Results Are In," 59–61. Most people used the free time for family or hobbies; the only "civic" activity explicitly mentioned is "volunteering at an animal shelter" (60).

63. On care work as a contribution to the social community, see Stuart White, *The Civic Minimum: On the Rights and Obligations of Economic Citizenship* (Oxford: Oxford University Press, 2003), 71–73.

64. In countries with a public retirement system, volunteer work could also be incentivized by providing "points" for the retirement system.

65. Another institutional approach that is sometimes suggested is a mandatory national service, which would bring individuals from different backgrounds together. It could be combined with forms of voluntary work as discussed here, but if it were to take a mandatory form it would require discussion beyond the space available here. See, for example, Debra Satz, "In Defense of a Mandatory Public Service Requirement," *Royal Institute of Philosophy Supplement* 91 (2022): 259–269.

66. Karin Jurczyk and Ulrich Mückenberger, eds., *Selbstbestimmte Optionszeiten im Erwerbsverlauf* (München: Deutsches Jugendinstitut, 2020).

67. For example, in the case of public security, proper training for everyone involved in the use of force is extremely important and there is also an important symbolic dimension to the question of who takes care of public security.

68. See, famously, Elinor Ostrom, *Governing the Commons: The Evolution of Institutions for Collective Action* (Bloomington: Indiana University Press, 1990).

69. BBC News, "Cameron and Clegg Set Out 'Big Society' Policy Ideas," May 18, 2010, http://news.bbc.co.uk/2/hi/uk_news/politics/8688860.stm.

70. Margaret Thatcher, Interview for *Woman's Own* ("no such thing [as society]"), September 23, 1987, https://www.margaretthatcher.org/document/106689.
71. See, for example, Andrew Williams, Mark Goodwin, and Paul Cloke, "Neoliberalism, Big Society, and Progressive Localism," *Environment and Planning A: Economy and Space* 46, no. 12 (2014): 2798–2815.
72. Or, for independent reasons, being raised, especially on the lower echelons of the wage scale. Chapter 4 explores this topic.
73. This could also be a way of cutting back the role of consultancies in public service, which is hugely expensive and has deeply undemocratic implications. See Mariana Mazzucato and Rosie Collington, *The Big Con: How the Consulting Industry Weakens Our Business, Infantilizes Our Government and Warps Our Economies* (London: Penguin, 2023).
74. Albert W. Dzur, *Democratic Professionalism: Citizen Participation and the Reconstruction of Professional Ethics, Identity, and Practice* (University Park: Pennsylvania State University Press, 2008); Albert W. Dzur, *Democracy Inside: Participatory Innovation in Unlikely Places* (New York: Oxford University Press, 2018). A similar approach is suggested in William M. Sullivan, *Work and Integrity: The Crisis and Promise of Professionalism in America* (San Francisco: Jossey-Bass, 2005).
75. Dzur, *Democratic Professionalism*, chaps. 2 and 3. Dzur discusses critics such as Eliot Freidson, Magali Sarfatti Larson, and Ivan Illich.
76. Dzur, *Democratic Professionalism*, 105.
77. See, for example, the contributions in Susanne Hecker, Muki Haklay, Anne Bowser, Zen Makuch, Johannes Vogel, and Aletta Bonn, eds., *Citizen Science: Innovation in Open Science, Society and Policy* (London: University College London Press, 2018). For my perspective, see Lisa Herzog and Robert Lepenies, "Citizen Science in Deliberative Systems: Participation, Epistemic Injustice, and Civic Empowerment," *Minerva* 60 (2022): 489–508.
78. Albert W. Dzur and Selen A. Ercan, "Participatory Democracy in Unlikely Places: What Democratic Theorists Can Learn from Democratic Professionals: Selen A. Ercan's Interview with Albert W. Dzur," *Democratic Theory* 3, no. 2 (2016): 94–113.
79. I here draw on Harry C. Boyte, "Constructive Politics and Public Work: Organizing the Literature," *Political Theory*, 39, no. 5 (2011): 630–660. Boyte builds on earlier work, including Forester's work on cooperative city planning: John Forester, *The Deliberative Practitioner: Encouraging*

Participatory Planning Processes (Cambridge, MA: MIT Press, 1999). A similar approach can be found in Benjamin Barber, *Strong Democracy: Participatory Politics for a New Age* (Berkeley: University of California Press, 1984), especially his notion of "common action" (209–211). Note, however, that I focus on voluntary forms of work.
80. Boyte, "Constructive Politics," 630.
81. Boyte, "Constructive Politics," 632–633.
82. Boyte, "Constructive Politics," 633.
83. John Kenneth Galbraith, *The Affluent Society* (Boston: Houghton Mifflin, 1998/1958), chap. 17.
84. Tocqueville, *Democracy in America,* chap. 12.
85. Putnam, *The Upswing.*
86. Putnam, *The Upswing,* chap. 4.
87. Putnam, *The Upswing,* 148–155.
88. Putnam, *The Upswing,* 156.
89. Putnam, *The Upswing,* 162–163.
90. Putnam, *The Upswing,* 163.
91. Putnam, *The Upswing,* esp. chap. 5.
92. Putnam, *The Upswing,* chap. 9.
93. Robert B. Talisse, *Overdoing Democracy: Why We Must Put Politics in Its Place* (New York: Oxford University Press, 2019).
94. Talisse, *Overdoing Democracy,* 163–164.
95. See, similarly, Anthony B. Atkinson, "The Case for a Participation Income," *Political Quarterly* 67, no. 1 (1996): 67–70.
96. Cynthia Estlund, *Working Together: How Workplace Bonds Strengthen a Diverse Democracy* (New York: Oxford University Press, 2003); Diana C. Mutz, *Hearing the Other Side: Deliberative versus Participatory Democracy* (Cambridge: Cambridge University Press, 2006).
97. Estlund, *Working Together.*
98. Would this proposal contradict the imperative of liberal states to remain neutral toward different conceptions of the good life? I do not think so, because there could be rather different kinds of projects, offering individuals different choices. Moreover, those who hold extremely individualist or materialist values, and therefore are not interested in participating, would not be forced to do so.
99. See, for example, Sebastian Engelbrecht and Manfred Götzke, "Das dysfunktionale Berlin. Wahl und Verwaltungschaos," *Deutschlandfunk,* January 28, 2023, https://www.deutschlandfunk.de/das-dyfunktionale-berlin-wahl-und-verwaltungschaos-dlf-09b41c3a-100.html.

100. One might certainly ask critically why this worked so much better in the case of refugees from Ukraine ("people like us") than in the case of refugees from further away—for example, from Afghanistan—who arrive at the borders of the European Union every day, or die on the way there. The point here is certainly not to glorify the European migration regime, but simply to emphasize how civil society actors played a decisive role in tackling a crisis.
101. Thomas S. Kuhn, *The Structure of Scientific Revolutions*. Chicago: University of Chicago Press, 1962.
102. See, for example, Aronoff et al., *A Planet to Win*, 22, 78–79.
103. Or, in the words of Frankfurt School sociologist Friedrich Pollock as early as 1963: "The introduction of a four-day working week will mean one more day for workers to waste watching Westerns on television." Quoted in Nicola Emery, "Friedrich Pollock Is a Crucial Guide to the Rise of Automation," *Jacobine*, August 30, 2023.
104. For an overview of numerous studies, see Daniel H. Pink, *Drive: The Surprising Truth About What Motivates Us* (Edinburgh: Canongate, 2009).
105. On reciprocity, see White, *The Civic Minimum*, chap. 4, esp. 90–91. On why this condition is often violated in the "Black Ghetto," see Tommie Shelby, "Justice, Work, and the Ghetto Poor," *Law & Ethics of Human Rights* 6, no. 1 (2012): 70–96.
106. See Autonomy Research, "Results Are In"; Klaus Dörre, *Die Utopie des Sozialismus: Kompass für eine Nachhaltigkeitsrevolution* (Berlin: Matthes & Seitz, 2022), 188–196. Shortening the workweek while also democratizing work can prevent increased pressures in the reduced hours. Chapter 2 of this book presents the arguments for democratization.
107. For an early proposal to introduce sabbaticals for everyone, see Louis Emmerij and J. A. E. Clobus, *Volledige werkgelegenheid door creatief verlof, naar een maatschappij van de vrije keuze* (Amsterdam: Kluwer, 1978).
108. The ecological transition might provide additional reasons for greater needs for retraining or other changes in people's lives, to adapt to a low-carbon economy.
109. Schor, *The Overworked American*.
110. For another view, see Boyte, "Constructive Politics," 11.

6: Repairing Democracy on the Open Sea

1. For another view, distinguishing "transformative" from "affirmative" change, see Nancy Fraser, "Reframing Justice in a Globalizing World," *New Left Review* 36 (2005): 69–88.
2. John Rawls, *A Theory of Justice* (Cambridge, MA: Belknap Press of Harvard University Press, 1971), 136–142.
3. For another criticism of lottocratic approaches on similar grounds, see Cristina Lafont, *Democracy without Shortcuts: A Participatory Conception of Deliberative Democracy* (New York: Oxford University Press, 2020).
4. In the context of the environmental crisis, see also Peter Docherty, Mari Kira, and A. B. Shami, eds., *Creating Sustainable Work Systems* (London: Routledge, 2009).
5. Plutarch reports that the effort to preserve the hero's storied ship over many decades meant that, eventually, every piece of it had decayed and been replaced—making of the ship "a standing example among the philosophers, for the logical question of things that grow; one side holding that the ship remained the same, and the other contending that it was not the same." Plutarch, *Life of Theseus*, trans. John Dryden (Boston: Little Brown and Co., 1906), 34.
6. Otto Neurath, *Empiricism and Sociology* (Dordrecht: D. Reidel, 1973), 199.
7. See, for example, Simon Sharpe and Timothy M. Lenton, "Upward-Scaling Tipping Cascades to Meet Climate Goals: Plausible Grounds for Hope," *Climate Policy* 21, no. 4 (2021): 421–433.
8. See, for example, Julie Battilana and Tiziana Casciaro, *Power, For All: How It Really Works and Why It's Everyone's Business* (New York: Simon & Schuster, 2021).
9. Hélène Landemore, *Open Democracy: Reinventing Popular Rule for the Twenty-First Century* (Princeton: Princeton University Press, 2020); Alexander Guerrero, *Lottocracy: Democracy Without Elections* (New York: Oxford University Press, 2024).
10. One example is the failure of constitutional reform (after a lottocratic rewriting process) in Iceland. See Björg Thorarensen, "Why the Making of a Crowd-Sourced Constitution in Iceland Failed," *Constitution Making & Constitutional Change,* February 26, 2014, https://www.constitutional-change.com/why-the-making-of-a-crowd-sourced

-constitution-in-iceland-failed/. Another is the failure by the French parliament to take up key provisions suggested by the Citizen Convention on Climate Change. See Sonia Phalnikar, "France's Citizen Climate Assembly: A Failed Experiment?" *DW*, February 16, 2021.
11. See, for example, Julia Cagé, *The Price of Democracy: How Money Shapes Politics and What to Do about It* (Cambridge, MA: Harvard University Press, 2020), Part III.
12. See, for example, Gordon Arlen and Enzo Rossi, "Must Realists Be Pessimists about Democracy? Responding to Epistemic and Oligarchic Challenges," *Moral Philosophy and Politics* 8, no. 1 (2021): 27–49; Elliot Bulmer and Stuart White, "Constitutions against Oligarchy," in *Wealth and Power: Philosophical Perspectives,* ed. Michael Bennett, Huub Brouwer, and Rutger Claassen (New York: Routledge, 2023), 274–294; Camilla Vergara, *Systemic Corruption: Constitutional Ideas for an Anti- Oligarchic Republic* (Princeton: Princeton University Press, 2020). For a historical-constitutional perspective in the United States, see Joseph Fishkin and William E. Forbath, *The Anti-Oligarchy Constitution* (Cambridge, MA: Harvard University Press, 2022).
13. See, for example, Andrew Dobson, "Representative Democracy and the Environment," *Democracy and the Environment: Problems and Prospects,* eds. W. M. Lafferty and J. Meadcroft (Cheltenham: Elgar, 1996), 124–139.
14. Kwame Anthony Appiah, *The Honor Code: How Moral Revolutions Happen* (London: Norton, 2011). I have drawn on his work in a previous short article: Lisa Herzog, "Il faut engager une révolution morale," *Le Monde,* December 13, 2018.
15. On experimental evidence for change of social conventions when tipping points are reached, see Damon Centola, Joshua Becker, Devon Brackbill, and Andrea Baronchelli, "Experimental Evidence for Tipping Points in Social Convention," *Science* 360, no. 6393 (2018): 1116–1119.
16. Social recognition is discussed in Chapter 4 of this book.
17. For a view of the progressive movement as "first and foremost, a moral awakening," see Robert D. Putnam with Shaylyn Romney Garrett, *The Upswing: How We Came Together a Century Ago and How We Can Do It Again* (New York: Simon & Schuster, 2020), 420.
18. For another example of recent successful norm change, this one concerning parental leave practices for fathers in Denmark, see Jennifer

Nedelsky and Tom Malleson, *Part-Time for All: A Care Manifesto* (New York: Oxford University Press, 2023), 21–23.
19. Adam Smith, *An Inquiry into the Nature and Causes of the Wealth of Nations,* 2 vols., ed. R. H. Campbell and A. S. Skinner, textual ed. W. B. Todd (Oxford: Clarendon Press, 1976 [1776]), book V, chap. III, para 7.
20. On financial intermediation and its problems see, for example, Diane-Laure Arjaliès, Philip Grant, Iain Hardie, Donald MacKenzie, and Ekaterina Svetlova, *Chains of Finance: How Investment Management Is Shaped* (Oxford: Oxford University Press, 2017).
21. See, for example, Michael Mechanic, *Jack Pot: How the Super-Rich Really Live—and How Their Wealth Harms Us All* (New York: Simon & Schuster, 2021).
22. See, for example, Andrew Cumbers, *The Case for Economic Democracy* (Cambridge: Polity, 2020), 80–95.
23. Chapter 3 includes a discussion of these inequalities.
24. See, for example, Gar Alperovitz and Lew Daly, *Unjust Deserts* (New York: New Press, 2008); Tom Malleson, *Against Inequality: The Practical and Ethical Case for Abolishing the Superrich* (New York: Oxford University Press, 2023).
25. See also Putnam, *The Upswing,* chap. 9.
26. See, for example, Alec Tyson and Brian Kennedy, "Two-Thirds of Americans Think Government Should Do More on Climate," Pew Research Center report, June 23, 2020, https://www.pewresearch.org/science/2020/06/23/two-thirds-of-americans-think-government-should-do-more-on-climate/.
27. See, for example, Frederic B. Bird, *The Muted Conscience: Moral Silence and the Practice of Ethics in Business* (Westport, CT: Quorum, 1996).
28. Mary C. Gentile, *Giving Voice to Values: How to Speak Your Mind When You Know What's Right* (New Haven, CT: Yale University Press, 2012).
29. Lisa Herzog, *Reclaiming the System: Moral Responsibility, Divided Labour, and the Role of Organizations in Society* (Oxford: Oxford University Press, 2019), chap. 8.
30. This term was first coined by Brian F. Yates and Celesa L. Horvath, "Social License to Operate: How to Get It, and How to Keep It," 2013 Summit Working Papers, Pacific Energy Summit 2013, https://www.nbr.org/wp-content/uploads/pdfs/programs/PES_2013_summitpaper_Yates_Horvath.pdf.

31. On meaningful work, see, for example, Ruth Yeoman, *Meaningful Work and Workplace Democracy: A Philosophy of Work and a Politics of Meaningfulness* (London: Palgrave Macmillan, 2014). The recent debate about "bullshit jobs" shows that there are many individuals searching for more meaningful work. David Graeber, *Bullshit Jobs: A Theory* (London: Allen Lane, 2018). For an empirical critique of Graeber, see Magdalena Soffia, Alex J. Wood, and Brendan Burchell, "Alienation Is Not 'Bullshit': An Empirical Critique of Graeber's Theory of BS Jobs," *Work, Employment and Society* 36, no. 5 (2021): 816–840.
32. Samuel Beckett, *Worstward Ho* (New York: Grove Press, 1983).
33. R. H. Tawney, "English Politics Today: We Mean Freedom," *Review of Politics* 8, no. 2 (1946): 223–239, at 230.
34. Jacob S. Hacker, *The Great Risk Shift: The New Economic Insecurity and the Decline of the American Dream* (New York: Oxford University Press, 2006).
35. See also Kate Aronoff, Alyssa Battistoni, Daniel Aldana Cohen, and Thea Riofrancos, *A Planet to Win: Why We Need a Green New Deal* (London: Verso, 2019), 187–188.
36. See, for example, Maxine Eichner, *The Free-Market Family: How the Market Crushed the American Dream (and How It Can Be Restored)* (New York: Oxford University Press, 2020), 35.
37. Sendhil Mullainathan and Eldar Shafir, *Scarcity* (New York: Penguin, 2013).
38. Michèle Lamont, "From 'Having' to 'Being': Self-Worth and the Current Crisis of American Society," *British Journal of Sociology* 70, no. 3 (2019): 660–707.
39. See the websites: Real Utopias Project, https://www.realutopias.org/the-real-utopias-project/; Participedia, https://participedia.net/; Global Atlas of Environmental Justice, https://ejatlas.org/.
40. See also Herzog, *Reclaiming the System*, chap. 7.
41. For a conceptual attempt, see Lisa Herzog, Frank Hindriks, and Rafael Wittek, "How Institutions Decay: Towards an Endogenous Theory," *Economics and Philosophy*, online first, https://www.cambridge.org/core/services/aop-cambridge-core/content/view/E5426C2B1BC11A6AF97C16165564C1C3/S0266267124000208a.pdf/div-class-title-how-institutions-decay-towards-an-endogenous-theory-div.pdf
42. For another view, see Joan C. Tronto, *Caring Democracy: Markets, Equality, and Justice* (New York: New York University Press, 2013), 28–31.

43. Francis Fukuyama, *The End of History and the Last Man* (New York: Free Press, 1992). A very similar sentiment was expressed by political scientist Louis Hartz, who expected, according to Samuel Bowles and Herbert Gintis, that when the Soviet Union was overcome, "the full harmony of the liberal system will be assured. The end of ideology is no less than the end of history." Samuel Bowles and Herbert Gintis, *Democracy and Capitalism: Property, Community, and the Contradictions of Modern Social Thought* (New York: Basic Books, 1986), 31.

Acknowledgments

These acknowledgments could be extremely long, or rather short—so I have decided to make them short. The reason they could be long is that this book is a synthesis of so much of the reading, thinking, discussing, and writing that I have done over the years, since entering university as a naive and idealistic student of philosophy and economics in 2002. If I have learned one thing, it is that we never think alone. Even those stereotypical lonely philosophers buried in their books are in dialogue with the ideas of others, whether from centuries ago or from present authors. For me, being in dialogue about philosophical ideas with real people—colleagues, students, critics, audience members at events, but also friends and family members—has been so important that I have sometimes wondered whether I was cut out for philosophy at all, given the dominance of the "lonely genius" cliché. The journey was not always easy, but thanks to many supportive colleagues, among them now some of my dearest friends, I stayed in the game. I am deeply grateful for the insights and inspirations I have gained by being part of various academic communities, and only wish that more scholars could enjoy this privilege as so many such communities remain haunted by inequities and exclusions. Together with my gratitude, I want to express my ongoing commitment to making academia a truly open and inclusive space.

There are some people I want to thank for the very concrete steps of bringing this book to market. David Johnson put me in touch with Sam Haselby, who helped me develop a proposal. Sam Stark took on the project as editor. Working with him was a wonderful experience and I am deeply grateful for his advice and guidance. I also want to thank two anonymous reviewers who gave me very valuable feedback, as well as Press editors Grigory Tovbis and Julia Kirby, who took over from Sam Stark in the production phase.

Finally, none of my academic work would ever have succeeded without the ongoing support of my husband, Georg. He knows this, but he does not like dedications very much. Therefore, I dedicate this book to the drivers of the many trains in which I sat working on it, and without whose work the interconnected European republic of letters would not be possible.

Index

advertising: regulation, and green values, 108, 109; truth in, 43
akrasia, 43–44
alternative work situations, 53, 54, 59–61
ancient Greece, 54
anti-poverty intuition, 78–81
anti-regulatory attitudes: of corporations and industries, 37–38; property rights focus, 29–30
antitrust enforcement, 41, 180n46
Appiah, Anthony Kwame, 149, 155
associational life, 18, 47, 121, 125–126, 139–141
Azmanova, Albena, 80

bankruptcy, 34
bargaining power: general workers, 85; labor unions, 36, 39, 70, 71, 127; skilled workers and unique talent, 55, 67, 83–84; for sustainability, 111

barriers to market entry, 26
basic needs, 79, 117, 161–162
behavior, human. *See* human and consumer behavior
Berman, Sheri, 2
black markets, 29, 45
Bourdieu, Pierre, 88–90
Boyte, Harry, 138–139
bureaucracy, 163
buyers and sellers, markets logic, 28–29, 42, 45, 46

Cameron, David, 136–137
campaign contributions, 12, 34, 89, 90, 195n43
"cannibal capitalism," 12
"capability approach," 116–117
capitalism: democracy relations, assumptions, and conflicts, 1–6, 12, 148, 150, 157–159, 162, 166; harms to families, 130–131; precarity, 80; revolution, 148; vs.

capitalism (*continued*)
  socialism, 12–13; time politics: care and community work, 23, 129–133, 147. *See also* markets
carbon emissions: lowered work hours effects, 134–135; taxation, 108, 109, 110–111, 112, 116; transitions to lower, 102–103, 107–112
Card, David, 97
care work and housework: pay and leave initiatives, 124, 129–130, 131, 210n42; time poverty, 125, 128, 129; valuing and reclaiming time, 125, 128, 129–133, 135, 147
Carnes, Nicholas, 125
CEO pay, 77, 81
citizen oversight, 72
citizen science, 138
Clark, Colin, 104
class stratification. *See* economic stratification
code switching, 91
codetermination, workers and owners, 71–72, 73–74
Cold War, 13, 102, 166, 220n43
collective organizations, 27, 136–137, 163
collusion, 37
colonialism, 7, 32, 35
"commons" values, 136
community benefits. *See* public good
competition: consumer choices, 46–47, 48, 49; economic theory, 41; elections, 14–15; human relations effects, 47, 119, 132–133; work options, 62–63, 65, 84

consumer behavior. *See* human and consumer behavior
consumer protections: property and contracts, 29, 40; weakness and lack of, 27, 40, 41. *See also* worker protections
contracts: consumer rights, 40; enforcement, for functioning markets, 29; labor, 55, 58–59, 60, 64
cooperatives, 70, 98–99
corporate legal personhood, 35
corporate social responsibility: vs. current realities, 36, 42–43, 137, 153, 159; public work opportunities, 146; representation and oversight for, 71–72, 74, 98–99
corporations and corporate power: control of markets, 27–28, 33, 36–37, 38–41; history, 35; income inequality, 77; labor hierarchies, 55–58, 69, 70, 74–75; lobbying and political influence, 34, 37–38, 39, 41, 149; logic of, 28, 33–38; negative effects to markets, 26, 27–28, 33, 36, 38–41, 42–43, 164–165; negative effects to workers, 52–53, 56–57, 58–61; structures, and inherent power, 27, 34, 35, 36. *See also* shareholders
Covid-19 pandemic: data reporting, 205n79; labor and workforce during and following, 52–53, 86, 94; supply chain effects, 38
"crony capitalism," 12, 179n35
cultural capital, 88–89
cultural shifts: arts and sciences, 96–97, 98, 121; associational and civic values, 126, 140–141;

Index

economic and social change, 23–24, 148–167; environmental over growth values, 108–109, 110–111, 115–116, 119–122, 144–145, 164; functional over growth values, 13, 21, 112–113, 115–116; human rights, 155, 166–167; identity politics, 20; paradigms, 144–145, 149, 155–156, 166–167; time politics effects, 125–126, 131–132, 147

Daly, Herman E., 102, 108, 115
deliberative democracy, 17, 139–140
democracy: advantages of structures, 14–15, 19, 69–70, 72, 91–92, 95–96, 98, 99, 115; capitalism and economic growth and, 1–6, 11–13, 101, 102–104, 107–113, 115, 203n47; citizens' agency and participation, 2, 5, 6, 12, 14–19, 88, 92–93, 94, 125–126, 129, 135–136, 137, 139, 142, 154, 196n45; economic theory of, 14–15, 16; elections, 14–15, 17, 146, 154; and environmental justice, 10, 110–111, 121, 164; forms, 17–19, 54, 72–74, 139–140, 154; human intermingling for, 5, 15, 18, 63–64, 64–65, 76, 95, 99, 140–142, 145, 147, 212n65; ideal market scenarios, 6, 7–8, 14, 37, 42–46, 48, 50–51, 53, 111, 120; and labor justice, 53, 54–55, 57, 58, 62–75, 114, 117, 125, 158–159; markets' anti-democratic aspects, 1–5, 11–13, 20, 25–51, 53, 88, 92–93; philanthropy as undemocratic, 88–89; post-democratic societies, 5, 14–15, 16–17; reclaiming time and care for, 5, 6, 133–147; repairing, 16–17, 23–24, 148–167; social norms and, 12, 15–17, 30–31, 42, 47; values of, and markets values, 2–3, 5–7, 16, 22, 26, 27–28, 30–32, 37, 39, 41, 45, 48–49, 103, 106, 108, 110–114, 150, 162; wavering national commitment, 1, 3, 41. *See also* inequality; political participation
democratic professionalism, 137–138
De-Shalit, Avner, 117
developing nations, carbon use, 102–103
Dewey, John, 3, 7, 16
distribution of wealth, 4, 9, 22–23, 80–81, 99, 101, 105, 114, 157–158
division of labor: labor markets, 85–86; technical vs. social, 63–64
Drucker, Peter, 202n34
Dzur, Albert, 137–138

"Easterlin paradox," 199n5
economic growth: debates on, 4, 5, 23, 101–103, 105–106, 107–119, 203n47; vs. finite resources and realities, 100, 102, 107, 122, 144–145; GDP and measurement, 5, 23, 103, 104–105, 106, 116–118, 120; government policy, 3–4, 102–104, 106, 110, 111, 113, 116–117, 120; postgrowth aims and conditions, 21, 101, 103–104, 107–112, 115, 118–119, 122; vs. social functions, 13, 103, 112–118, 120
economic mobility, 65–66, 192n10

economics. *See* economic growth; economic theory

economic stratification: CEOs and superrich, 77, 81–82, 88–90, 94, 102; class pressures, 11–12, 92–94, 98, 123–125, 149; class signs and symbols, 76, 79–80, 90–91, 92–93, 99; cultural and social capital, 88–89; financial insecurity, 26, 80–82, 96, 161–162; generational wealth, 77, 82, 89, 94–95; individual and class differences, 2, 26, 46, 48, 79–81, 88, 128–129; opportunity gaps, 79, 86, 97, 129, 130; work and leisure time, 123–125, 128; workers, jobs, and training, 61, 62–64, 65–66, 79, 81, 116. *See also* inequality; poverty

economic theory: academic discipline and modeling, 6–7, 8; capability approach, 116–117; classical theory and theorists, 5–6, 37, 42, 62, 70, 101, 119; competition, 14, 41, 47, 62–63; efficiency, reconsidered, 9–11; growth values, reconsidered, 4, 102–103, 107–114; human behavior and utility, 36, 116–117; incorporation/corporations, 35–36; labor-market dynamics, 62–63, 65; markets logic, 25, 28–29, 42, 45; national income, 104–105; rents, 33, 45; social theory shortcomings, 92, 97; statistics shortcomings, 105–106

education: democratic professionalism, 137–138; higher education costs, 105–106, 161; human nature and curiosity, 118, 119, 151; personal success and capital, 89, 92; as publicly-provided good, 3, 95, 98, 99; system failures, 149, 161

efficiency: care and caring work judgments, 132–133; "democratic work" values and assumptions, 68–69, 150; environmental hopes and shortcomings, 4, 10, 107–108, 109, 156, 159; functions, 11, 45, 114, 118, 119; "new work" ideas and terms, 73; over-focus and shortcomings, 2, 3, 4, 8–11, 12, 45, 156–157; rebound effect, 107–108

Eichner, Maxine, 129, 131–132

elections, 14–15, 17, 146, 154

Elliot, Kevin J., 212n61

emergency response work, 143–144, 215n100

emergency savings, 80, 193n14

endowment effect, 95

environmental values: commons care, 136; of consumers, 109, 111, 118, 155–156; vs. consumption and extraction harms, 4, 31–32, 42–43, 45–46, 92, 102, 105, 108–109, 120; efficiency thought shortcomings, 4, 10, 107–108, 109, 156, 159; egalitarian societies, 10, 99, 109; environmental data tracking, 118, 164; industries vs., 120, 153; lowered work hours for, 134–135, 211n57, 211n59; and market externalities, 42–43, 102, 108, 111; nature's lack of representation, 27; public opinion, 120–121, 151; public provision for, and green transition economies, 50, 102–103, 107–112, 115–122, 154, 164;

regulation and reform, 43, 46, 108–109, 110–112, 120, 121–122; of stakeholders, 72, 74
equilibrium, 5, 29, 84–85
ethics and morals. *See* moral issues
exchange: corporations, 35; market examples, 25, 26, 31, 32, 42, 105; price mechanism, 28–29
exploitation: corporate power, 36, 39, 59; forms and accounts, 126, 148, 177n17; informal labor, 61, 64; labor agreements, 58–59, 60, 64; market transactions, 11, 31–32, 33; rent-seeking, 33, 45; unpaid labor, 177n17
extraction: corporate power, 36, 39, 42–43, 158; crony capitalism, 179n35; market transactions, 31–32, 45, 105; paying for environmental harms, 105, 108–109

factor markets, 39
facts and truth, 16, 37
fairness and justice: anti-poverty "sufficientarianism," 78–80; economic values and, 3, 44–45, 46–47; environmental buy-in, 103, 116, 120, 122; functional logic, 113–114, 117; inequality and "deservingness," 77–78, 81–87, 95, 158; theories, 19, 150; workers' labor and conditions, 52–53, 54, 60–61, 62–63, 64–65, 85, 86, 122, 145–146, 158–159. *See also* moral issues
fear, 96, 98, 161, 162
feminism, 129–130, 131
financial insecurity, 26, 80–81, 96, 161–162

"fissured workplace," 58–59, 64
four-day work week, 133–134, 146, 215n103
freedoms: individual, and democracy, 2, 5, 19, 26, 43, 91, 94–99, 115, 125; individual, and markets, 2, 26, 43–44, 46–47, 158; individual, vs. community ties, 141, 145; of mobility, at work, 65–66; of opinion, at work, 54, 55–57, 67, 69–70, 74–75, 159–160; reducing inequality for, 94–99
Friedman, Benjamin, 116

Galbraith, John Kenneth, 139
GDP (gross domestic product): alternatives for measurement, 5, 106, 117–118, 120; as life quality measure, 106, 120; as traditional growth measure, 23, 103, 104–105, 106
gendered work, 85, 129–130, 131
gender pay gap, 85, 195n34
generational wealth, 77, 82, 89, 94–95
gig economy, 59–61
Greek democracy, 54, 154
growth. *See* economic growth
guaranteed jobs and income, 66–67, 74, 96, 98, 116, 162, 191n94

happiness, 199n5
Hartz, Louis, 220n43
health care and health insurance: access, 88; costs, 74, 80, 161; mental health, 92, 130, 162; as publicly-provided good, 3, 95, 98, 161

heterodox economics, 4, 102–103, 110
Hickel, Jason, 102, 106, 108, 109, 200n6, 211n57
hierarchies: societal, 5, 7, 11–12, 13–15, 18, 57; workplace alternatives, 68–75, 98–99; workplaces and roles, 54–56, 57–58, 67, 69, 75
homo oeconomicus, 36
honor, 30–31, 114, 149, 155, 156
household work. *See* care work and housework
human and consumer behavior: consumer choice and power, 14, 26, 128–129, 155–156; consumption shifts, 109, 111, 118, 155–156; democratic intermingling, 5, 15, 18, 63–64, 64–65, 76, 95, 99, 140–142, 145, 147, 212n65; financial advantage, 46–47, 48–49; *homo oeconomicus*, 36; human nature, 7, 13–14, 17, 118–119, 162, 166; justice and fairness, 19, 44–45, 46–47, 150–151; personal relationships, 15, 18, 47, 51, 91, 128, 132–133; scarcity mindset, 9, 162; self-identity, 5, 67, 90–91, 117, 145; social norms, 30–31, 47, 109, 127–128, 159–160; social tensions, 7, 116, 140, 142, 165–166; weakness and self-control, 43–44; work ethic, 52–53, 55, 81, 96–97, 114, 119, 127–128; work social activity, 54, 55, 56, 57, 61, 63–64, 65, 67, 75, 142–143. *See also* cultural shifts; leisure time; work-life balance
Human Development Index, 118

human rights: public provision for, 50; values and norms, 2, 7, 18, 155, 166–167; workplace abuses, 58, 60–61; workplace protection, 64–65

identity issues: class identity and communication, 90–91, 92–93, 141–142; identity politics, 19–20, 142; jobs and work, 67, 117, 129, 130, 145; self-actualization, 5, 91, 117, 129, 130, 145
immigrant labor, 61
inequality: anti-democratic outcomes, 3–5, 11–13, 18, 27, 28, 31, 38, 39, 46, 87–94; corporations' powers and, 27, 34, 36, 38, 39; and "deservingness," 77–78, 81–87, 95, 158; distribution of wealth, 4, 9, 22–23, 80–81, 99, 101, 105, 114, 157–158; exploitation scenarios, 3–4, 31–33, 39, 45; income and material, 76–77, 79–80, 81–87, 119, 153–154, 157–158, 192n10, 193n14; as market social ill, 3, 11–12, 26, 38, 39; purchasing power, 26, 46, 48, 79–80, 88, 128–129; reducing and repairing, 7, 8, 12, 14, 75, 78, 94–99, 115–116, 146, 153–155, 161, 163–164; rent-seeking outcomes, 33, 45, 86, 114; research on, 76–77, 81–82, 86, 97, 105; societal comparisons, 7–8, 46, 77, 79, 92–94, 99, 102–103, 130; time resources, 5, 124–125, 128–129, 142; unionization to combat, 71. *See also* economic stratification; hierarchies

Index

informal labor, 61, 64
innovation: egalitarian societies and systems, 78, 95, 96–97, 97–98, 109, 121–122; green policy and, 109, 111–112, 119, 121–122, 164; "new work" ideas, 73; in successful markets, 51, 96; via economic growth, 101
intellectual property rights, 33

Jackson, Tim, 102
Jevons, William Stanley, 107
job guarantee programs, 66–67, 74, 96, 98, 116, 162, 191n94
joint-stock companies, 35
justice. *See* fairness and justice

Kaldor-Hicks efficiency, 9
Keynes, John Maynard, 123
Kogelmann, Brian, 202n40
Kuhn, Thomas, 144
Kuznets, Simon, 104–105

labor. *See* work and workers; worker protections
labor unions: bargaining power vs. corporations, 36, 39, 70, 71; Europe, 70, 71, 127; opposition and demise, 3; protest methods, 52; unionization, 71; working time demands, 126–127; workplace democracy and, 70. *See also* worker protections
Lamont, Michèle, 162
Latin American resource exploitation, 32
legal structures: corporate legal personhood, 35; corporations' nature, 34; forms, 29, 34; functioning markets needs, 29–30; platform work, 60–61; preventing exploitation and extraction, 32–33; unsupportive of economic and social change, 148–149, 163
Le Grand, Julian, 10–11
leisure time: past's conditions and predictions, 123, 126; personal choices and responsibility, 123, 127–128, 135, 145, 212n62, 215n103; time politics and justice, 23, 50, 124–125, 128. *See also* work-life balance
life expectancy, 2, 106, 187n59
lobbying: anti-environmental, 120; corporate influence, 34, 37–38, 39, 41, 88, 89; reform needs, 39, 41, 149
"lottocracy," 73–74, 154, 216n10

Malleson, Tom, 194n26, 210n42
Mankiw, Greg, 81–82, 83, 193n19
market equilibrium, 5, 29, 85
marketization, 26, 28, 38–41
markets: alternatives, 49–50, 95; anti-democratic aspects, 1–5, 11–13, 20, 22, 25–51, 53, 88; assumptions about: market economies, 25–26, 42, 150; corporations' negative effects in, 26, 27–28, 33, 36, 38–41, 42–43, 164–165; exchanges descriptions, 25, 26, 28–29, 31, 105; forms and types, 27, 31, 32, 39, 46; historical views, 2, 28, 42, 104–105; illegal, 29, 45; within institutional frameworks, 28, 42–43, 47–50; labor

markets (*continued*)
  market organization, 52–53, 84–86; logic of, 3, 28–33, 42, 45, 46–47, 48–49, 50, 84; perils of excessive choice, 2, 26, 128–129; regulation sources, powers, and effects, 3, 13, 27, 28, 33, 37. *See also* capitalism
market societies: development and declines, 39–40; vs. market economies, 47; regulation and corporate power, 40–41; social aspects, 48–49, 81
Marx, Karl, 126–127
Marxist theory, 148, 153
medical care. *See* health care and health insurance
mental health, 92, 130, 133, 134, 162
meritocracy, 158, 194n26
microwork, 59–61
Mill, John Stuart, 70, 101, 119
minimum wage, 97
modeling, economic, 6–7
money in politics. *See* campaign contributions; lobbying; personal political influence; political participation
moral issues: anti-poverty "sufficientarianism," 78–80; business ethics, 159–160; democratic work obligations, 145–146, 212n62; economic "deservingness," 77–78, 81–87, 95, 158; environmental degradation and waste, 108, 109, 120–121, 155–156; human rights and value, 2, 7, 155, 166–167; market success and virtue, 48–49, 81–82, 86–87, 158; meritocracy, 194n26; revolution and change, 149, 155–156, 159–160; work duty, 62, 67; work types, 63, 86

national incomes, 104–105
national service programs, 212n65
natural resources: commons, 136; extraction and abuse, 4, 31–32, 42–43, 45–46, 120–121; lack of representation, 27; market externalities, 42, 108; public provision for, 50, 107–112, 119, 154; use data tracking, 118
Nedelsky, Jennifer, 210n42
neoliberalism, 21–22, 27, 137, 161, 162
Neurath's Boat metaphor, 151–152
New Deal era, 116
norms. *See* social norms
Nussbaum, Martha, 116–117

oligopoly, 41
O'Neil, Cathy, 105–106
opportunity gaps: capitalist rat race as, 92, 93, 98, 124–125, 130–131; political influence, 18; remedying, 146; in youth, 79, 86, 97, 129, 130
outsourcing: effects on workers, 11, 54, 58–59; types and descriptions, 58–61

paradigm shifts, 21–22, 144–145, 149
Pareto efficiency, 9
parliamentary systems, 17–18, 154
participatory democracy, 17–19, 72–74, 139–140, 154

personal political influence: candidates' time and money privilege, 125, 146–147, 154; for economic and social change, 148–149; money's power, 88, 89, 149. *See also* political participation
personal vs. productive property, 30, 157–158
Petty, William, 104
philanthropy, 89–90, 137. *See also* volunteerism
Philippon, Thomas, 40–41, 195n43
philosophical schools and traditions, 6, 7–8
planned obsolescence, 108, 109
platform work, 59–61
Plutarch, 216n5
Polanyi, Karl, 47, 49
political participation: citizens' abilities, time, money, and agency, 2, 5, 6, 12, 14–19, 88, 92–93, 94, 125–126, 129, 135–136, 137, 139, 142, 154, 196n45; democracy basics, 1, 2–3, 14–15, 18–19, 146–147; identity politics and, 20, 142; participatory democracy, 17, 72–74, 139–140, 154; power of money in politics, 12, 88, 89, 125, 146–147, 154; workplace democracy and, 188n64. *See also* lobbying
political reform, 23, 149–150, 154–155
post-democratic societies, 5, 14–15, 16–17
poverty: anti-poverty intuition, 78–81; "deservingness" issue, 77–78; focus on uplifting from, 77, 79, 80, 101; time, 128–129

"precarity capitalism," 80
predistribution policies, 95
price mechanisms: corporations and, 35; equilibrium, 29; within markets, 28–29, 84; measuring GDP, 105
pricing: benefits and fairness beliefs, 45; consumer choices, 46–47; environmental goods and services, 10
privacy rights: data collection and analysis, 118, 205n83; platform workers, 60–61
private property: personal vs. productive property, 30, 105; personal vs. public property, 139
privilege, economic, 95–96; bureaucratic, 163; campaign financing, 125, 146–147, 154; care work issues, 131; changemaking power, 160; and economic pressures, 11; education and training, 66, 88, 89; income and wealth, 82–83, 87, 97. *See also* inequality
"productive" vs. "reproductive" work, 129–130, 135
productivity: vs. care and caring work, 132–133; democratic work efficiency, 68–69, 70, 191n89; union density and, 70; worker attitude shifts, 52–53; worker motivation, 57–58; work hours and, 6, 124, 126–127, 133–135
product offerings, and excessive choice, 2, 26, 128–129
professionalism, democratic, 137–138
property assets, 77, 114, 153

property rights: anti-regulatory views on, 29–30; functional logic, 113–114; functioning markets, 29, 30; history, and inequality, 2, 30, 157–158; personal vs. productive property, 30, 157–158

public assistance. *See* welfare systems

public good: associational and civic values, 47, 121, 125–126, 139–141; citizens' work and volunteering for, 135–136, 137, 138–139, 142–144; corporate social responsibility, 36, 137, 153; markets' orientation toward, 5–6, 28, 136; philanthropy considered, 89–90, 137; property considered, 30, 114, 157; public goods and services, 3, 95, 136, 141, 144, 161, 163; regulations for, 37–38; social safety nets, 48, 78–79, 95, 130, 131–132, 161–162

public jobs and public work: democratic societies and values, 135–136, 138–139, 143–144, 145–147, 212n67; guaranteed job concept, 66–67, 74, 96, 98, 116, 191n94; training, 212n67

purchasing power: market exclusion based on, 26, 46, 48, 80, 88; poverty classifications, 79–80; time's value, in decision making, 128–129

Putnam, Robert, 126, 140–141

quality of life: basic needs, 79, 117, 161–162; health and life expectancy, 2, 66, 88, 106, 120, 187n59; income and happiness, 128, 130, 199n5; mental health, 130, 133, 134; self-actualization and -determination, 5, 91, 117, 129, 130, 135; social functioning, 106, 117, 120, 127–128; surveys, 130; time resources and, 122, 123–147. *See also* work-life balance

"quiet quitting," 52–53, 67

racial justice issues, 32, 95, 131, 141, 167

rankings statistics, 105–106

Rawls, John, 19, 150, 165

Reagan, Ronald, 3

real estate assets, 77, 157

reality, shared, 16

"rebound effect," 107–108

redistribution vs. predistribution, 95

refeudalization of economy, 22, 28, 38–41, 88

refugee responses, 143–144, 215n100

regulation: anti-regulatory attitudes, 3, 29–30, 37–38; environmental, 43, 46, 108–109, 110–112, 120; labor agreements, 60–61, 64; labor market, 64, 66, 67, 97, 133; legal rules, 29–30; market shaping, 3, 13, 27, 28, 45–46, 49–50, 67, 88; paperwork and red tape, 163; poor and absent regulation effects, 3, 28, 32–33, 37–39, 40–41, 49, 60–61, 64, 88; sources and powers, 12, 13, 27, 33, 37; worker health and safety, 29, 64, 65

rents: economic theory, 33; functional logic, 114; prevention, 45, 86

representative democracy, 17, 72

Index

"reproductive" vs. "productive" work, 129–130, 135
retirement supports: pension fund investments, 157; as publicly-provided good, 98; volunteering credit, 212n64
revolution, 148, 149, 155–156, 167
risk management, corporate, 35, 40
role hierarchy, 55–56
Rose, Julie, 124–125

safety nets, economic. *See* privilege, economic; welfare systems
savings, households, 80, 193n14
scarcity mindset, 9, 162
Schor, Juliet, 124, 208n23, 211n60
Schumpeter, Joseph A., 13
scientific research, 144
self-provision, 50, 53, 211n60
sellers and buyers, markets logic, 28–29
Sen, Amartya, 116–117
service contracts, 40
sex discrimination, 85, 167
shareholders: co-representation with workers, 71–72, 98–99; corporations' ultimate value, 27, 35–36, 53, 68, 70–71; power, ownership, and liability, 34–35, 40; shareholder theory and efficiency, 68–69
Ship of Theseus story, 151–152, 216n5
small businesses: consumer choices, 46–47, 48, 49; vs. corporations, 34, 38–39; examples and exchange, 25, 26, 31, 32

Smith, Adam, 5–6, 37, 42, 62, 65, 79, 119, 157
smoking, 37–38
social capital, 88–89, 125–126, 132–133, 155
social choice theory, 14
social division of labor, 63–64, 85–86
social functions of economy, 23, 112–118, 119, 120
socialist systems, 12–13, 114
social norms: associational life, 140–141; class structures, 90–91; cultural shifts, 144–145, 149, 155–156; democratic and market ideals, 12, 15–17, 30–31, 42, 47, 122; fairness, 44; green transitions, 109, 122; infrastructure's influence, 109, 121, 122; as market shapers, 30–31, 42, 47; social capital's power, 89, 132–133, 155; work motivation, 119, 127–128. *See also* human and consumer behavior
social stratification. *See* economic stratification
statistics, over-reliance, 105–106
subcontracting. *See* outsourcing
"sufficientarianism," 78–80
supply and demand: markets logic and price mechanisms, 28–29, 45, 46, 84; work, social contributions, and income, 83–85, 86
"survival mode," 162

Talisse, Robert, 142
Tawney, R. H., 104, 113–115, 118, 161

tax system and taxation: carbon taxes, 108, 109, 110–111, 112, 116; market regulation, 29, 43; property rights and, 29, 30, 157, 158; taxation and reduced inequality, 94–95, 101, 158; taxation vs. philanthropy, 89–90
technical division of labor, 63–64
technological innovations: environmental, 107–108, 109, 111–112, 121, 164; markets logic and price mechanisms, 84; "new work" ideas and change, 73, 183n7, 191n89; platform work, 60–61; poverty and economic justice, 79–80, 96
Terzi, Alessio, 107, 108, 202n46, 203n50
Thatcher, Margaret, 3, 136–137
time: for care work, 125, 128, 129–133, 135, 147; for democracy, 5, 6, 133–147; "time politics," 23, 50, 125–126, 127–128, 135–147, 211–212n61; as valuable human resource, 122, 123, 124–125, 126–127, 128–129, 135. *See also* work-life balance
time-inconsistent preferences, 43–44
tobacco industry, 37–38
Tocqueville, Alexis de, 125–126, 139
traditional work situations, 53, 54–56
truth and facts, 16, 37

ultimatum games, 44
unconditional basic income, 161–162, 191n94
unemployment, 66, 98, 161–162

unionization, 71
unions. *See* labor unions
unpaid labor: care and housework, 125, 128, 129–133; exploitation, 177n17; scope and importance, 53, 129, 130–131
upward mobility. *See* economic mobility
utility, human, 36, 171n20

volunteerism: national service programs, 212n65; public and civic contributions, 135–136, 137, 142, 145; refugee and emergency response work, 143–144, 215n100

weakness of will, 43–44
Weil, David, 58, 64
welfare systems: child and family care, 130, 131; descriptions and offerings, 3–4, 78, 94–96, 98, 116, 130, 131, 136, 161–162; labor in societies without, 124–125, 130–131; public provision, 50, 136, 137
Wolff, Jonathan, 117
work and workers: employer-employee relations, 52–53, 54, 55–59, 64–65, 66–67, 69–70, 71–74, 84–85, 111, 126, 133–134, 159; freedom of opinion, 54, 55–57, 67, 69–70, 74–75, 159–160; gendered work, 85, 129–130, 131; green transitions buy-in, 116, 120, 122; labor market realities, 3, 11, 52–53, 54–61, 62–68, 97, 126, 148, 158–159; "new work" ideas and terms, 73; organizing demo-

cratic work, 68–75, 133–147, 191n89; part-time issues, 124, 128, 210n42; rat race traps, 11–12, 92–94, 98, 123–125, 130–131, 149; social relationships, 54, 55, 56, 57, 61, 63–64, 65, 67, 75, 142–143; training, 66, 116, 212n67; work as democratic contribution, 62–68, 114, 117, 158–159; workplace and type choices, 53, 54, 59–61, 62–63, 65–66, 67, 69–70, 124–125, 127, 131, 135. *See also* labor unions; public jobs and public work; unpaid labor; worker protections; work ethic notions; work-life balance
worker cooperatives, 70
worker protections: vs. corporate power, 36, 38; as democratic necessity, 5, 55, 58, 64–65; vs. exploitation, 11, 31–32, 36, 39, 58, 59–61, 64; health and safety regulation, 29, 64, 65; vs. unemployment fear, 98, 161–162; weakness or lack of, 3, 27, 58–59, 61, 64. *See also* consumer protections; labor unions
work ethic notions: attitude shifts, 52–53, 67; deserved incomes, 81, 86; functional logic, 114, 117; innovation drivers, 96–97; motivation, 55, 114, 119, 127–128; purpose of work, 55, 62, 67, 117
work-life balance: alternative work and precarity, 53, 54, 55–56, 59–61; civic work and environmental values, 122, 126, 131–132; economic mobility, 65–66; hours worked, 54, 123–124, 126–127, 133–135, 146; modern work, nature of, 55, 67, 123–124, 130–131; reform thought and experiments, 133–147; values and protests, 52–53; work scheduling problems, 58, 184n20. *See also* leisure time; time
work week length, 133–135, 146, 215n103